Dr. Ron &

The WATCHMAN ON THE WALL

Volume 4

Daily Devotions for
Praying God's Word
Over Those You Love

XARIS PUBLICATIONS

Copyright © 2020 Dr. Ron & Marsha Harvell

The WATCHMAN on the WALL—VOLUME 4
Daily Devotions for Praying God's Word Over Those You Love

All Rights Reserved. This book is protected by the copyright laws of the United States of America. This book may not be copied or reprinted for commercial gain or profit. The use of short quotations is permitted. Permission will be granted upon request. The author guarantees all contents are original and do not infringe upon the legal rights of any other person or work.

Printed in the USA

Cover Design & Layout by Wendy K. Walters | www.wendykwalters.com

ISBN (Hardcase): 978-1-7327271-5-1
ISBN (Paperback): 978-1-7327271-6-8
ISBN (Kindle): 978-1-7327271-7-5
ISBN (ePub): 978-1-7327271-8-2
Library of Congress Control Number: 2020916459

Published By
Xaris Publications
Moncks Corner, South Carolina

Unless otherwise noted, Scripture quotations are taken from the *New American Standard Bible*®, Copyright © 1960, 1962, 1963, 1968, 1971, 1972, 1973, 1975, 1977, 1995 by The Lockman Foundation. Used by permission. www.Lockman.org

Portions of scripture taken from the *King James Version* are marked KJV. Originally published in 1611, this Bible is in the public domain.

To Contact the Authors:
www.GodsGreaterGrace.com

DEDICATION

To our grandchildren:
Nathan, Adilynn, Kik, Daniel, Kyro, Caleb, and Abigail

We love watching you grow to love Jesus,
inviting Him to live in your life
as your LORD and Savior. We pray you
will walk with Jesus all the days
of your life, loving Him more than anyone
or anything else on earth.

We love you and thank Jesus for you~
Papa and Mutti.

*May my prayer be counted as incense before You,
the lifting up of my hands as the evening offering.*
—PSALM 141:2

*Another angel came and stood at the altar,
holding a golden censer; and much
incense was given to him, so that he might add
it to the prayers of all the saints on
the golden altar which was before the
throne. And the smoke of the incense,
with the prayers of the saints, went up before
God out of the angel's hand.*
—REVELATION 8:3-4

CONTENTS

vii	INTRODUCTION
1	JANUARY
35	FEBRUARY
67	MARCH
101	APRIL
135	MAY
169	JUNE
201	JULY
235	AUGUST
269	SEPTEMBER
303	OCTOBER
337	NOVEMBER
369	DECEMBER
403	SCRIPTURE INDEX
405	TOPICAL INDEX
411	ABOUT THE AUTHORS

INTRODUCTION

Wow! What a journey! We never dreamt in 2014, when *The Watchman on the Wall, Vol. 1* was published, that three more volumes would follow. Now every chapter of the Bible has a prayer devotional written for it—that's 1,189 chapters and 1,189 prayers from those chapters. The LORD is so good, and we are grateful for His Word and His faithfulness.

You may have read and prayed through the first three volumes of *The Watchman on the Wall*, or perhaps you are starting with volume 4. Either way, we are excited you are taking seriously God's call to be a watchman on the wall for those you love. Isaiah 62:6-7 says God has appointed watchmen who all day and all night never keep silent. They keep talking and talking to God about Jerusalem. They remind God of His promises, His good Word, and His good name. They refuse to back down or take a break, and they do not give God rest. These watchmen tirelessly pray until God establishes Jerusalem, making her a praise in the earth. The LORD is an establisher, and He not only wants to establish Jerusalem, He wants to establish you and those you love in His faithfulness, holiness, and steadfastness. Do not grow weary, prayer warrior. Take courage and encouragement from what God's Word says about prayer:

*The LORD listened to me that time also; the
LORD was not willing to destroy you.*
—DEUTERONOMY 10:10B

*Then the LORD appeared to Solomon at night
and said to him, "I have heard
your prayer and have chosen this place for
Myself as a house of sacrifice."*
—2 CHRONICLES 7:12

*When he was in distress, he entreated the
LORD his God and humbled himself
greatly before the God of his fathers. When
he prayed to Him, He (God) was
moved by his entreaty and heard his supplication
and brought him again to
Jerusalem to his kingdom. Then Manasseh
knew that the LORD was God.*
—2 CHRONICLES 33:12-13

*So Peter was kept in the prison, but prayer for him was
being made fervently by the church to God. On the very
night when Herod was about to bring him forward,
Peter was sleeping between two soldiers, bound with two
chains, and guards in front of the door were watching over
the prison. And behold, an angel of the LORD suddenly
appeared, and a light shone in the cell; and he struck Peter's
side and woke him up, saying, "Get up quickly."
And his chains fell off his hands. And the angel said to
him, "Gird yourself and put on your sandals."
And he did so. And he said to him, "Wrap your
cloak around you and follow me."
And he went out and continued to follow, and he
did not know that what was being done by the angel
was real, but thought he was seeing a vision.*

When they had passed the first and second guard, they came to the iron gate that leads into the city, which opened for them by itself; and they went out and went along one street, and immediately the angel departed from him. When Peter came to himself, he said, "Now I know for sure that the LORD has sent forth His angel and rescued me from the hand of Herod and from all that the Jewish people were expecting."
—ACTS 12:5-11

Now while I (Daniel) was speaking and praying, and confessing my sin and the sin of my people Israel, and presenting my supplication before the LORD my God in behalf of the holy mountain of my God, I was still speaking in prayer, then the man Gabriel, whom I had seen in the vision previously, came to me in my extreme weariness about the time of the evening offering. He gave me instruction and talked with me and said, "O Daniel, I have now come forth to give you insight with understanding. At the beginning of your supplications the command was issued, and I have come to tell you, for you are highly esteemed; so give heed to the message and gain understanding of the vision.
—DANIEL 9:20-23

Then he said to me, "Do not be afraid, Daniel, for from the first day that you set your heart on understanding this and on humbling yourself before your God, your words were heard, and I have come in response to your words."
—DANIEL 10:12

*Devote yourselves to prayer, keeping alert in
it with an attitude of thanksgiving.*
—COLOSSIANS 4:2

*With all prayer and petition, pray at all times
in the Spirit, and with this in
view, be on the alert with all perseverance
and petition for all the saints.*
—EPHESIANS 6:18

The effective prayer of a righteous man can accomplish much.
—JAMES 5:16B

So, armed with God's Word, let's get started. As you read the Bible, look for verses you want God to fulfill in those you love. You may want to write their names in the margin of your Bible next to the verses you are praying. It is exciting to look back days, months, and years later and reflect on how God is answering those prayers. This will be an exciting year for you and those you love.

We pray Philippians 1:9-11 over you:

*"LORD, let the love of these watchmen on the
wall, these prayer warriors, abound
still more and more in real knowledge and all
discernment, so they may approve
the things that are excellent in order to be sincere
and blameless until the day of Christ.
Fill them with the fruit of righteousness which
comes through You, Jesus Christ.
To Your glory and praise, God~"*

We are praying with you on the Wall~

Ron and Marsha Harvell

January

*On your walls, O Jerusalem,
I have appointed watchmen;
All day and all night they
will never keep silent.
You who remind the LORD,
take no rest for yourselves;
And give Him no rest until He establishes
And makes Jerusalem a
praise in the earth.*
Isaiah 62:6-7, NASB

JANUARY 1

Please read Psalm 118.

Meditate on verse 24.

> *This is the day which the LORD has made;
> let us rejoice and be glad in it.*

Psalm 118 is probably the hymn Jesus and His disciples sang after drinking the last cup of wine at the Passover, the cup representing Christ's blood to be poured out for the forgiveness of sins (Matthew 5:28)[1] Can you imagine Jesus singing these words, knowing He is the psalm's fulfillment?

- The Gate the righteous enter to come to God (v. 20; John 10:7, 9)
- Salvation (v. 21; Luke 2:25-30)
- The Stone the builders rejected who became the chief corner stone (v. 22; 1 Peter 2:6-7)
- The blessed One, coming in the name of the LORD (v. 26; John 12:12-13)
- The Light of the world (v. 27; John 8:12)
- The Passover festival sacrifice (v. 27; 1 Corinthians 5:7)

As Christians, we rejoice in each day the LORD makes, thankful for our salvation through Him.

As a faithful, prayerful watchman (Isaiah 62:6-7), start this New Year praising Jesus with Psalm 118. Verses 1-4 and 24 are written below to get you started.

> *"Thank You, LORD, for You are good; Your lovingkindness is everlasting. Oh, let _____ say, 'Your lovingkindnes is everlasting.' Oh, let everyone in my house say, 'Your lovingkindness is everlasting.' I fear You, LORD, and I say, 'Your lovingkindness is everlasting.' LORD, this is the day which You have made; I will rejoice and be glad in it.
> In Your name, Jesus~"*

---

1. Retrieved from http://hallel.info/psalm-113-118-the-hallel-and-the-passover/

JANUARY 2

Please read 1 Thessalonians 1.

Meditate on verse 8.

> *For the Word of the LORD has sounded forth from you, not only in Macedonia and Achaia, but also in every place your faith toward God has gone forth, so that we have no need to say anything.*

Paul established the church at Thessalonica amid much persecution (Acts 17:1-9). Because of false accusations and physical violence by the Jews, he was sent away from the city (Acts 17:10), and as he journeyed through the rest of Greece, he heard about the faith of this Thessalonian church (vs. 8-10). What an encouragement for Paul to know these persecuted believers were boldly living their faith in Christ! Paul wrote this letter to let them know he knew about their faithfulness and to exhort them to excel still more as they walked with Jesus (1 Thessalonians 4:1).

More than 2,000 years later, Christians are still under severe opposition and persecution. Let Paul's letter to the Thessalonians be God's letter of encouragement to you as you walk with Christ, waiting for His return (v. 10).

Pray 1 Thessalonians 1:7-10 over yourself and those for whom you stand guard as a faithful, prayerful watchman (Isaiah 62:6-7).

> *"LORD, let _____ and me be an example to all the believers and to those who need to believe. Let Your Word sound forth from us in every place our faith toward You has gone forth. We serve You, the living and true God, as we wait for Your Son from heaven, whom You raised from the dead, that is Jesus, who rescues us from the wrath to come. And in Whose name, we pray-"*

JANUARY 3

Please read 1 Thessalonians 2.

Meditate on verse 19.

> *For who is our hope or joy or crown of exultation? Is it not even you, in the presence of our LORD Jesus at His coming?*

Prior to coming to Thessalonica, Paul was beaten and put in prison at Philippi for sharing God's Word (Acts 16:11-24). After his miraculous release, he made his way to this city, where he reasoned with the Thessalonians from the Scriptures, explaining Jesus is the Christ. The result was the same as at Philippi; some were persuaded to follow Jesus, and some persecuted him (Acts 17:1-9).

Why would Paul continue to share God's Word amid such opposition? There was no doubt in Paul's mind that God's Word applied to one's life changes that life for eternity. And, when Christ returns, He will bring with Him those who have believed in Him. Paul's crown of exultation is those who believe in Jesus because he shared God's Word with them.

Will you have a crown of exultation when Christ returns?

Pray 1 Thessalonians 2:12-13 and 19 over yourself and those for whom you stand guard as a faithful, prayerful watchman (Isaiah 62:6-7).

> *"LORD, please help _____ and me walk in a manner worthy of You who calls us into Your own kingdom and glory. Please let _____ receive Your Word which they have heard. Let them accept it, not as the word of men, but for what it really is, Your Word, God, which performs its work in those who believe. May they be our hope and joy and crown of exultation in Your presence, LORD Jesus, when You come. For the glory of Your name~"*

JANUARY 4

Please read 1 Thessalonians 3.

Meditate on verse 8.

For now we really live, if you stand firm in the LORD.

Paul was concerned the Thessalonian Christians were discouraged in their faith and tempted by the deceiver, so he sent Timothy to check on them (vs. 5-7). Imagine Paul's relief to know they were doing well in the LORD (vs. 8-9).

What joy to know those you help grow in Christ are standing firm in Christ! As a faithful, prayerful watchman, do not grow weary in praying for them. Teach them how to walk with Jesus, so they are not lacking in their faith (v. 10). You will really live when you hear and see those you love standing firm in the LORD.

Pray 1 Thessalonians 3:8-13 over yourself and those for whom you stand guard as a faithful, prayerful watchman (Isaiah 62:6-7).

"LORD, I will really live if _____ stands firm in You. I rejoice before You, God, on their account. Please let me see their face and complete what is lacking in their faith. God and Father and Jesus our LORD, please direct my way to them. Cause them to increase and abound in love for one another and for all people, just as I do for them. Establish their hearts without blame in holiness before You, God and Father, at Your coming, LORD Jesus, with all Your saints. For the sake of Your name, Jesus~"

JANUARY 5

Please read 1 Thessalonians 4.

Meditate on verse 13.

> *But we do not want you to be uninformed, brethren, about those who are asleep, so that you will not grieve as do the rest who have no hope.*

As I write this devotional, our entire world is in turmoil because of a virus wreaking havoc in the lives of millions. For those who do not know Jesus, what a truly horrific time it is, for this tiny microbe can infect one's lungs and take one's life in a matter of days, if not hours. Scary, if you do not understand the difference between dying and falling asleep in Jesus. God's Word refers to the bodily death of Christians as:

- Absent from the body and at home with the LORD (2 Corinthians 5:8)
- Asleep in Jesus (1 Thessalonians 4:14)
- Laying aside the earthly dwelling (2 Peter 1:14)

Jesus promises those who believe in Him will live and never die spiritually (John 11:25-26).

God wants you to know what happens when a Christian departs this earth and what happens when Christ returns with His bride, the church (Revelation 19:5-14). Thankfully, we have God's Word to teach us these truths. As you continue to read the devotionals in *The Watchman on the Wall, Vol. 4,* you will read and pray many of the books in the Bible which address The Day of the LORD and Christ's return. What an amazing treasure hunt it will be!

Pray 1 Thessalonians 4:14 over yourselves and those for whom you stand guard as a faithful, prayerful watchman (Isaiah 62:6-7).

> *"Jesus, I believe You died and rose again and will bring with You those who have fallen asleep in You. Please let _____ believe, so they will be with You when You return. In Your name, Jesus."*

JANUARY 6

Please read 1 Thessalonians 5.

Meditate on verses 1-2 and 4.

> *Now as to the times and the epochs, brethren, you have no need of anything to be written to you. For you yourselves know full well that the day of the LORD will come just like a thief in the night. But you, brethren, are not in darkness, that the day would overtake you like a thief.*

The Christians in Thessalonica knew about the day of the LORD, but Paul reminded them of some key truths (v. 1). Observe what a contrast the day will be for believers and nonbelievers:

CHRISTIANS AND THE DAY OF THE LORD	NONCHRISTIANS AND THE DAY OF THE LORD
✧ Will not overtake them like a thief (v. 4)	✧ Comes just like a thief in the night (v. 2)
✧ Light and day (v. 5)	✧ Night and darkness (v. 5)
✧ Alert and sober (v. 6)	✧ Asleep and drunk (v. 7)
✧ Salvation through Jesus Christ (v. 9)	✧ Destruction and wrath (vs. 3, 9)

Who do you know that the day of the LORD would overtake them like a thief in the night? Invite them to join you under the column on the left.

Pray 1 Thessalonians 5:23-24 over yourself and those for whom you stand guard as a faithful, prayerful watchman (Isaiah 62:6-7).

> *"God of peace, sanctify _____ and me entirely and may our spirit and soul and body be preserved complete, without blame at Your coming, LORD Jesus Christ. LORD, You are faithful who calls us, and You will bring it to pass. In Your name, Jesus~"*

JANUARY 7

Please read 2 Thessalonians 1.

Meditate on verses 6-7.

> *For after all, it is only just for God to repay with affliction those who afflict you and to give relief to you who are afflicted, and to us as well, when the LORD Jesus will be revealed from heaven with His mighty angels in flaming fire.*

Paul wrote a second letter to the persecuted church in Thessalonica, continuing to comfort them with descriptions of what will occur on the day of the LORD (v. 7):

- God afflicts those who afflict Christians (v. 6).
- God relieves afflicted believers, revealing the LORD Jesus with His mighty angels in flaming fire (v. 7).
- God deals out retribution to those who do not know Him and do not obey the Gospel of Jesus Christ (v. 8).
- Those who do not know the LORD pay the penalty of eternal destruction away from the presence of God and the glory of His power (v. 9).
- God is glorified in His saints and marveled at among all who believe (10).

What a glorious day for Christians! What a horrific day for unbelievers! Who do you need to tell before it is too late?

Pray 2 Thessalonians 1:11-12 over yourself and those for whom you stand guard as a faithful, prayerful watchman (Isaiah 62:6-7).

> *"LORD, count _____ and me worthy of our calling and fulfill every desire for goodness and work of faith with power, so Your name, LORD Jesus, will be glorified in us, and us in You, according to Your grace, God and LORD Jesus Christ. In Whose name, I pray~"*

JANUARY 8

Please read 2 Thessalonians 2.

Meditate on verses 1-2.

> *Now we request you, brethren, with regard to the coming of our LORD Jesus Christ and our gathering together to Him, that you not be quickly shaken from your composure or be disturbed either by a spirit or a message or a letter as if from us, to the effect that the day of the LORD has come.*

The believers in Thessalonica needed reassurance. False rumors floated around that the day of the LORD had come. The believers feared they missed being gathered to Him, and now faced God's wrath and destruction (1Thessalonians 4:17; 5:3, 9). Paul reassured them of what must occur prior to that day. Keep these truths in mind, so you can correctly recognize the coming of the day of the LORD.

Before the day of the LORD, two things will happen. The apostasy, a worldwide rebellion and falling away from the faith, occurs (v. 3; 1 Timothy 4:1-3; 2 Timothy 3:1-5; 4:3-4). And, the man of lawlessness, the son of destruction, is revealed (v. 3; Daniel 11:36-45). This man of sin acts on behalf of Satan, exalting himself as God and taking his seat in God's temple to be worshiped (vs. 4, 8-10; Revelation 13:1-6).

Look around. Do you see any evidence the day of the LORD may be near?

Pray for those who need to receive the love of the truth before it is too late, using the words from 2 Thessalonians 2:10 and 13-14 as their faithful, prayerful watchman (Isaiah 62:6-7).

> *"LORD, please let _____ receive the love of the truth to be saved. God, choose them for salvation. Sanctify them by the Spirit and faith in the truth. Call them through Your Gospel, that they may gain Your glory, By Your name, LORD Jesus Christ~"*

JANUARY 9

Please read 2 Thessalonians 3.

Meditate on verse 1.

> *Finally, brethren, pray for us that the Word of the LORD will spread rapidly and be glorified, just as it did also with you.*

With the day of the LORD on Paul's mind and on the minds of his readers, he knew it was crucial for God's Word to spread rapidly, bringing salvation to those who would hear and receive it. Paul wrote this letter 2,000 years ago; just imagine how much closer the day of the LORD is to those of us reading it today. "LORD, let Your Word spread rapidly and be glorified in the lives of people before it is too late!"

It is no accident God wanted the prayer devotionals for *Daniel, Joel, Amos, Zephaniah, Malachi, Matthew, 1 & 2 Thessalonians, 1 & 2 Timothy, 1 & 2 Peter,* and *Revelation* written for *The Watchman on the Wall, Volume 4*. They all speak about the day of the LORD. (We did not make this connection until we started writing this fourth volume.) Our world is in the labor pains of Christ's return. Recognize the signs, share the Gospel, and pray with fervency as a faithful, prayerful watchman (Isaiah 62:6-7).

Pray 2 Thessalonians 3:1-3 over those you love.

> *"LORD, let Your Word spread rapidly and be glorified! Please rescue _____ and me from perverse and evil men for not all have faith. But, LORD, You are faithful, and You will strengthen and protect us from the evil one. In Your name, Jesus~"*

JANUARY 10

Please read Numbers 1.

Meditate on verse 53a.

> *But the Levites shall camp around the tabernacle of the testimony, so that there will be no wrath on the congregation of the sons of Israel.*

The LORD commanded Moses and Aaron to number the men of Israel, twenty years and older, who were able to go to war (vs. 2-3). The Levites, however, were exempt from earthly battle (v. 47). Their job was to set up, care for, and guard the tabernacle, the holy place of God's presence in the center of the camp. It was crucial for a Levite to faithfully execute his God-given duties, camping around the tabernacle, so the wrath of God would not be poured out on the Israelites.

As a Christian, God also gives you the high Levitical calling to His priesthood:

> *You also, as living stones, are being built up as a spiritual house for a holy priesthood, to offer up spiritual sacrifices acceptable to God through Jesus Christ... so that you may proclaim the excellencies of Him who has called you out of darkness into His marvelous light.*
> —1 PETER 2:5,9B

As you continue to read the book of Numbers, notice God's instructions to the Levites, making practical applications to your life. Stay faithfully camped around those you love, praying for them and proclaiming the LORD's excellencies to them, so they will choose to be part of the holy priesthood of Christ, rather than experience His wrath.

Use the words from Numbers 1:53-54 to pray over yourself and those for whom you stand guard as a faithful, prayerful watchman (Isaiah 62:6-7).

> *"LORD, I will faithfully camp around others, so there will be no wrath on them. As a spiritual Levite, I shall keep charge of Your Testimony, sharing it with them. Help _____ and me do according to all which You command.*
> *In Your name, Jesus~"*

JANUARY 11

Please read Numbers 2.

Meditate on verse 2.

> *The sons of Israel shall camp, each by his own standard, with the banners of their fathers' households; they shall camp around the tent of meeting at a distance.*

The Israelites set up camp with the tabernacle, the tent of meeting, in the center of camp. God's presence and the worship of Him was at the center of Israelite life. Each tribe had a standard or a flag representing it, and each family in the tribe had a banner. The banner was the sign, the distinguishing mark, of that household.

Think about your life. What would others say is the center of your life? Is there a banner—evidence, proof, a distinguishing mark—that God is the center of your life, and you live to worship Him?

The Hebrew word translated "at a distance" in the meditation verse is *neged*, and it also means: "what is conspicuous, before your face, and in your view."[1] Ask the LORD to be the conspicuous, distinguishing mark on your life.

Use the words from Number 2:2 to pray over yourself and those for whom you stand guard as a faithful, prayerful watchman (Isaiah 62:6-7).

> *"LORD, let _____ and me camp by Your standard, with banners— miraculous signs—of You in our household. Let us camp around Your presence, not at a distance, but in sight of all You are doing. In Your name, Jesus~"*

---

1. Retrieved from www.blueletterbible.org/lang/lexicon/lexicon.cfm?Strongs=H5048&t=NASB

JANUARY 12

Please read Numbers 3.

Meditate on verses 6 and 15.

> *Bring the tribe of Levi near and set them before Aaron the priest, that they may serve him. Number the sons of Levi by their fathers' households, by their families; every male from a month old and upward you shall number.*

Recall God commanded Moses to number all the sons of Israel, twenty years old and older, for the purpose of going to war, with the exception of the Levites (Numbers 1:1-3). Interestingly, God numbered the Levites, starting at the tender age of one month, not twenty years, for the purpose of serving Him.

As a Christian family, a family of spiritual priests and Levites (Revelation 1:6; 5:10), think about the practical applications from Numbers 3. The LORD numbers you from birth to be set before Him to serve Him all the days of your life (v. 6, Galatians 1:15). You are called to serve and care for His congregation, His people (v. 7). Be mindful of the little ones in your family, even those a month old, teaching them what it means to belong to God (vs. 12, 15).

Pray Numbers 3:6-10 over yourself and those for whom you stand guard as a faithful, prayerful watchman (Isaiah 62:6-7).

> *"LORD, bring _____ and me near and set us before You that we may serve You. Let us perform the duties before You and for the whole congregation before the tent of meeting, to do the service of the tabernacle. Let us keep all the furnishings of the tent of meeting, along with the duties of being Your child, to do the service of the tabernacle. As Christians, thank You that You have wholly given us the privilege of being Your priests. Let us faithfully keep Your priesthood.*
> *In Your name, Jesus~"*

JANUARY 13

Please read Numbers 4.

Meditate on verse 49.

> *According to the commandment of the LORD through Moses, they were numbered, everyone by his serving or carrying; thus, these were his numbered men, just as the LORD had commanded Moses.*

God gave 8,580 Levites from the Kohath, Gershon, and Merari families the holy task of carrying (vs. 47-48). They carried things like firepans, forks, shovels, curtains, boards, bars, pillars, and sockets (vs. 14, 31). God devoted 100 verses to their job descriptions and to numbering these servants set apart for Him (Numbers 3:1-4:49). God takes very seriously the carrying of His things.

What or whom has the LORD asked you to carry? Perhaps it is an aging parent or a child who needs special nurturing. Perhaps He has tasked you with carrying the chairs to set up for a Bible study or worship event. Or, maybe He has called you to carry the trash out of your church or home. Be encouraged by the emphasis God places in His Word on numbering the Kohathites, Gershonites, and Merarites for the express purpose of carrying.

Using the words from Numbers 4:49, commit yourself to be one of God's servers and carriers. Pray the words over yourself and those for whom you stand guard as a faithful, prayerful watchman (Isaiah 62:6-7).

> *"LORD, according to Your commandment, please include _____ and me in Your number to serve and carry just as You command.*
> *In Your name, Jesus~"*

JANUARY 14

Please read Numbers 5.

Meditate on verses 5-7.

> *Then the LORD spoke to Moses, saying, "Speak to the sons of Israel, 'When a man or woman commits any of the sins of mankind, acting unfaithfully against the LORD, and that person is guilty, then he shall confess his sins which he has committed, and he shall make restitution in full for his wrong and add to it one-fifth of it and give it to him whom he has wronged.'"*

What an interesting chapter in God's Word! Suffice it to say, you may think you can get away with your sins; however, God knows when you go astray, are unfaithful, harbor jealousy, and defile yourself. And, He has ways to make your sins and guilt known; therefore, be quick to confess, quick to repent, and quick to make restitution. Come to God, asking Him to reveal areas where you have gone astray and defiled yourself. Let Him wash you clean with His forgiveness and keep you from sinning. Let the LORD free you of your guilt.

As a faithful, prayerful watchman (Isaiah 62:6-7), pray for God to keep you and those you love from going astray and being unfaithful to Him (v. 12) and use the words from Numbers 5:6-7 to start your personal prayer of confession.

> *"LORD, do not let _____ and me go astray and be unfaithful to You and our spouse. Please forgive me for committing the sins of mankind, specifically for committing the sin of _____. I have acted unfaithfully against You, LORD. I am guilty. I confess my sins that I have committed, and I will make restitution in full for my wrong and add one-fifth to it, and I will give it to the person I have wronged. Thank You for forgiveness in Your name, Jesus~"*

JANUARY 15

Please read Numbers 6. Notice the repeated words: *dedicate and separate*. Meditate on verse 8.

> *All the days of his separation, he is holy to the LORD.*

Men and women in Israel could choose to dedicate themselves to the LORD (v. 2). This separation to God came with promises to behave in ways indicative of being holy and belonging to Him.

Ask the LORD to convict you of areas where you need to separate yourself from the ways of the world and dedicate yourself to God, for this Old Testament passage addressing holiness is applied to New Testament believers.

> *Do not be bound together with unbelievers; for what partnership have righteousness and lawlessness, or what fellowship has light with darkness? Or what harmony has Christ with Belial (Satan), or what has a believer in common with an unbeliever? Or what agreement has the temple of God with idols? For we are the temple of the living God; just as God said, "I WILL DWELL IN THEM AND WALK AMONG THEM; AND I WILL BE THEIR GOD, AND THEY SHALL BE MY PEOPLE. Therefore, COME OUT FROM THEIR MIDST AND BE SEPARATE," says the LORD. "AND DO NOT TOUCH WHAT IS UNCLEAN; and I will welcome you. And I will be a Father to you, and you shall be sons and daughters to Me," says the LORD Almighty.*
> —2 CORINTHIANS 6:14-18

Pray Numbers 6:8 and 24-27 over yourself and those for whom you stand guard as a faithful, prayerful watchman (Isaiah 62:6-7).

> *"LORD, keep _____ and me separate and holy to You all our days. LORD, bless us and keep us. LORD, make Your face shine on us and be gracious to us. LORD, lift up Your countenance on us and give us peace. LORD, put Your name on us and bless us. Because of Your name, Jesus~"*

JANUARY 16

Please read Numbers 7.

Meditate on verse 11.

> *Then the LORD said to Moses, "Let them present their offering, one leader each day, for the dedication of the altar."*

Perhaps as you read the 89 verses of Numbers 7, you thought Moses could have summarized the 12-day offering event, since each day consisted of the exact same offering; the only difference was the leader and the tribe from whom the offering came. Keep in mind, Moses wrote what God told him to write; therefore, this lengthy chapter gives insight into God and how important offerings are to Him. God wanted the details of each day carefully recorded. Thankfully Moses obeyed.

The word translated as "offering" in this chapter is the Hebrew word, *qorban*. It is used 28 times in Numbers 7 and means "a sacrificial present."[1]

Think about what you offer the LORD in terms of time, talent, money, belongings, etc. Would the LORD call your offerings, *qorban*, a sacrificial present? Ponder this exhortation from the New Testament:

> *Therefore, I urge you, brethren, by the mercies of God, to present your bodies a living and holy sacrifice, acceptable to God, which is your spiritual service of worship.*
> —ROMANS 12:1

As the temple of the Holy Spirit and a faithful, prayerful watchman (1 Corinthians 3:16; Isaiah 62:6-7), dedicate yourself to the LORD, using the words from Numbers 7:1 and 11.

> *"LORD, as Your tabernacle, anoint[2] and consecrate[3] me. I present myself as the offering in dedication to You. Because of Your name, Jesus~"*

---

1. Retrieved from www.blueletterbible.org/lang/lexicon/lexicon.cfm?page=2&strongs=H7133&t=NASB#lexResults
2. Anoint means to besmear or cover.
3. Consecrate means to set apart, dedicate, and prepare for special purpose.

JANUARY 17

Please read Numbers 8.

Meditate on verses 15-16. The LORD is speaking.

> *"Then after that the Levites may go in to serve the tent of meeting. But you shall cleanse them and present them as a wave offering, for they are wholly given to Me from among the sons of Israel. I have taken them for Myself instead of every first issue of the womb, the firstborn of all the sons of Israel."*

Chosen by God to serve in the tent of meeting, the Levites were responsible for setting up the tabernacle and caring for its furniture and utensils. God set them apart for Himself to serve Him.

When you become a Christian, God also chooses you and sets you apart for Himself:

> *So as those who have been chosen of God…do your work heartily, as for the LORD rather than for men, knowing that from the LORD you will receive the reward of the inheritance. It is the LORD Christ whom you serve.*
> —COLOSSIANS 3:12, 23-24

Wholly give yourself to the LORD (v. 16), asking Him to qualify you to perform every act of service faithfully in His name (v. 11).

As a faithful, prayerful watchman (Isaiah 62:6-7), use the words from Numbers 8:6, 11, and 16 to dedicate yourself and those you love to the LORD.

> *"LORD, take _____ and me and cleanse us and present us before You as an offering that we may qualify to perform service for You. We give ourselves wholly to You; please take us for Yourself. In Your name, Jesus~"*

JANUARY 18

Please read Numbers 9.

Meditate on verse 23.

> *At the command of the LORD, they camped, and at the command of the LORD, they set out; they kept the LORD's charge, according to the command of the LORD through Moses.*

"At the command of the LORD" is a repeated phrase in this chapter. The Israelites moved, set-up camp, remained camped, and set out at the LORD's command. They didn't presume upon God's will; they waited to hear from Him about where and when to go. God literally gave the marching orders. "Even when the cloud lingered over the tabernacle for many days, the sons of Israel would keep the LORD's charge and not set out" (v. 19).

Can the same be said about you and your loved ones? Do you obey the LORD and set out when He says, "Move," or do you become impatient with God's timing, rushing ahead of His plans for your life?

Ask the LORD to spiritually tune you to hear His commands and obey what He says. As you wait for God's move, embrace the time by lingering in His presence, learning more about Him and gaining strength for the journey.

Commit yourself and those you love to the LORD's command by praying Numbers 9:22-23 as a faithful, prayerful watchman (Isaiah 62:6-7).

> *"LORD, whether it is two days or a month or a year, let _____ and me linger in Your presence. May we remain camped with You and not set out without You. At Your command, we will camp, and at Your command, we will set out. We will keep Your charge according to Your command. In Your name, LORD Jesus~"*

JANUARY 19

Please read Numbers 10.

Meditate on verse 33.

> *Thus, they set out from the mount of the LORD three days' journey, with the ark of the covenant of the LORD journeying in front of them for the three days, to seek out a resting place for them.*

Notice the repeated phrase "set out" in Numbers 10. The LORD gave specific instructions for setting out or journeying with Him. After leaving Egypt, the children of Israel remained camped at Mount Sinai for over a year; they were not to set out on a journey unless led by the LORD. Finally, on the twentieth day of the second month of the second year, after leaving Egypt, the Israelites moved out according to the LORD's command with His presence leading them (vs. 11-13, 33).

It is important to journey with God leading you, being careful to set out at His command rather than your own whims and desires. Journeying with the LORD brings confidence as He guides your steps and protects you along the way. Ask Him to make it as obvious as the blowing of a trumpet for when and where you are to go every moment of the day.

Pray Numbers 10:35, Moses' prayer for God's protection, over yourself and those for whom you stand guard as a faithful, prayerful watchman (Isaiah 62:6-7).

> *"Rise up, O LORD, as _____ and I set out with You! And let Your enemies be scattered and let those who hate You flee before You. We follow in Your name, Jesus~"*

JANUARY 20

Please read Numbers 11.

Meditate on verse 1.

> *Now the people became like those who complain of adversity in the hearing of the LORD, and when the LORD heard it, His anger was kindled, and the fire of the LORD burned among them and consumed some of the outskirts of the camp.*

Oh, the whining and complaining in this chapter! Despite being miraculously freed from slave-owners, the Israelites wistfully longed for Egyptian fish (v. 5). Despite being hand-picked by God to lead His people, Moses bemoaned God's calling, making it a personal burden (v. 11). Despite the refreshing sound of prophecy amongst a grumbling camp, a young man complained to Moses about the Spirit-led act (vs. 26-29). And, the chapter ends with a bunch of grumblers greedily gathering God's generous provision of quail, angering the LORD to such a degree He struck and killed them (v. 33). This place of grumbling and greed was named Kibroth-hattaavah, which means "graves of greediness" (v. 34).[1] What a poignant picture of greediness being an open grave desiring to consume you!

Allow God's Word to examine you for areas of greed and grumbling. Repent quickly and determine to live in continual praise and thanksgiving to God for His provision and calling on your life and the lives of those around you.

Pray for Numbers 11:1 not to describe you and those for whom you stand guard as a faithful, prayerful watchman (Isaiah 62:6-7).

> *"Do not let _____ and me become like those who complain of adversity in Your hearing, LORD. We do not want Your anger kindled and Your fire to burn among us and consume us. We will praise You by Your Spirit, Jesus~"*

---

1. Retrieved from *The New Inductive Study Bible* @ 2000 Precept Ministries International. pg. 242.

JANUARY 21

Please read Numbers 12.

Meditate on verses 1-2.

> *Then Miriam and Aaron spoke against Moses because of the Cushite woman whom he had married (for he had married a Cushite woman); and they said, "Has the LORD indeed spoken only through Moses? Has He not spoken through us as well?" And the LORD heard it.*

Oops! The LORD heard Miriam and Aaron grumble against Moses, and He held them responsible for their sinful words. Amazingly, faithful, humble Moses interceded on behalf of those who spoke ill of him. "Oh, LORD, give us a faithful, humble heart like Moses!"

The LORD hears what we say. The LORD sees what we do. The LORD knows what we think. I wonder if Miriam and Aaron knew God was listening when they complained about Moses. I wonder if they would have stopped themselves from saying the regrettable if they had thought about what was said in the presence of God. I wonder… I wonder if knowing this story will make a difference in your life and mine. Will knowing God hears, sees, and cares, cause us to pause and consider the consequences the next time we are tempted to grumble about others? I pray it does! I pray it will keep us from sinning with our mouths (Psalm 39:1).

Use the words from Numbers 12:11 and 13, asking God to forgive and heal you and those for whom you stand guard as a faithful, prayerful watchman (Isaiah 62:6-7).

> *"Oh, my LORD, I beg You, do not account this sin to _____ and me in which we have acted foolishly and in which we have sinned. O God, heal us, I pray! In Your name, Jesus~"*

JANUARY 22

Please read Numbers 13.

Meditate on verses 27-28 and 30.

> *Thus, they told him, and said, "We went into the land where you sent us; and it certainly does flow with milk and honey, and this is its fruit. Nevertheless, the people who live in the land are strong, and the cities are fortified and very large; and moreover, we saw the descendants of Anak there." Then Caleb quieted the people before Moses and said, "We should by all means go up and take possession of it, for we will surely overcome it."*

With whom do you relate to more in this story—confident Caleb or the spineless spies? The very first words of the story are from God's lips, promising to give the Israelites this incredible land (vs. 1-2). Yet, after spying out the land, the men returned with their eyes fixed on giants instead of Almighty God. The consequences of their faithless report were disastrous.

What has God told you to do that makes you squirm in fear because it requires you to function in His strength and not your own? Has God given you a vision for your family that is impossible to achieve without Him? Ask God to make you a faith-filled, Christ-confident Caleb. Ask Him to give you His perspective on His will for your life. Do not make decisions based on fear; make them based on God's promises, knowing nothing is too difficult for Him (Jeremiah 32:17).

As a faithful, prayerful watchman (Isaiah 62:6-7), pray Numbers 13:30 over yourself and those you love to be obedient to God's commands.

> *"LORD, at Your command, _____ and I should by all means go up and take possession of what You tell us, for we will surely overcome it. With Your power, Jesus~"*

JANUARY 23

Please read Numbers 14.

Meditate on verse 11.

> *The LORD said to Moses, "How long will this people spurn Me? And how long will they not believe in Me, despite all the signs which I have performed in their midst?"*

The consequences of grumbling disobedience were severe for the Israelites. Instead of taking possession of God's abundant promised land, He sentenced them to wander in the wilderness for 40 years, until every male, twenty years old and older, died (vs. 28-29). Only Joshua and Caleb were spared God's judgment because they did not complain and distrust the LORD. Imagine the women and children burying their husbands, brothers, fathers, and grandfathers for 40 years, until all of the unfaithful complainers were dead. What a needless tragedy—the children suffered for 40 years because of their fathers' unfaithfulness (v. 33)!

As you take God's Word to heart, commit to living in thankful obedience with the LORD instead of in discontented rebellion to Him. Ask God to make you like Joshua and Caleb, so your family does not suffer for your unfaithfulness.

This chapter is rich with verses to pray over yourself and your loved ones. Pray Numbers 14:9, 17, 24, and 33, plus other verses you find, as a faithful, prayerful watchman (Isaiah 62:6-7).

> *"LORD, do not let _____ and me rebel against You. Do not let us fear the people of the land. LORD, You are with us; do not let us fear people. Now I pray, let Your power be great in my family, just as You have declared! Make us like Your servant Caleb who had a different spirit and followed You fully. Make us faithful, so our children do not suffer for our unfaithfulness. Because You are faithful, Jesus~"*

JANUARY 24

Please read Numbers 15.

Meditate on verse 39. The LORD is speaking.

> *"It shall be a tassel for you to look at and remember all the commandments of the LORD, so as to do them and not follow after your own heart and your own eyes, after which you played the harlot."*

Have you ever been given this advice: "Follow your heart"? Or have you ever said, "My heart told me to…"? This is what God says about the heart:

> *The heart is more deceitful than all else and is desperately sick; who can understand it?*
> —JEREMIAH 17:9

> *Yet they did not obey or incline their ear but walked in their own counsels and in the stubbornness of their evil heart, and went backward and not forward.*
> —JEREMIAH 7:24

God says **do not** follow your heart because it is deceitful. However, when you delight yourself in God and His Word, He will give your heart His desires (Psalm 37:4), so you can move forward with Him instead of backward.

Pray Numbers 15:39-41 over yourself and those for whom you stand guard as a faithful, prayerful watchman (Isaiah 62:6-7).

> *"LORD, help _____ and me remember all Your commandments so as to do them and not follow after our own heart and our own eyes. Do not let us play the harlot but help us remember to do all Your commandments and be holy to You, God. You are the LORD our God who brought us out from slavery to sin to be our God. You are the LORD our God, Jesus~"*

JANUARY 25

Please read Numbers 16.

Meditate on verses 4, 22a, and 45b.

> *When Moses heard this, he fell on his face. But they fell on their faces. Then they fell on their faces.*

Three times in this chapter you see Moses facedown before the LORD. He fell on his face because people spoke evil, threatening words to him, and twice, he and Aaron fell on their faces when God threatened to destroy the Israelites (vs. 1-4, 20-22, 41-45). This face to the ground prayer position says, "LORD, I really need Your help!" Moses knew he needed to speak God's words to rebellious Korah not his own retaliatory comments. Moses knew to approach God in humility on behalf of the people, begging God to spare them.

What is your first response to someone who is threatening you or your loved ones? Fall on your face before God, seeking His help and wisdom in the distressful situation. Fall on your face before God, asking Him to help you and your family repent and live holy to Him.

As a faithful, prayerful watchman (Isaiah 62:6-7), fall on your face and start praying with Numbers 16:22.

> *"O God, God of the spirits of all flesh, when one man sins, will You be angry with the entire congregation? God, please do not be angry with _____ and me. (Stay on your face and continue talking to God about your life situations.) For the sake of Your name, Jesus~"*

JANUARY 26

Please read Numbers 17.

Meditate on verses 7-8.

> *So, Moses deposited the rods before the LORD in the tent of the testimony. Now on the next day Moses went into the tent of the testimony; and behold, the rod of Aaron for the house of Levi had sprouted and put forth buds and produced blossoms, and it bore ripe almonds.*

Imagine 12 rods, 12 lifeless walking sticks, being placed in the tabernacle for a day; within 24 hours, one of those dead rods miraculously sprouts and produces ripe almonds. Incredible! That is exactly what happened to Aaron's rod when it was placed in the presence of God. There could be no doubt among the Israelites whom God had chosen to lead His people.

Aaron's rod is a picture of your soul. Apart from Christ, you are lifeless and dead, but when you encounter the presence of God, you are made miraculously alive—sprouting, putting forth buds, producing blossoms, and bearing ripe almonds. Amazing!

Ask the LORD to make you and those you love like Aaron's rod, producing fruit for His glory. Pray Numbers 17:7-8 and 11 over yourself and those for whom you stand guard as a faithful, prayerful watchman (Isaiah 62:6-7).

> *"LORD, I deposit _____ and me before You. Please make us sprout, put forth buds, and produce blossoms. Let us bear ripe almonds. May it be said of us: 'They did just as the LORD commanded, so they did.' For the glory of Your name, Jesus~"*

JANUARY 27

Please read Numbers 18.

Meditate on verse 5.

> *So, you shall attend to the obligations of the sanctuary and the obligations of the altar, so that there will no longer be wrath on the sons of Israel.*

Aaron and his sons were Levites, the tribe of Israel chosen by God to serve as priests and workers in the tabernacle. God told them to attend to their obligation He had given them (vs. 3-5). He expected the Levites to be watchmen, guarding and protecting the people and ministries He placed in their care. What a sacred obligation!

As a Christian, God considers you to be one of his priests (Revelation 1:6), a watchman guarding and protecting those He places in your care. What a sacred obligation!

Ask the LORD to help you attend well to your obligations with His kind, caring, and selfless heart.

Pray Numbers 18:5 over yourself and other "Levites," asking God to help you attend to your obligations as faithful, prayerful watchmen (Isaiah 62:6-7).

> *"LORD, help _____ and me attend to the obligations of our family and the obligations of Your other ministries, so there will no longer be wrath on my family and others. In Your name, Jesus~"*

JANUARY 28

Please read Numbers 19.

Meditate on verses 1-4.

> *Then the LORD spoke to Moses and Aaron, saying, "This is the statute of the law which the LORD has commanded, saying, 'Speak to the sons of Israel that they bring you an unblemished red heifer in which is no defect and on which a yoke has never been placed. You shall give it to Eleazar the priest, and it shall be brought outside the camp and be slaughtered in his presence. Next Eleazar the priest shall take some of its blood with his finger and sprinkle some of its blood toward the front of the tent of meeting seven times.'"*

Before the people came to the tabernacle to offer an unblemished lamb as a sacrifice for sins, God required a red heifer be sacrificed outside the camp. The people needed a red heifer before they could even come close to the tabernacle, the dwelling place of God. As you ponder this requirement to come near to God, read these words from the book of *Hebrews*:

> *Therefore, Jesus also, that He might sanctify the people through His own blood, suffered outside the gate. So, let us go out to Him outside the camp, bearing His reproach.*
> —HEBREWS 13:12-13

Jesus, the Lamb of God who takes away the sin of the world (John 1:29), is also the red heifer you need to even begin drawing near to God. Jesus fulfilled all of the sacrificial requirements of the Law. As you spend this day walking with the LORD, thank Him for all He did to make your relationship with Him possible.

As a faithful, prayerful watchman (Isaiah 62:6-7), thank Jesus for fulfilling the sacrificial requirements of Numbers 19:2-3 and pray for those who need Jesus to be their red heifer.

> *"Jesus, thank You for being the red heifer slaughtered outside the camp. LORD, _____ needs to You to be their red heifer, so they can come near to God through You.*
> *Please save them in Your name, Jesus~"*

JANUARY 29

Please read Numbers 20.

Meditate on verse 12.

> *But the LORD said to Moses and Aaron, "Because you have not believed Me, to treat Me as holy in the sight of the sons of Israel, therefore you shall not bring this assembly into the land which I have given them."*

This was not the first time the Israelites grumbled about their water situation. The first was recorded in Exodus 17 when God told Moses to strike the rock once with his rod (Exodus 17:2-6). Now, more than a year later, God told Moses to speak to the rock; Moses disobeyed, striking it twice. Moses' disobedience had severe consequences: he would not be allowed to enter the Promised Land, and he marred God's picture of Messiah.

> *For I do not want you to be unaware, brethren, that our fathers ... all drank the same spiritual drink, for they were drinking from a spiritual rock which followed them; and the rock was Christ.*
> —1 CORINTHIANS 10:1, 4

> *By this will we have been sanctified through the offering of the body of Jesus Christ once for all.*
> —HEBREWS 10:10

This rock was to be struck only once for the people to receive life-giving water because according to God's Word, the rock was Christ, who would only need to die once for the forgiveness of sins. When Moses struck the rock twice, he gave the Jewish people an unholy picture of Messiah, that His once for all sacrifice was not enough to take away sins.

Let these amazing truths from God's Word soak in and pray Numbers 20:12 over yourself and those for whom you stand guard as a faithful, prayerful watchman (Isaiah 62:6-7).

> *"LORD, may _____ and I always believe You and treat You as holy in the sight of all people. Because You are holy, Jesus~"*

JANUARY 30

Please read Numbers 21.

Meditate on verse 8.

> *Then the LORD said to Moses, "Make a fiery serpent and set it on a standard; and it shall come about, that everyone who is bitten, when he looks at it, he will live."*

Thankfully, Moses obeyed God's instructions for providing a cure to the calamity caused by sin. He made a bronze image of the thing killing the people. All they had to do was look at it in order to live. In human reasoning, it seems an odd thing to do, but God's ways are not our ways (Isaiah 55:8), and just like the life-giving rock in Numbers 20, this serpent on a stick was actually a foreshadowing picture of Messiah.

> *As Moses lifted up the serpent in the wilderness, even so must the Son of Man be lifted up; so that whoever believes will in Him have eternal life.*
> —JOHN 3:14-15

> *He made Him who knew no sin to be sin on our behalf, so that we might become the righteousness of God in Him.*
> —2 CORINTHIANS 5:21

In obedient faith, the people had to look up at the serpent, the thing killing them, in order to live. In obedient faith, you must look up at Jesus, who became the sin that will kill you, in order to be saved.

Ponder the enormity of God becoming your sin and taking the punishment. Then, look to Him, and as a faithful, prayerful watchman (Isaiah 62:6-7), confess your sins by praying Numbers 21:7.

> *"LORD, I have sinned because I have spoken against You and against _____. Jesus, please intercede for me and remove these sins from me. (Continue confessing your sins to the LORD.) Thank You for forgiveness in Your name, Jesus~"*

JANUARY 31

Please read Numbers 22.

Meditate on verse 12.

> *God said to Balaam, "Do not go with them; you shall not curse the people, for they are blessed."*

What a convicting chapter from God's Word! Have you ever known what God wanted you to do, yet you hoped to tweak His plans? So, you started saying and doing things disobedient to God, convincing yourself He was okay with what you were doing, but in the end, God was not okay at all; in fact, He was angry, encountering you as an adversary (vs. 19-22). And, when you came to your senses, asking forgiveness and hoping to get back into the LORD's plan, God made you stay on your self-willed path and finish the course (vs. 34-35). "LORD, forgive us! Keep us from sinning!"

You may want to reread this chapter, noticing when Balaam started disobeying God and what enticed him to sin. Learn well from Balaam's rebellion, asking the LORD to keep you on His path for your life.

Use the words from Numbers 22:12, 20, 22, and 34 to pray over yourself and those for whom you stand guard as a faithful, prayerful watchman (Isaiah 62:6-7).

> *"LORD, help _____ and me obey when You say, 'Do not go with them.' Please let us be blessed by You; let no one curse us. Help us do only the word which You speak to us. God, we do not want You to be angry with us and become an adversary against us. LORD, we have sinned; please allow us to turn back from what displeases You. In Your name, Jesus~"*

FEBRUARY

*On your walls, O Jerusalem,
I have appointed watchmen;
All day and all night they
will never keep silent.
You who remind the LORD,
take no rest for yourselves;
And give Him no rest until He establishes
And makes Jerusalem a
praise in the earth.*
ISAIAH 62:6-7, NASB

FEBRUARY 1

Please read Numbers 23.

Meditate on verses 19-20.

> *God is not a man, that He should lie, nor a son of man, that He should repent; has He said, and will He not do it? Or has He spoken, and will He not make it good? Behold, I have received a command to bless; when He has blessed, then I cannot revoke it.*

King Balak really wanted Balaam to curse the Israelites for him. But, no matter how much he begged and bribed Balaam, Balaam knew he could not speak a word against God's people.

Be encouraged by the story of God, Balaam, Balak, and Israel. A human cannot "curse whom God has not cursed nor denounce what the LORD has not denounced" (v. 8). If you belong to Jesus, you cannot be cursed by man. God does not want you to be afraid of people; He wants you living confidently in Him (Proverbs 14:26).

> *In God I have put my trust; I shall not be afraid.*
> *What can mere man do to me?*
> —PSALM 56:4B

Pray Numbers 23:8, 10, 12, and 19 over yourself and those for whom you stand guard as a faithful, prayerful watchman (Isaiah 62:6-7).

> *"LORD, please let _____ and me never be cursed or denounced by You or anyone. Let us die the death of the upright. Make us careful to speak what You put in our mouths. God, thank You that You are not a man that You should lie, not a son of man, that You should repent. You have said, and You will do it. You have spoken, and You will make it good. Because of Your name, Jesus~"*

FEBRUARY 2

Please read Numbers 24.

Meditate on verse 13.

> *Though Balak were to give me his house full of silver and gold,*
> *I could not do anything contrary to the command of*
> *the LORD, either good or bad, of my own accord.*
> *What the LORD speaks, that I will speak.*

Balaam spoke what God commanded him to speak, but, recall he did not do what the LORD first commanded. God told him not to go with King Balak's men (Numbers 22:12). However, Balaam badgered God until God let him get what he wanted. For three chapters, you have read the frustrating conversation between Balaam and Balak. Finally, Balak bullies Balaam by saying he would have honored him greatly, yet God has withheld that honor from Balaam (v. 11). Isn't it interesting that Balak's words are often echoed today against Christians refusing to compromise God's Word.

Learn well from the story of Balaam. When God says, "Do not go there," obey immediately and do not be tempted to get God to change His mind. When people try to make you say or do things contrary to the Bible, do not succumb to their bullying tactics; ask God to give you His strength to stand firm in His Word.

Pray Numbers 24:1 and 13 over yourself and those for whom you stand guard as a faithful, prayerful watchman (Isaiah 62:6-7).

> *"LORD, may it please You to bless _____ and*
> *me. Do not let us go where You do not want us to go. Keep*
> *our faces set toward You! Even if someone were to give us*
> *his house full of silver and gold, do not let us do anything*
> *contrary to Your command, LORD, either good or bad, of*
> *our own accord. What You speak, that we will speak!*
> *In Your name, Jesus~"*

FEBRUARY 3

Please read Numbers 25.

Meditate on verses 1-2 and Revelation 2:14.

> *While Israel remained at Shittim, the people began to play the harlot with the daughters of Moab. For they invited the people to the sacrifices of their gods, and the people ate and bowed down to their gods.*

> *"But I (Jesus) have a few things against you, because you have there some who hold the teaching of Balaam, who kept teaching Balak to put a stumbling block before the sons of Israel, to eat things sacrificed to idols and to commit acts of immorality."*

Balaam may not have spoken a curse against Israel, but he taught King Balak how to make the people sin. Numbers 25 is the graphic picture of God's judgment poured out on the Israelites. As the leaders were executed for worshiping Baal and 24,000 Israelites were dying by plague, Zimri, the son of a prominent Israelite leader, had the audacity to publicly engage in sexual immorality with Cozbi, the daughter of a prominent Midianite leader. Phineas, the grandson of Aaron the priest, speared the couple to death as they committed their affair. God was pleased with Phineas and pronounced a great blessing over him because he took an obvious stand for God and His holiness.

As you take God's Word to heart, ask the LORD to not let you be a Balaam, causing people to sin. Ask God to make you a Phineas, making a bold stand for Christ and His Word.

Pray Numbers 25:12-13 over yourself and those for whom you stand guard as a faithful, prayerful watchman (Isaiah 62:6-7).

> *"LORD, as _____ and I act like Phineas, please give us Your covenant of peace. Let it be for us and our descendants, a covenant of a perpetual priesthood because we are jealous for You, God. You are our atonement, Jesus~"*

FEBRUARY 4

Please read Numbers 26.

Meditate on verses 63-65.

> *These are those who were numbered by Moses and Eleazar the priest, who numbered the sons of Israel in the plains of Moab by the Jordan at Jericho. But among these there was not a man of those who were numbered by Moses and Aaron the priest, who numbered the sons of Israel in the wilderness of Sinai. For the LORD had said of them, "They shall surely die in the wilderness." And not a man was left of them, except Caleb the son of Jephunneh and Joshua the son of Nun.*

Nearly 40 years passed since God had Moses number the males twenty years old and older—those men able to go to war (Numbers 1:1-3; 26:2). Tragically, the men in the first census (except for Joshua and Caleb) were not included in this second census because they were dead:

> *"Say to them, 'As I live,' says the LORD, 'just as you have spoken in My hearing, so I will surely do to you; your corpses will fall in this wilderness, even all your numbered men, according to your complete number from twenty years old and upward, who have grumbled against Me.'"*
> —NUMBERS 14:28-29

And, because those men died, Israel had 1,820 fewer men than when they left Egypt 40 years earlier (Numbers 1:46; 26:51). Oh, the consequences of sin!

Notice in the first census, the Levites were not numbered at all because their job was to care for the tabernacle rather than go to war (Numbers 1:47-53). In the second census, every Levite male from a month old was numbered (v. 62). As a faithful, prayerful watchman (Isaiah 62:6-7), pray for God to number your loved ones from the time they are born as belonging to Him, using the words from Numbers 26:62.

> *"LORD, please number _____ and me as Yours. Because You are our inheritance, Jesus~"*

FEBRUARY 5

Please read Numbers 27.

Meditate on verses 12-14.

> *Then the LORD said to Moses, "Go up to this mountain of Abarim, and see the land which I have given to the sons of Israel. When you have seen it, you too will be gathered to your people, as Aaron your brother was; for in the wilderness of Zin, during the strife of the congregation, you rebelled against My command to treat Me as holy before their eyes at the water." (These are the waters of Meribah of Kadesh in the wilderness of Zin.)*

Kadesh—it was there the Israelites chose to doubt God and focus on giants (Numbers 13:25-14:38). God punished them severely for their unbelief (Numbers 26:64-65). It was also at Kadesh that Moses did not believe God nor treat Him as holy, twice striking the rock to get water for the people instead of speaking to it (Numbers 20:7-13). God severely punished Moses for his disobedient unbelief as well; he was not allowed to lead the Israelites into the promised land (vs. 12-14).

Be mindful when God brings you to "Kadesh," the place of decision to believe and obey Him. It will be a place requiring you to wholeheartedly trust God despite overwhelming circumstances. It will be a place requiring you to humbly acknowledge God's holiness, so others can see that salvation comes from Him.

Notice Moses' heart for the people. If Moses could not lead them into the land, he wanted God to give them a good leader to take his place. Pray Moses' prayer from Numbers 27:16-17 over a church for whom you stand guard as a faithful, prayerful watchman (Isaiah 62:6-7).

> *"LORD, the God of the spirits of all flesh, appoint a man over the congregation who will go out and come in before them and who will lead them out and bring them in, so that the congregation of the LORD will not be like sheep which have no shepherd. For the sake of Your church, Jesus~"*

FEBRUARY 6

Please read Numbers 28.

Meditate on verses 3 and 6.

> *This is the offering by fire which you shall offer to the LORD: two male lambs one year old without defect as a continual burnt offering every day. It is a continual burnt offering which was ordained in Mount Sinai as a soothing aroma, an offering by fire to the LORD.*

God required the Israelites to daily present two perfect, unblemished lambs as a continual burnt offering. This offering was to be made to God at all times, without interruption.

Picture yourself living under that law, daily finding two faultless lambs to offer to God to cover your sins. As the enormity of that task sinks in, thank Jesus for being the perfect Lamb of God who takes away the sin of the world (John 1:29).

> *For the Law… can never, by the same sacrifices which they offer continually year by year, make perfect those who draw near. But in those sacrifices, there is a reminder of sins year by year. We have been sanctified through the offering of the body of Jesus Christ once for all. He, having offered one sacrifice for sins for all time, … has perfected for all time those who are sanctified.*
> —HEBREWS 10:1, 3, 10, 12, 14

As a faithful, prayerful watchman (Isaiah 62:6-7), pray Numbers 28:22 over those who need Jesus to be their sin offering and thank Him for making atonement[1] for you.

> *"LORD, thank You for being my sin offering to make atonement for me. Please let _____ receive You as their sin offering to make atonement for them. Because You are the perfect sin offering, Jesus~"*

---

1. Atonement is the Hebrew word *kaphar*, and it means "to cover, to cancel, to appease, to cleanse sin with the blood of a sacrifice." Retrieved from www.blueletterbible.org/lang/lexicon/lexicon.cfm?Strongs=H3722&t=NASB

FEBRUARY 7

Please read Numbers 29.

Meditate on verse 7.

Then on the tenth day of this seventh month you shall have a holy convocation, and you shall humble yourselves; you shall not do any work.

Have you ever thought about rest being an act of humility? Pride motivates people to work all the time, doing more than those around them and resenting those not as productive as they.

Rest is important to God. After creating the world in six days, He rested on the seventh day, setting an example for us to obey.

Remember the sabbath day, to keep it holy. Six days you shall labor and do all your work, but the seventh day is a sabbath of the LORD your God; you shall not do any work… For in six days the LORD made the heavens and the earth, the sea and all that is in them, and rested on the seventh day; therefore, the LORD blessed the sabbath day and made it holy.
—EXODUS 20:8-11

Ask the LORD to show you areas where pride drives you to work laboriously rather than rest in Him. Do you ever cancel your daily quiet time with God because your to-do list is long? Do you work an extra hour hoping to get ahead instead of giving your family the attention they desperately crave? Do you justify the world's way of keeping the sabbath, working to get caught up, participating in sporting events, getting the shopping and laundry done…?

Pray Numbers 29:7 over yourself and those for whom you stand guard as a faithful, prayerful watchman (Isaiah 62:6-7).

"LORD, help _____ and me humble ourselves and not do any work when You give the command to rest. In Your name, Jesus~"

FEBRUARY 8

Please read Numbers 30.

Meditate on verses 1b-2.

> *This is the word which the LORD has commanded.*
> *"If a man makes a vow to the LORD, or takes an oath to*
> *bind himself with a binding obligation, he shall not*
> *violate his word; he shall do according to all*
> *that proceeds out of his mouth."*

Perhaps you are surprised when others keep their word, doing what they say they will do. Perhaps you struggle with carrying through on promises, leaving others disappointed. Meditate on these Bible verses:

> *For my mouth will utter truth; and wickedness is an*
> *abomination to my lips. All the utterances of my mouth are in*
> *righteousness; there is nothing crooked or perverted in them.*
> —PROVERBS 8:7-8

> *The mouth of the righteous is a fountain of life,*
> *but the mouth of the wicked conceals violence.*
> —PROVERBS 10:11

> *The LORD is my portion; I have promised to keep Your words.*
> —PSALM 119:57

Ask the LORD to help you be a person of integrity who keeps His Word and as a result, keeps your word, bringing righteousness, truth, and life to those around you.

Pray Numbers 30:2b over yourself and those for whom you stand guard as a faithful, prayerful watchman (Isaiah 62:6-7).

> *"LORD, please make _____ and*
> *me people who do not violate our word.*
> *Help us do according to all that proceeds out of our mouths.*
> *In Your name, Jesus~"*

FEBRUARY 9

Please read Numbers 31.

Meditate on verses 15-16.

> *And Moses said to them, "Have you spared all the women? Behold, these caused the sons of Israel, through the counsel of Balaam, to trespass against the LORD in the matter of Peor, so the plague was among the congregation of the LORD."*

Numbers 31 tells the rest of the story of Balaam being hired by King Balak to curse Israel, so they would not be able to destroy the pagan nations surrounding their promised land (Numbers 22:1-7). The Midianites were part of that group who hoped Israel would be destroyed. Taking Balaam's advice, the women seduced the Israelites into adulterous idolatry by joining themselves to Baal through sexual intimacy (Numbers 25:1-9). God had already punished the Israelites for their foolishness; now He commanded the Midianites be destroyed, so they could not seduce His people into unfaithfulness again.

Are there things in your life seducing you from faithfulness to God? Spend time asking God to reveal them to you, even the "little ones" (v. 17). Ask God to help you remove them, so they do not hinder your walk with Christ.

As a faithful, prayerful watchman (Isaiah 62:6-7), use the words from Numbers 31:15-17 to ask God to help you and those you love remove unfaithfulness from your midst.

> *"LORD, do not let _____ and me spare anything that causes us to trespass against You. We do not want a plague among us. Help us to kill every little thing that keeps us from intimately knowing You, LORD.*
> *In Your name, Jesus~"*

FEBRUARY 10

Please read Numbers 32.

Meditate on verses 11-13.

> *None of the men who came up from Egypt,*
> *from twenty years old and upward,*
> *shall see the land which I swore to Abraham, to Isaac and to*
> *Jacob; for they did not follow Me fully, except Caleb the son*
> *of Jephunneh the Kenizzite and Joshua the son of Nun,*
> *for they have followed the LORD fully.*
> *So, the LORD'S anger burned against Israel, and He made*
> *them wander in the wilderness forty years, until the entire*
> *generation of those who had done evil in the*
> *sight of the LORD was destroyed.*

Observe the contrast between the Israelite men and Joshua and Caleb. God described the men as not fully following Him; however, Joshua and Caleb followed the LORD fully. These two men were allowed to enter the promised land, but the rest were not. That generation of men was destroyed because of their evil deeds.

Have you ever thought about not fully following God as evil? The LORD expects total allegiance to Him; not remaining loyal to Him is evil and invites calamity into one's life.

Evaluate your walk with Christ. Would He describe you as following Him fully? Confess areas where you do not wholeheartedly walk with Him and ask Him to help you give Him your unwavering loyalty.

Pray Numbers 32:12 over yourself and those for whom you stand guard as a faithful, prayerful watchman (Isaiah 62:6-7).

> *"LORD, please make _____ and me like*
> *Caleb and Joshua; may we follow You fully.*
> *In Your name, Jesus~"*

FEBRUARY 11

Please read Numbers 33.

Meditate on verses 55-56. The LORD is speaking.

> "But if you do not drive out the inhabitants of the land from before you, then it shall come about that those whom you let remain of them will become as pricks in your eyes and as thorns in your sides, and they will trouble you in the land in which you live. And as I plan to do to them, so I will do to you."

The Israelites made forty stops in forty years before finally landing on the plains of Moab (vs. 5-48). As they prepared to enter the promised land of Canaan, the LORD gave them these instructions:

> "When you cross over the Jordan into the land of Canaan, then you shall drive out all the inhabitants of the land from before you, and destroy all their figured stones, and destroy all their molten images and demolish all their high places; and you shall take possession of the land and live in it, for I have given the land to you to possess it."
> —NUMBERS 33:51B-53

The Canaanites were idolatrous people; they and everything they worshiped had to be removed so the Israelites would not be tempted to worship their gods, practicing their sinful lifestyle.

What tempts you away from God? Remove it so you can live the plans God has for you.

Pray the opposite of Numbers 33:55 over yourself and those for whom you stand guard as a faithful, prayerful watchman (Isaiah 62:6-7).

> "LORD, let _____ and me drive out sin from before us. Let none of it remain so that it becomes as pricks in our eyes and as thorns in our sides. Do not let sin trouble us as we live with You, LORD. In Your name, Jesus~"

FEBRUARY 12

Please read Numbers 34.

Meditate on verses 1-2.

> *Then the LORD spoke to Moses, saying, "Command the sons of Israel and say to them, 'When you enter the land of Canaan, this is the land that shall fall to you as an inheritance, even the land of Canaan according to its borders.'"*

In this chapter, God laid out the borders for the land promised to the Israelites; the land was their inheritance from Him. When you became a Christian, you, too, received a precious inheritance from God:

> *Blessed be the God and Father of our LORD Jesus Christ, who according to His great mercy has caused us to be born again to a living hope through the resurrection of Jesus Christ from the dead, to obtain an inheritance which is imperishable and undefiled and will not fade away, reserved in heaven for you, who are protected by the power of God through faith for a salvation ready to be revealed in the last time.*
> —1 PETER 1:3-5

Think about your precious God-given inheritance described as undecaying, unsoiled, and unfading, carefully guarded in heaven for you. And not only is your inheritance protected; you are eternally kept and saved by God's power. These are important truths to remember and to tell others who need to know they, too, can receive an eternal inheritance when they belong to Jesus.

Using the words from Numbers 34:29, pray to be the one God uses to apportion the inheritance of salvation to those for whom you stand guard as a faithful, prayerful watchman (Isaiah 62:6-7).

> *"LORD, I will obey Your command to apportion the inheritance of salvation by telling others about You. In Your name, Jesus~"*

FEBRUARY 13

Please read Numbers 35.

Meditate on verse 19.

> *The blood avenger himself shall put the murderer to death; he shall put him to death when he meets him.*

Consider how the LORD Jesus Christ fulfilled this chapter, being both the city of refuge and the blood avenger. He is the blood avenger; His death and resurrection defeated the murderer Satan whose end is eternity in the Lake of Fire (John 8:44; Revelation 20:10). Jesus is the city of refuge. Anyone who runs to Him will not die in their sins. Jesus took the punishment for the sins of the whole world (1 John 2:1-2). And just like the manslayer had to flee to the city of refuge in order not to be killed by the blood avenger, every person must choose to flee to Jesus as their city of refuge, so they will not face Him as the blood avenger in death (Proverbs 18:10; Revelation 20:11-15).

Thank Jesus for being your City of Refuge. Pray for those who need to make Him their City of Refuge, so they do not face Him as the Blood Avenger. Use the words from Numbers 35:26-28 and 34 to pray as a faithful, prayerful watchman (Isaiah 62:6-7).

> *"LORD Jesus, You are _____ and my City of Refuge. Let us never go beyond You. We do not want You to find us as the Blood Avenger. Please let _____ make You their City of Refuge. LORD, dwell in our midst. In Your name, Jesus~"*

FEBRUARY 14

Please read Numbers 36.

Meditate on verses 5-6 and 10.

> *Then Moses commanded the sons of Israel according*
> *to the word of the LORD, saying,*
> *"The tribe of the sons of Joseph are right in their statements. This is what the LORD has commanded concerning the daughters of Zelophehad, saying, 'Let them marry whom they wish; only they must marry within the family of the tribe of their father.'"*
> *Just as the LORD had commanded Moses, so*
> *the daughters of Zelophehad did.*

What a great chapter for leaders and followers! When the brothers of Zelophehad perceived a problem with the plan for their nieces' inheritance, they brought their concerns to Moses. Moses listened, acknowledging the validity of their concerns; then, after getting God's wisdom on the situation, he offered the solution to the problem.

Ask the LORD to make you a humble leader who listens to the concerns of others and prayerfully seeks God's solutions. Ask the LORD to make you a great follower who presents concerns to your leaders instead of passively letting problems grow and cause harm to you and those around you.

Pray Numbers 36:5 and 10 over yourself and those for whom you stand guard as a faithful, prayerful watchman (Isaiah 62:6-7).

> *"LORD, help _____ and me command according to*
> *Your Word and let us do just as You command.*
> *In Your name, Jesus~"*

FEBRUARY 15

Please read Deuteronomy 1.

Meditate on verse 3.

> *In the fortieth year, on the first day of the eleventh month,*
> *Moses spoke to the children of Israel, according to all that*
> *the LORD had commanded him to give to them.*

You will spend the next 34 days reading the last words of Moses before his death. They are the words God commanded him to speak to the children of Israel before they entered the promised land. The words might sound familiar to you because Moses spoke them 40 years earlier as recorded in Exodus and Leviticus, but they had to be repeated because the members of this audience were children, or not yet born, when they were first spoken. And, the fathers and grandfathers who should have taught these words to their families were dead because of disobedience (vs. 26-36).

As you take God's words to heart, ask Him to bring to your remembrance His faithfulness throughout your life. Teach the younger ones in your realm of influence about God, His Word, and how to live pleasing to Him.

Moses prayed a blessing over this younger generation (v. 11). Pray it over those for whom you stand guard as their faithful, prayerful watchman (Isaiah 62:6-7).

> *"LORD, You are God of _____ and me.*
> *Please increase us a thousand-fold and bless*
> *us just as You have promised.*
> *In Your name, Jesus~"*

FEBRUARY 16

Please read Deuteronomy 2.

Meditate on verse 15.

> *Moreover, the hand of the LORD was against them,*
> *to destroy them from within the camp until they all perished.*

What a sobering meditation verse! "LORD, please do not let Your hand ever need to be against us to destroy us until we perish." God wanted these young Israelites to know well the story of why their fathers and grandfathers died, so they would not repeat mistakes from the past. God expected them to obey Him, conquering where and when He commanded (vs. 2-6, 9, 19, 37). Thankfully, we have their story as well, so we do not repeat others' mistakes, learning to fully obey God.

This chapter has several verses with words you can use to pray over yourself and those you love. Start with Deuteronomy 2:3, 7, 9, 15, 30, and 37 as a faithful, prayerful watchman (Isaiah 62:6-7).

> *"LORD, _____ and I have been going in*
> *circles long enough; now tell us where to turn.*
> *Please bless us in all we do; You know our wanderings.*
> *You have been with us; we have not lacked a thing.*
> *Do not let us harass _____ or provoke them.*
> *Please, do not let Your hand be against us to destroy us until*
> *we perish. Do not harden our spirit and make our heart*
> *obstinate. LORD, we want to go wherever You command us.*
> *In Your name, Jesus~"*

FEBRUARY 17

Please read Deuteronomy 3.

Meditate on verse 21. Moses is speaking.

> *"I commanded Joshua at that time, saying, 'Your eyes have seen all that the LORD your God has done to these two kings, so the LORD shall do to all the kingdoms into which you are about to cross.'"*

Deuteronomy 3 records conquering land east of the Jordan River given to the tribes of Reuben, Gad, and Manasseh. It was the prequel to conquering the rest of the promised land west of the Jordan River. Moses would not live to see those victories, but he wanted Joshua confident in the LORD they would come. Moses really desired to be a part of those conquests, but just as God would keep His word about the land, He would keep His word about Moses not entering the land because of disobedience. God did let Moses climb to the top of Mount Pisgah for a bird's eye view of the amazing land that would become Israel, and interestingly, Moses actually set foot in the land 1,400 years later with Elijah, Peter, James, and John on a mountain where Jesus was transfigured before his eyes (Mark 9:2-8).

Be confident in the LORD and His plans for you and those you love. Do not fear the future, knowing God is faithful.

Pray Deuteronomy 3:22, 24, and 28 over yourself and those for whom you stand guard as a faithful, prayerful watchman (Isaiah 62:6-7).

> *"LORD our God, do not let _____ and me fear, for You are the one fighting for us. O LORD God, You have begun to show us, Your servants, Your greatness and Your strong hand, for what god is there in heaven or on earth who can do such works and mighty acts as Yours? Please encourage and strengthen us in Your name, Jesus~"*

FEBRUARY 18

Please read Deuteronomy 4.

Meditate on verses 15-16a.

> *So watch yourselves carefully, since you did not see any form on the day the LORD spoke to you at Horeb from the midst of the fire, so that you do not act corruptly and make a graven image for yourselves in the form of any figure.*

Why did God not bodily reveal Himself nor show His face in the Old Testament? And why is He so adamantly opposed to graven images? Because Jesus is "the image of the invisible God," and "the knowledge of the glory of God is in the face of Christ" (Colossians 1:15; 2 Corinthians 4:6). Jesus, God in the flesh, is the only image of the Almighty. Humans are incapable of making an image of God and any attempt to do so misrepresents Him.

Fix your eyes on Jesus (Hebrews 12:2) and pray Deuteronomy 4:4-6, 9, and 23 over yourself and those for whom you stand guard as a faithful, prayerful watchman (Isaiah 62:6-7).

> *"LORD our God, let _____ and me hold fast to You. Let us keep and do Your statutes and judgments, for that is our wisdom and understanding. Make us wise and understanding people. Help us give heed to ourselves and keep our souls diligently so that we do not forget the things which our eyes have seen, and those things do not depart from our hearts all the days of our lives, but, let us make them known to our children and grandchildren. Let us watch ourselves that we do not forget Your covenant, LORD our God. Do not let us make a graven image in the form of anything against You. In Your name, Jesus~"*

FEBRUARY 19

Please read Deuteronomy 5.

Meditate on verse 1.

> *Then Moses summoned all Israel and said to them: "Hear, O Israel, the statutes and the ordinances which I am speaking today in your hearing, that you may learn them and observe them carefully."*

Words spoken by God 40 years earlier, Moses faithfully taught to the next generation for they, too, must hear, learn, and do them. Hear the cry of God's heart for His people:

> *"Oh, that they had such a heart in them, that they would fear Me and keep all My commandments always, that it may be well with them and with their sons forever!"*
> —DEUTERONOMY 5:29

Is that the cry of your heart for those you love? Faithfully teach them God's Word and pray Deuteronomy 5:24, 29, and 31-33 as their faithful, prayerful watchman (Isaiah 62:6-7).

> *"Behold, LORD our God, You have shown us Your glory and Your greatness, and we have heard Your voice, and we have seen that You speak with people. Oh, that _____ and I may have such a heart in us that we would fear You and keep all Your commandments always, that it may be well with us and our children forever! As we stand here by You, speak to us all the commandments and the statutes and the judgments which we will teach to others that they may observe them. LORD our God, help us observe to do just as You have commanded us; do not let us turn aside to the right or to the left. Let us walk in all the way which You have commanded that we may live and that it may be well with us and that we may prolong our days in the land which we will possess. In Your name, Jesus~"*

FEBRUARY 20

Please read Deuteronomy 6.

Meditate on verse 17.

> *You should diligently keep the commandments of the LORD your God, and His testimonies and His statutes which He has commanded you.*

As Christians, does God still expect us to keep His commandments? Hear His Words from the New Testament:

> *"If you love Me, you will keep My commandments."*
> —JOHN 14:15

> *By this we know that we have come to know Him, if we keep His commandments. The one who says, "I have come to know Him," and does not keep His commandments, is a liar, and the truth is not in him.*
> —1 JOHN 2:3-4

Christ did not abolish the Law; rather He fulfilled it by accomplishing all of the sacrificial commandments and teaching us how to observe the rest of the 613 laws (Matthew 5:17, 27-48).

As you continue reading Deuteronomy, take God's Words to heart, applying them to your life and praying them over yourself and those you love. Pray Deuteronomy 6:4-7, 12, and 17-18 as a faithful, prayerful watchman (Isaiah 62:6-7).

> *"LORD, You are God; You are one! May _____ and I love You with all our heart, soul, and might. May the words You are commanding us be on our heart. Let us teach them diligently to our children and talk of them when we sit in our houses and when we walk by the way and when we lie down and when we rise up. May we watch ourselves that we do not forget You, LORD. Help us diligently keep Your commandments, testimonies, and statutes. Help us do what is right and good in Your sight, LORD, that it may be well with us. In Your name, Jesus~"*

FEBRUARY 21

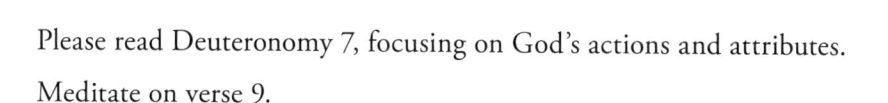

Please read Deuteronomy 7, focusing on God's actions and attributes. Meditate on verse 9.

> *Know therefore that the LORD your God, He is God, the faithful God, who keeps His covenant and His lovingkindness to a thousandth generation with those who love Him and keep His commandments.*

Take confidence in these facts about God:

- He brings people where He needs them, clearing, delivering, and defeating obstacles (vs. 1-2).
- He chooses people and sets His love on them (vs. 6-7).
- He keeps His oaths and brings people out by His mighty hand, redeeming them (v. 8).
- He is faithful, keeping His covenant and lovingkindness with those who love and obey Him (v. 9).
- He loves, blesses, and multiplies (v. 13).
- He removes sickness and diseases (v. 15).
- He is great and awesome (v. 21).

Pray for the great and awesome God to do these things in the lives of those you love. Pray Deuteronomy 7:6, 9, 13, and 15 as a faithful, prayerful watchman (Isaiah 62:6-7).

> "LORD, make _____ and me holy people to You, chosen for Your own possession. LORD, You are the faithful God who keeps Your covenant and Your lovingkindness to a thousandth generation with those who love You and keep Your commandments. May we love You and keep Your commandments. Please love, bless, and multiply us. Please bless the fruit of our womb, the fruit of our ground, our grain and new wine and oil, the increase of our herd, and the young of our flock. LORD, please remove all sickness from us and do not put on us any of the harmful diseases. In Your name, Jesus~"

FEBRUARY 22

Please read Deuteronomy 8.

Meditate on verse 3b.

> *Man does not live by bread alone, but man lives by everything that proceeds out of the mouth of the LORD.*

As you hold the Bible, the Words that proceed from the mouth of the LORD, ponder His desire to strengthen and sustain you with every word in it. Think about your favorite food, something you crave, something that instantly makes your stomach growl. Ask God to give you the same craving hunger for His Word. Ask Him to awaken you every morning with the insatiable desire to feed on His Words. And just as you eat food throughout the day, meditate on verses from the Bible throughout the day.

There is a lot to chew from this chapter. As you do, pray Deuteronomy 8:3, 6, 10-14, and 16-18 over yourself and those for whom you stand guard as a faithful, prayerful watchman (Isaiah 62:6-7).

> *"Make _____ and me understand we do not live by bread alone, but we live by everything that proceeds out of Your mouth, LORD. Help us keep Your commandments to walk in Your ways and fear You. When we eat and are satisfied, let us bless You for the good You give us. Do not let us forget You, LORD our God, by not keeping Your commandments and Your ordinances and Your statutes. When we eat and are satisfied, and build good houses and live in them, and when our herds and flocks multiply, and our silver and gold multiply, and all we have multiplies, do not let our heart become proud and forget You, LORD our God. You brought us out of slavery to sin. As You humble and test us to do good for us in the end, let us never say in our heart, 'My power and the strength of my hand made me this wealth.' Let us remember that You, LORD our God, give us power to make wealth.*
> *For the glory of Your name, Jesus~"*

FEBRUARY 23

Please read Deuteronomy 9.

Meditate on verses 6-7.

> *Know then it is not because of your righteousness that the LORD your God is giving you this good land to possess, for you are a stubborn people. Remember, do not forget how you provoked the LORD your God to wrath in the wilderness; from the day that you left the land of Egypt until you arrived at this place, you have been rebellious against the LORD.*

Three times in this chapter the people were told they provoked the LORD to wrath, and three times they were reminded it was not because of their righteousness the LORD worked on their behalf (vs. 4-8, 22). We have a similar story. Our hard hearts provoke God, and our righteous deeds are filthiness in His sight (Hebrews 3:8; Isaiah 64:6). Only Jesus Christ can be our righteousness; through Him we can be filled with the fruit of righteousness (1 Corinthians 1:30; Philippians 1:11).

For whom are you praying for God to save from His wrath through the righteousness of Jesus? Take heart that God listened to Moses when he prayed for the Israelites as they experienced God's "anger and hot displeasure" (v. 19). Continue to be a faithful, prayerful watchman (Isaiah 62:6-7) and pray Deuteronomy 9:19-21 over yourself and those you love.

> *"LORD, please listen to me again this time. Spare _____ and me from Your anger, hot displeasure, and wrath that would destroy us. LORD, You are angry enough with _____ to destroy them; please save them instead. Please help us take our sinful things, burn them with fire, crush them, grind them very small until they are as fine as dust and throw them away.*
> *In Your name, Jesus~"*

FEBRUARY 24

Please read Deuteronomy 10.

Meditate on verse 10b.

> *The LORD listened to me that time also; the*
> *LORD was not willing to destroy you.*

Does prayer make a difference? God did not destroy Aaron and the Israelites after they made and worshiped the golden calf because Moses begged God to spare them (Deuteronomy 9:18-20). Do not lose heart in prayer because your prayers move the heart of God on behalf of those you love. Deuteronomy 10 is full of verses to pray; pray verses 8-10, 12-17, and 20-21 as a faithful, prayerful watchman (Isaiah 62:6-7).

> *"LORD, set apart _____ and me to stand before You to serve You and to bless Your name. LORD, You are our inheritance. Please listen to me this time also; do not destroy us. Help us do what You require from us: to fear You, LORD our God, to walk in all Your ways and love You, and to serve You, LORD our God, with all our heart and with all our soul, and to keep Your commandments and Your statutes which You command for our good. Behold, to You, LORD our God, belong heaven and the highest heavens, the earth and all that is in it. Yet, You set Your affection to love us and our descendants after us. So, circumcise our hearts; let us stiffen our necks no longer. For LORD, You are the God of gods and the LORD of lords, the great, the mighty, and the awesome God who does not show partiality nor take a bribe. Let us fear You, LORD our God, and serve You and cling to You. You are our praise, and You are our God who has done great and awesome things for us which our eyes have seen. Thank You, in Your name, Jesus~"*

FEBRUARY 25

Please read Deuteronomy 11.

Meditate on verse 7.

> *But, your own eyes have seen all the great*
> *work of the LORD which He did.*

As Moses recounted the miracles and disciplines of the LORD over the past 40 years, he reminded the older generation that they, too, were eyewitnesses to these works of God, and they were to tell their children about God and His mighty deeds (v. 19). Then, their children would see with their own eyes the work of the LORD and teach their children how to recognize God and His ways.

Ask God to help you see with your own eyes all the great work He is doing in your life and the lives of those you love. Tell others what He has done, so they, too, can recognize His hand on their lives.

Pray Deuteronomy 11:7, 13, and 18-22 over yourself and those for whom you stand guard as a faithful, prayerful watchman (Isaiah 62:6-7).

> *"LORD, please help _____ and me see with our own*
> *eyes all the great work You are doing. Help us listen obediently*
> *to Your commandments to love You and to serve You with all*
> *our heart and soul. Help us impress Your Words on our heart*
> *and on our soul. Let us bind them as a sign on our hand and*
> *as frontals on our forehead. Let us teach them to our children,*
> *talking of them when we sit in our house and when we walk*
> *along the road and when we lie down and when we rise up. Let*
> *us write them on the doorposts of our house and on our gates, so*
> *that our days and the days of our children may be multiplied. Let*
> *us be careful to keep all this commandment to love You, LORD*
> *our God, to walk in all Your ways and to hold fast to You.*
> *In Your name, Jesus~"*

FEBRUARY 26

Please read Deuteronomy 12. Notice the repeated words, "the place." Meditate on verse 5.

> *But, you shall seek the LORD at the place which the LORD your God will choose from all your tribes, to establish His name there for His dwelling, and there you shall come.*

Six times in this chapter Moses talks about the place God will choose to establish His name (vs. 5, 11, 14, 18, 21, 26). Interestingly, he never names a geographical location. God did that on purpose because He had a very special place in mind for His name to dwell. Although the tabernacle would be erected in Gilgal, Shiloh, and Gibeon, and the temple would eventually be built in Jerusalem (Joshua 4:19; 18:1; 1 Chronicles 21:29; 2 Chronicles 3:1), an even more incredible place would be home for God's name.

> *Do you not know that you are a temple of God and that the Spirit of God dwells in you?*
> —1 CORINTHIANS 3:16

The place is you!

God always knew His name would be established and dwell in you. He purposely called it the place because you are the place God chose for His name to dwell. God had you on His mind when He gave Moses these words nearly 3,500 years ago. Amazing!

Pray for those you love who still need to give themselves to God as His dwelling place. Pray for them to desire to be the place. As their faithful, prayerful watchman (Isaiah 62:6-7), pray for them using Deuteronomy 12:5.

> *"LORD, please let _____ seek You and be the place which You will choose to establish Your name for Your dwelling. In Your name, Jesus~"*

FEBRUARY 27

Please read Deuteronomy 13.

Meditate on verses 4 and 17a.

You shall follow the LORD your God and fear Him, and you shall keep His commandments, listen to His voice, serve Him, and cling to Him. Nothing from that which is put under the ban shall cling to your hand.

In this chapter, God contrasts clinging to Him and clinging to things that take your allegiance from Him. He commands the purging of evil and putting to death things which seduce you away from Him (vs. 5, 10). This is strong language, demanding serious attention.

Think about your life. To what or whom do you cling besides Almighty God? Who and what seduces you not to wholeheartedly walk with Christ and love Him with all your heart, soul, mind, and strength? Ask God to help you purge things distracting you from Him.*

Pray Deuteronomy 13:4-5 and 17-18 over yourself and those for whom you stand guard as a faithful, prayerful watchman (Isaiah 62:6-7).

"LORD, help _____ and me follow You and fear You. Help us keep Your commandments, listen to Your voice, serve You, and cling to You. Let us put to death anything counseling rebellion against You, LORD our God, for You redeemed us from the house of slavery to sin. Help us put to death anything that seduces us from the way in which You command us to walk. Purge the evil from among us. Let nothing which You have banned cling to our hands. LORD, please turn from Your burning anger and show mercy to us. Have compassion on us and make us increase as we listen to Your voice, keep Your commandments, and do what is right in Your sight. In Your name, Jesus~"

---

*Prayerfully consider relationships, music, media, books, habits, etc. that God wants to you to purge.

FEBRUARY 28

Please read Deuteronomy 14.

Meditate on verse 2.

> *For you are a holy people to the LORD your God, and the LORD has chosen you to be a people for His own possession out of all the peoples who are on the face of the earth.*

God not only chose Israel to be His people; He chose people who are born again through the resurrection of Jesus Christ (1 Peter 1:3).

> *But you are a chosen race, a royal priesthood, a holy nation, a people for God's own possession, so that you may proclaim the excellencies of Him who has called you out of darkness into His marvelous light; for you once were not a people, but now you are the people of God; you had not received mercy, but now you have received mercy.*
> —1 PETER 2:9-10

Holy people, chosen by Almighty God, behave differently from the rest of the world. By obeying the commands in Deuteronomy 14, the Israelites set themselves apart from those not belonging to God. Do your behaviors make it obvious you belong to God instead of the world?

As a faithful, prayerful watchman (Isaiah 62:6-7), use the words from Deuteronomy 14:2 and 29, praying for God to choose and bless those you love.

> *"LORD, please make _____ a holy people to You. Choose them to be a people for Your own possession out of all the peoples who are on the face of the earth. LORD our God, please bless us in all the work of our hands, so the Levite, the alien, the orphan, and the widow can come to us and eat and be satisfied. In Your name, Jesus~"*

FEBRUARY 29

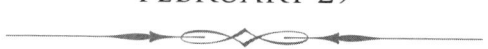

Please read Deuteronomy 15.

Meditate on verse 9a.

> *Beware that there is no base thought in your heart.*

What an amazing verse to meditate on today! Think about a few of the words.

- Beware means "to guard and observe; to keep watch and protect; to keep oneself from."[1]
- Base means "worthless, good for nothing, unprofitable, wicked, destructive."[2]
- Thought means "word, thing, matter, utterance."[3]
- Heart means "mind, inner being, thinking, inclination, seat of appetites."[4]

Ask the LORD to make you aware of every time your mind wanders to worthless things. Train your mind to immediately "take every thought captive to the obedience of Christ" (2 Corinthians 10:5).

Pray Deuteronomy 15:9a over yourself and those for whom you stand guard as a faithful, prayerful watchman (Isaiah 62:6-7).

> *"LORD, please make _____ and me beware that there is no base thought in our heart. In Your name, Jesus~"*

---

[1]. Retrieved from www.blueletterbible.org/lang/lexicon/lexicon.cfm?Strongs=H8104&t=NASB
[2]. Retrieved from www.blueletterbible.org/lang/lexicon/lexicon.cfm?Strongs=H1100&t=NASB
[3]. Retrieved from www.blueletterbible.org/lang/lexicon/lexicon.cfm?Strongs=H1697&t=NASB
[4]. Retrieved from www.blueletterbible.org/lang/lexicon/lexicon.cfm?Strongs=H3824&t=NASB

March

*On your walls, O Jerusalem,
I have appointed watchmen;
All day and all night they
will never keep silent.
You who remind the LORD,
take no rest for yourselves;
And give Him no rest until He establishes
And makes Jerusalem a
praise in the earth.*
Isaiah 62:6-7, NASB

MARCH 1

Please read Deuteronomy 16.

Meditate on verses 2-3a.

> *You shall sacrifice the Passover to the LORD your God from the flock and the herd, in the place where the LORD chooses to establish His name. You shall not eat leavened bread with it.*

As you read Deuteronomy, notice God continues to talk about the place He will choose to establish His name. Recall from Deuteronomy 12 He never names a geographical location because ultimately people are the place where God dwells through faith in the sacrifice of Jesus Christ for our sins.

> *Christ our Passover also has been sacrificed. Therefore, let us celebrate the feast, not with old leaven, nor with the leaven of malice and wickedness, but with the unleavened bread of sincerity and truth.*
> —1 CORINTHIANS 5:7B-8

As a Christian, you no longer sacrifice the Passover to the LORD your God because Christ your Passover lives inside of you—the place—where the LORD chose to establish His name—Amazing!

In sincerity and truth, thank God for choosing you and ask Him to choose those you know who still need to invite Him to establish His name in them as His dwelling place.

Pray Deuteronomy 16:15 over yourself and those for whom you stand guard as a faithful, prayerful watchman (Isaiah 62:6-7).

> *"LORD my God, I celebrate that I am the place You choose. Please choose _____ to also be the place. Please bless _____ and me in all our produce and in all the work of our hands, so that we will be altogether joyful. In Your name, Jesus~"*

MARCH 2

Please read Deuteronomy 17.

Meditate on this phrase from verses 7 and 12.

Purge the evil...

God knows allowing evil to remain in the land corrupts people, desensitizing them to callously continue sinning. In this chapter, the LORD tells you how to stop sinning.

- Purge the evil from your midst (v. 7).
- Write God's Word, making a copy for yourself of verses you need to remember (v. 18).
- Keep it with you, reading God's Word every day of your life, that you may learn to fear the LORD your God by carefully observing all His Words (v. 19).

Ask the LORD to search and purge you of evil thoughts and actions. Fill your mind with God's Word: write it; read it; memorize it; tell it, so others can know how to please God.

Pray Deuteronomy 17:7 and 18-20 over yourself and those for whom you stand guard as a faithful, prayerful watchman (Isaiah 62:6-7).

> *"LORD, please purge the evil from _____ and me. Help us write a copy of Your Word and keep it with us. Let us read it all the days of our life that we may learn to fear You by carefully observing all the words of Your law and statutes, that our hearts will not be lifted up above others and that we may not turn aside from the commandments to the right or the left, so that our children may continue long in Your Kingdom, Jesus~"*

MARCH 3

Please read Deuteronomy 18.

Meditate on verse 2.

> *They (the Levites) shall have no inheritance among their countrymen; the LORD is their inheritance, as He promised them.*

There is a sense of relief in not receiving an earthly inheritance—no worries about what a family member did or did not leave you in their will—no worries about what you will or will not leave family members in your will. There are no worries about squabbling with family members because of an inheritance—no worries about destroying family relationships over an inheritance. Thankfully, if you are a Christian, you are considered a priest by God, a spiritual Levite (Revelation 1:6). And, like the Levites in Deuteronomy, the LORD is your inheritance. There is no inheritance on earth that compares to Him; He is more than enough.

Ponder what it means to have the LORD as your inheritance. If you are concerned about an earthly inheritance, let it go. Nothing you inherit on this earth is eternal, but the people you might be tempted to fight with because of a will are eternal. Don't risk your relationship with them and the opportunity to share the Gospel with them for a paltry sum of money, piece of land, or stuff.

Pray Deuteronomy 18:5 and 13 over yourself and those for whom you stand guard as a faithful, prayerful watchman (Isaiah 62:6-7).

> *"LORD my God, please choose _____ and me to stand and serve in Your name forever. Make us blameless before You. In Your name, Jesus, our inheritance~"*

MARCH 4

Please read Deuteronomy 19.

Meditate on verse 7.

> *Therefore, I command you saying, "You shall set aside three cities for yourself."*

God made provision for those who unintentionally killed another to have a place to flee, a city of refuge, a place where the blood avenger could not stalk and kill them. It was the only safe place for manslayers; they must run to the city of refuge and remain there in order not to die.

As God made provision for the Israelites to have cities of refuge, He was giving them foreshadowing pictures of Messiah. Jesus is both the city of refuge and the blood avenger. Jesus came to earth the first time as the city of refuge, the place of salvation for all who run to Him. Remarkably, He welcomes not only those who sin unintentionally but those of us who are intentional sinners. "Thank You, Jesus!"

When you run to Him in repentance, He becomes your city of refuge where you can remain and never die (Psalm 31:1). He is your only safe place because a day is coming when He will return to earth as the blood avenger, slaying everyone who did not choose Him to be their city of refuge (Revelation 19:11-21).

Pray Deuteronomy 19:9 and 12 over yourself and those for whom you stand guard as a faithful, prayerful watchman (Isaiah 62:6-7).

> *"LORD, please let _____ and me carefully observe all this commandment that You command us today, to love You, LORD our God and to walk in all Your ways always. You are our city of refuge. Please let _____ choose You to be their city of refuge so they will not be delivered into Your hand, Blood Avenger, so that they die. Save them in Your name, Jesus~"*

MARCH 5

Please read Deuteronomy 20.

Meditate on verse 1.

> *When you go out to battle against your enemies and see horses and chariots and people more numerous than you, do not be afraid of them; for the LORD your God, who brought you up from the land of Egypt, is with you*

Whether you are an actual military member or a member of God's army, engaged in spiritual battle, Deuteronomy 20 contains great advice for approaching a battle. The chapter can be summed up with three exhortations:

- Do not be afraid for the LORD your God is with you.
- Do not be distracted.
- Stay focused on the battle.

As a Christian, you are fighting a spiritual battle. The enemy, Satan, wants to destroy those you love, so they do not have the opportunity to know Jesus. He wants to distract you from praying for them and sharing the Gospel with them. Be aware of his tactics and do not be fooled by his strategies. Devote yourself to prayer, keeping alert in it (Colossians 4:2). Stay focused on opportunities to tell others about Jesus. When the LORD returns will there be people worshiping around His throne because you shared the Gospel with them?

Spiritual warfare is real. Pray like a well-trained soldier, using God's Word as your weapon (Ephesians 6:13-20).

Pray Deuteronomy 20:3-4 over yourself and those for whom you stand guard as a faithful, prayerful watchman (Isaiah 62:6-7).

> *"LORD, as _____ and I approach the battle against our enemies today, do not let us be fainthearted. Do not let us be afraid, or panic, or tremble before them, for You, LORD our God, are the one who goes with us to fight for us against our enemies to save us. LORD, please save _____ .*
> *In Your name, Jesus~"*

MARCH 6

Please read Deuteronomy 21.

Meditate on verses 18-19 and 21.

> *If any man has a stubborn and rebellious son who*
> *will not obey his father or his mother, and when they*
> *chastise him, he will not even listen to them,*
> *then his father and mother shall seize him,*
> *and bring him out to the elders of his city at the gateway of his*
> *hometown. Then all the men of his city shall stone him to death;*
> *so, you shall remove the evil from your midst,*
> *and all Israel will hear of it and fear.*

Do these verses make you squirm? They should because God has not changed His mind about stubborn, rebellious children. It is grievous in the sight of God for children to rebel against their parents, and on the cross, Jesus took our deserved stoning for stubborn rebellion.

Teach your children what the Bible says about honoring and respecting parents (Exodus 20:12; 21:15; Leviticus 20:9; Deuteronomy 21:18-21; Matthew 15:4; Ephesians 6:1-3; Colossians 3:20). Pray for their salvation, so their punishment will be paid by the death of Jesus. Teach your children what Jesus did for them, so they can choose to follow Him instead of dying in their sins.

Pray Deuteronomy 21:8-9 and 21 over yourself and those for whom you stand guard as a faithful, prayerful watchman (Isaiah 62:6-7).

> *"O LORD, please forgive _____ and*
> *me, Your people, whom You have redeemed.*
> *Help us do what is right in Your eyes, forgive our*
> *bloodguiltiness, and remove the guilt of innocent blood*
> *from our midst. Remove the evil from our midst.*
> *May others hear and fear You, LORD.*
> *In Your name, Jesus~"*

MARCH 7

Please read Deuteronomy 22.

Meditate on verses 1 and 3-4.

> *You shall not see your countryman's ox or his sheep straying away and pay no attention to them; you shall certainly bring them back to your countryman. Thus, you shall do with his donkey, and you shall do the same with his garment, and you shall do likewise with anything lost by your countryman, which he has lost and you have found. You are not allowed to neglect them. You shall not see your countryman's donkey or his ox fallen down on the way, and pay no attention to them; you shall certainly help him to raise them up.*

These verses address the sin of doing nothing. All three verses contain the Hebrew word *alam*, translated as "pay no attention" and "to neglect." *Alam* literally means "to hide yourself."[1]

Let that soak in for a moment—neglecting a noticed need, deliberately hiding rather than assisting is sin. Ouch! God's Word is convicting, making us evaluate our attitudes. Do we really care, or do we turn the other way, pretending not to see?

Ask the LORD to give you His heart for others, and when He does, ask Him to strengthen and equip you to help.

As a faithful, prayerful watchman (Isaiah 62:6-7), pray for yourself and those you love not to be people who *alam*, using the words from Deuteronomy 22:1 and 3-4.

> *"LORD, help _____ and me not see others straying away and pay no attention to them. Help us bring them back to You. LORD, do not let us be people who neglect. Help us pay attention and help others, raising them up. In Your name, Jesus~"*

---

1. Retrieved from www.blueletterbible.org/lang/lexicon/lexicon.cfm?Strongs=H5956&t=NASB

MARCH 8

Please read Deuteronomy 23.

Meditate on verse 14.

> *Since the LORD your God walks in the midst
> of your camp to deliver you and to
> defeat your enemies before you; therefore,
> your camp must be holy; and
> He must not see anything indecent among
> you, or He will turn away from you.*

Deuteronomy 23 contains many rules for maintaining cleanliness and holiness among the Israelites. Purity and integrity are very important to the LORD, and His commands for holy behavior are not only in the Old Testament; they are throughout the New Testament as well. Consider these exhortations from Ephesians, noticing their similarity to the Old Testament law:

> *But immorality or any impurity or greed must not even be named
> among you, as is proper among saints; and there must be no
> filthiness and silly talk, or coarse jesting, which are not fitting, but
> rather giving of thanks. For this you know with certainty, that no
> immoral or impure person or covetous man, who is an idolater,
> has an inheritance in the kingdom of Christ and God. Let no
> one deceive you with empty words, for because of these things the
> wrath of God comes upon the sons of disobedience. Therefore, do
> not be partakers with them, for you were formerly darkness, but
> now you are Light in the LORD; walk as children of Light.*
> —EPHESIANS 5:3-8

As Light in the LORD, pray Deuteronomy 23:14 over yourself and those for whom you stand guard as a faithful prayerful watchman (Isaiah 62:6-7).

> *"LORD my God, may _____ and I walk as children
> of Light as You walk in our midst to deliver us and to defeat
> our enemies before us. LORD, make us holy, so You will not
> see anything indecent among us. Do not turn away from us.
> In Your name, Jesus~"*

MARCH 9

Please read Deuteronomy 24.

Meditate on verses 1-4.

> *When a man takes a wife and marries her, and it happens that she finds no favor in his eyes because he has found some indecency in her, and he writes her a certificate of divorce and puts it in her hand and sends her out from his house, and she leaves his house and goes and becomes another man's wife, and if the latter husband turns against her and writes her a certificate of divorce and puts it in her hand and sends her out of his house, or if the latter husband dies who took her to be his wife, then her former husband who sent her away is not allowed to take her again to be his wife, since she has been defiled; for that is an abomination before the LORD, and you shall not bring sin on the land which the LORD your God gives you as an inheritance.*

The meditation verses, a single sentence, illustrate the messy confusion of divorce. Jesus explained these verses when asked why there were laws permitting divorce and can a divorce be granted for any reason at all (Matthew 19:3-7). Jesus answered God intends a husband and wife never be separated; the laws for divorce were given because of people's hard hearts, and the only reason for divorce is sexual immorality (Matthew 19:8-9).

Pray for the opposite of Deuteronomy 24:1-2 to happen in the marriages you are guarding as a faithful, prayerful watchman (Isaiah 62:6-7).

> *"LORD, thank You for the marriage of*
> *_____ and _____ .*
> *Let them find favor in each other's eyes.*
> *Let there be no indecency in their marriage.*
> *Let a certificate of divorce never be written and placed in their hands.*
> *May they never send each other out of their house.*
> *May they never become the spouse of another.*
> *In Your name, Jesus~"*

MARCH 10

Please read Deuteronomy 25.

Meditate on verses 13-16.

> *You shall not have in your bag differing weights, a large and a small. You shall not have in your house differing measures, a large and a small. You shall have a full and just weight; you shall have a full and just measure, that your days may be prolonged in the land which the LORD your God gives you. For everyone who does these things, everyone who acts unjustly is an abomination to the LORD your God.*

God established standard weights and measures because using differing weights (a set of weights in one's favor for buying but a different set for selling) is an abomination to the LORD. God wants people to have integrity in their dealings and relationships with others. There should be no deceit and no cheating of one another, for that is wicked in the sight of God and should be to us as well.

Take time to examine your dealings with others. Do you treat people fairly and with integrity? Ask the LORD to reveal areas that you might not even be aware. Thankfully, Christ the Just died for us the unjust to bring us to God (1 Peter 3:18). Thank Him for His sacrifice and pray Deuteronomy 25:15-16 over yourself and those for whom you stand guard as a faithful, prayerful watchman (Isaiah 62:6-7).

> *"LORD, help _____ and me treat others with a full and just measure. May our days be prolonged in the land You give us. Do not let us act unjustly; we do not want to be an abomination to You, LORD our God. In Your name, Jesus~"*

MARCH 11

Please read Deuteronomy 26.

Meditate on verse 18.

> *The LORD has today declared you to be His people,*
> *a treasured possession, as He promised you, and that*
> *you should keep all His commandments.*
>
> *Our great God and Savior, Christ Jesus, gave Himself for us*
> *to redeem us from every lawless deed and to purify for Himself*
> *a people for His own possession, zealous for good deeds.*
> —TITUS 2:13B-14

As God spoke to Israel in these verses, keep in mind He speaks to you as well. You are God's treasured possession, bought with the life of Christ. His death on the cross paid the necessary price to become a person called by His name. And, while good deeds cannot pay any part of the great cost of redemption, keeping His commandments and doing good deeds are the supernatural actions of one who is the blessed recipient of this great salvation.

Commit yourself to the LORD and pray for others to do the same by praying Deuteronomy 26:14 and 16-18 over yourself and those for whom you stand guard as a faithful, prayerful watchman (Isaiah 62:6-7).

> *"LORD my God, may _____ and I listen to Your*
> *voice. Let us do according to all that You have commanded us.*
> *LORD, You command us to do these statutes and ordinances;*
> *therefore, help us be careful to do them with all our heart*
> *and with all our soul. Please let _____ want*
> *You to be their God and walk in Your ways and keep Your*
> *statutes, Your commandments, and Your ordinances and*
> *listen to Your voice. Thank You for declaring us to be Your*
> *people, a treasured possession, as You promised us.*
> *Help us keep all Your commandments.*
> *In Your name, Jesus~"*

MARCH 12

Please read Deuteronomy 27.

Meditate on verses 9-10.

> *Then Moses and the Levitical priests spoke to all Israel, saying, "Be silent and listen, O Israel! This day you have become a people for the LORD your God. You shall therefore obey the LORD your God and do His commandments and His statutes which I command you today."*

Proof of belonging to God is obedience to Him. This principle is taught throughout Scripture in both the Old and the New Testaments. Jesus Himself said:

> *"Therefore, go and make disciples of all nations, baptizing them in the name of the Father and the Son and the Holy Spirit, teaching them to obey everything I have commanded you. And remember, I am with you always, to the end of the age."*
> —MATTHEW 28:19-20 (NIV)

In a week, you will begin praying the book of Matthew, noticing the commands of Christ. Moses told the people to write all the law of God on stones (vs. 2-3, 8). Consider getting a journal and writing His commands when you see them in Matthew.

Pray Deuteronomy 27:8-10 over yourself and those for whom you stand guard as a faithful, prayerful watchman (Isaiah 62:6-7).

> *"LORD, write on _____ and my heart all the words of Your law very distinctly. Let us be silent and listen to You because we are a people for You, LORD our God. Help us obey You and do Your commandments and statutes which You command us. In Your name, Jesus~"*

MARCH 13

Please read Deuteronomy 28.

Meditate on verse 2.

> *All these blessings will come upon you and overtake you if you obey the LORD your God.*

This is a sobering chapter in God's Word, a chapter to be pondered with the help of the Holy Spirit and prayed with an obedient heart, desiring God's blessings, not the world's. Matthew 5:3-11 is a good place to start thinking about God's blessings. Jesus defined them as:

- Blessed are the poor in spirit, for theirs is the kingdom of heaven.
- Blessed are those who mourn, for they shall be comforted.
- Blessed are the gentle, for they shall inherit the earth.
- Blessed are those who hunger and thirst for righteousness, for they shall be satisfied.
- Blessed are the merciful, for they shall receive mercy.
- Blessed are the pure in heart, for they shall see God.
- Blessed are the peacemakers, for they shall be called sons of God.
- Blessed are those who have been persecuted for the sake of righteousness, for theirs is the kingdom of heaven.
- Blessed are you when people insult you and persecute you, and falsely say all kinds of evil against you because of Me.

Pray Deuteronomy 28:1-2, 9-10, and 47 over yourself and those for whom you stand guard as a faithful, prayerful watchman (Isaiah 62:6-7).

> *"LORD my God, please help _____ and me diligently obey You, being careful to do all Your commandments which You command us. May Your blessings come upon us and overtake us when we listen to Your voice. LORD, establish us as a holy people to Yourself. May we keep Your commandments and walk in Your ways, so all the peoples of the earth will see that we are called by Your name, LORD our God. Help us serve you with joy and a glad heart— For the abundance of all things and the sake of Your name, Jesus~"*

MARCH 14

Please read Deuteronomy 29.

Meditate on verse 29.

> *The secret things belong to the LORD our God, but the things revealed belong to us and to our sons forever, that we may observe all the words of this law.*

It is amazing the LORD our God chooses to reveal Himself to us. What a privilege to have His Words written to read, hear, ponder, memorize, and live! God does not take lightly those who hear His Word yet walk in the stubbornness of their heart (vs. 19-21).

As you continue to read the Bible, learn from the Old Testament who God is, noticing what makes Him happy and what makes Him angry. Desire to live pleasing to Him.

Pray Deuteronomy 29:2-4, 9-13, 25-26, and 29 over yourself and those for whom you stand guard as a faithful, prayerful watchman (Isaiah 62:6-7).

> *"LORD, please give _____ and me a heart to know, eyes to see, and ears to hear all You have done and are doing before our eyes, the great trials and Your great signs and wonders. Help us keep the words of Your covenant to do them that we may prosper in all we do. Let us stand before You, today, and enter into the covenant with You and into Your oath that You may establish us as Your people that You will be our God. Do not let us forsake Your covenant and serve and worship other gods. The secret things belong to You, LORD our God, but the things revealed belong to us and our sons forever, that we may observe all Your Words. For the sake of Your name, Jesus~"*

MARCH 15

Please read Deuteronomy 30.

Meditate on verses 19b-20a.

> *So, choose life in order that you may live, you and your descendants, by loving the LORD your God, by obeying His voice, and by holding fast to Him, for this is your life and the length of your days.*
>
> *When Christ, who is our life, is revealed, then you also will be revealed with Him in glory.*
> —COLOSSIANS 3:4

God gave His people choices in this chapter: life or death; prosperity or adversity; the blessing or the curse. The choice seems easy; however, history and the Bible record that many in Israel chose to disobey the LORD rather than obey, resulting in the curse, adversity, and death.

Now 3,500 years later, the LORD still offers the same life or death choice to people, with the added insight that Jesus Christ is Life, and apart from Him is adversity and the curse of death. The choice seems easy; however, many choose not to follow Him, but rather they follow a path leading to destruction.

As a faithful, prayerful watchman (Isaiah 62:6-7), pray Deuteronomy 30:2-3, 6, and 14 over those you love to make the right choice.

> *"LORD my God, may _____ return to You and obey You with all their heart and soul. Restore them from captivity to sin and have compassion on them and gather them to Yourself, LORD. Circumcise their heart to love You with all their heart and with all their soul, so they may live. Let Your Word be very near them, in their mouth and in their heart, that they may observe it. May they choose Life in Your name, Jesus~"*

MARCH 16

Please read Deuteronomy 31.

Meditate on verse 8.

> *The LORD is the one who goes ahead of you; He will be with you. He will not fail you or forsake you. Do not fear or be dismayed.*

The Israelites were led around the wilderness for 40 years by their faithful leader, Moses, but now he is about to die and will not be the one to lead them into the Promised Land. Can you imagine the emotions running through the Israelite camp as it sank in that the biggest adventure of their life would be without the man upon whom they depended? Moses reminded the people the LORD their God would cross ahead of them; He would go ahead of them; He would be with them (vs. 3, 6, 8). God would be the Leader of Israel.

The same God who led Israel 3,500 years ago wants to lead you. He is a faithful Leader who will never leave or forsake you. Do not fear, even if a person you thought was leading has been removed from that role. The LORD is the One who goes ahead of you in the journey. He is the One who will always be with you.

Pray Deuteronomy 31:6 over yourself and those for whom you stand guard as a faithful, prayerful watchman (Isaiah 62:6-7).

> *"LORD, help _____ and me be strong and courageous. Do not let us be afraid or tremble. LORD, our God, thank You that You go with us and will not fail us or forsake us. Because of Your name, Jesus~"*

MARCH 17

Please read Deuteronomy 32.

Meditate on verses 2-4.

> *Let my teaching drop as the rain, my speech distill as the dew, as the droplets on the fresh grass and as the showers on the herb. For I proclaim the name of the LORD; ascribe greatness to our God! The Rock! His work is perfect, for all His ways are just; a God of faithfulness and without injustice, righteous and upright is He.*

Interestingly, Moses' last words were a teaching song. He wanted the Israelites to remember God's faithfulness and their past unfaithfulness, in hopes they would take his words to heart, observing God's law and teaching it to their children because their lives depended on it. Look for opportunities to teach God's Word, even if it is with your dying breath, because the eternal lives of others are at stake.

Moses' final words began with a prayer for his teaching to impact his hearers like rain impacts vegetation, causing it to flourish, thrive, and reproduce. It is a perfect prayer to pray over yourself when the LORD gives you the opportunity to speak about Him.

Pray it (Deuteronomy 32:2-4) now as a faithful, prayerful watchman (Isaiah 62:6-7).

> *"LORD, please let my teaching drop as the rain and my speech distill as the dew, as the droplets on the fresh grass and as the showers on the herb. For I proclaim Your name, LORD, and ascribe greatness to You, God. You are the Rock! Your work is perfect, for all Your ways are just. You are a God of faithfulness and without injustice. You are righteous and upright. You are Jesus, in whose name I pray~"*

MARCH 18

Please read Deuteronomy 33.

Meditate on verses 3 and 29a.

> *Indeed, He (God) loves the people; all Your holy ones are in Your hand, and they followed in Your steps; everyone receives of Your words. Blessed are you, O Israel; who is like you, a people saved by the LORD!*

As a Christian, you, too, are God's holy one, saved by the LORD. And while the blessings in this chapter were spoken over the tribes of Israel, they are great blessings to pray over those you love as well. Treasure hunt this chapter for verses you would like to see the LORD fulfill in the lives of your loved ones. Below are some we pray over our family.

Pray Deuteronomy 33:3, 12-16, 23, and 27 over yourself and those you love as a faithful, prayerful watchman (Isaiah 62:6-7).

> *"LORD, thank You for loving _____ and me, Your people. Thank You for making us Your holy ones and keeping us in Your hand. May we follow in Your steps and receive of Your Words. As Your beloved, let us dwell in security by You. Shield us all the day and let us dwell between Your shoulders. Bless our land with the choice things of heaven, with the dew from the deep lying beneath, with the choice yield of the sun, with the choice produce of the months, with the best things of the ancient mountains, with the choice things of the everlasting hills, with the choice things of the earth and its fullness, and with Your favor, LORD. Let us be satisfied with favor and full of the blessing of You, LORD. Eternal God, You are our dwelling place and underneath are Your everlasting arms. Drive out the enemy before us. Because of Your name, Jesus~"*

MARCH 19

Please read Deuteronomy 34.

Meditate on verse 5.

> *So, Moses the servant of the LORD died there in the land of Moab, according to the Word of the LORD.*

Many things could have been written on Moses' tombstone:

- Moses: Survivor of Infanticide (Exodus 1:22-2:4)
- Moses: Son of Pharaoh's Daughter (Exodus 2:5-10)
- Moses: Murderer of an Egyptian (Exodus 2:11-14)
- Moses: Herder of Sheep (Exodus 3:1)
- Moses: Maker of Excuses (Exodus 3:10-4:14)
- Moses: Leader of Israel (Exodus 32:34)
- Moses: Prophet in Israel (Deuteronomy 34:10)
- Moses: Performer of Signs and Wonders (Deuteronomy 34:11)
- Moses: Disqualifier for Entering the Promised Land (Numbers 20:12)

But instead, God gave him this epitaph: Moses: Servant of the LORD (v. 5). Ponder God's description of Moses, asking Him how He would describe you. Desire to be His faithful servant.

Pray Deuteronomy 34:5, 7, and 9 over yourself and those for whom you stand guard as a faithful, prayerful watchman (Isaiah 62:6-7).

> *"LORD, may _____ and I die as
> Your servants, according to Your Word.
> Please let our eyes not dim, nor our vigor abate
> as we serve You to our dying day.
> Fill us with Your Spirit of wisdom.
> In Your name, Jesus~"*

MARCH 20

Please read Matthew 1.

Meditate on verses 20 and 24 and on Jesus' command in Matthew 28:19-20.

> *But when he had considered this, behold, an angel of the LORD appeared to him in a dream, saying, "Joseph, son of David, do not be afraid to take Mary as your wife; for the Child who has been conceived in her is of the Holy Spirit. And Joseph awoke from his sleep and did as the angel of the LORD commanded him and took Mary as his wife.*
>
> *"Go therefore and make disciples of all the nations, baptizing them in the name of the Father and the Son and the Holy Spirit, teaching them to observe all that I commanded you."*

The book of *Matthew* ends with Jesus' command to "make disciples" (Matthew 28:19). And, He said the way to disciple a new believer was to teach them to obey ALL of His commandments (Matthew 28:20). As you read and pray *Matthew*, look for Jesus' commands. You may want to underline them in your Bible and/or write them in a journal.

Interestingly, the book begins with a command followed by obedience. Joseph was commanded to not be afraid and take Mary as his wife (v. 20). Joseph obeyed immediately (v. 24).

Ask the LORD to help you read Matthew with obedient eyes. Use the words from Matthew 1:20 and 24 to pray over yourself and those for whom you stand guard as a faithful, prayerful watchman (Isaiah 62:6-7).

> *"LORD, help _____ and me hear You say, 'Do not be afraid.' Help us obey this first command in Matthew. LORD, teach us to do all You command. In Your name, Jesus–"*

MARCH 21

Please read Matthew 2.

Meditate on verses 12-14.

> *And having been warned by God in a dream not to return to Herod, the magi left for their own country by another way. Now when they had gone, behold, an angel of the LORD appeared to Joseph in a dream and said, "Get up! Take the Child and His mother and flee to Egypt, and remain there until I tell you, for Herod is going to search for the Child to destroy Him." So, Joseph got up and took the Child and His mother while it was still night and left for Egypt.*

Joseph and the magi are great examples for how to obey God—unquestioningly quickly! As soon as the LORD said, "Go!" they went without hesitation. Delayed obedience could have resulted in deadly disobedience.

How would the LORD describe your obedience? Ask Him to make you a quick-to-obey wise person who knows the LORD's commands and does not hesitate to do them.

Pray Matthew 2:10-12 over yourself and those for whom you stand guard as a faithful, prayerful watchman (Isaiah 62:6-7).

> "LORD, I have seen You, the bright morning star (Revelation 22:16), and I rejoice exceedingly with great joy. I fall to the ground and worship You. I present to You the gift of my life. May _____ give You their life and worship You. Help us hear when You warn us and go the way You want us to go. In Your name, Jesus~"

MARCH 22

Please read Matthew 3.

Meditate on verses 15-17.

> *But Jesus answering said to him, "Permit it at this time; for in this way it is fitting for us to fulfill all righteousness." Then he permitted Him. After being baptized, Jesus came up immediately from the water; and behold, the heavens were opened, and he saw the Spirit of God descending as a dove and lighting on Him, and behold, a voice out of the heavens said, "This is My beloved Son, in whom I am well-pleased."*

When John tried to prevent Jesus from being baptized, Jesus said He needed to be baptized to "fulfill all righteousness" (v. 15). The Greek word for fulfill is *pleroo*, and it means "to cause God's will to be obeyed as it should be."[1] God took pleasure in Jesus as He obeyed Him fully.

Joseph, the wisemen, and Jesus—three examples of obedience to emulate as we continue reading *Matthew*, looking for Christ's commands. When you find those commands, ask the LORD to give you His heart to obey His will as it should be—wholeheartedly, faithfully, and quickly.

Pray Matthew 3:15-17 over yourself and those for whom you stand guard as a faithful, prayerful watchman (Isaiah 62:6-7).

> *"LORD, help _____ and me do what is fitting to fulfill all righteousness. Spirit of God, You have descended on us and have lighted in us. Father, we want to be children in whom You are well-pleased. For the sake of Your name, Jesus~"*

---

1. www.blueletterbible.org/lang/lexicon/lexicon.cfm?Strongs=G4137&t=NASB

MARCH 23

Please read Matthew 4.

Meditate on verse 17.

> *From that time, Jesus began to preach and say,*
> *"Repent, for the kingdom of heaven is at hand."*

The first command of Christ as recorded by Matthew is: "Repent, for the kingdom of heaven is at hand." Repent. It is the first command every human must obey in order to become a Christian. Repent is the Greek word *metanoeo*, and it means "to change one's mind for better; heartily to amend, with abhorrence of one's past sins."[1] Have you wholeheartedly obeyed Jesus' command to repent?

The second command of Christ is also in this chapter. "Follow Me" (v. 19). Follow is the Greek word *deute*, and it is an imperative command that says, "Come now!"[2] No wonder Peter and Andrew immediately left their nets and followed Jesus (v. 18-20). No wonder James and John immediately left their boat and their father to follow Christ (v. 21-22). When the Master gives a command, it must be obeyed straightway.

Ask the LORD to give you His abhorrence for sin and the willingness to follow Him everywhere He wants you to go.

Pray Matthew 4:17 and 19-20 over yourself and those for whom you stand guard as a faithful, prayerful watchman (Isaiah 62:6-7).

> *"LORD, I repent, for the kingdom of heaven is at hand. Please let _____ repent for the sake of Your kingdom. You command us to follow You. Help us immediately leave whatever we are doing and follow You. Make us fishers of men. In Your name, Jesus~"*

---

1. www.blueletterbible.org/lang/lexicon/lexicon.cfm?Strongs=G3340&t=NASB
2. www.blueletterbible.org/lang/lexicon/lexicon.cfm?Strongs=G1205&t=NASB

MARCH 24

Please read Matthew 5.

Meditate on verse 12.

> *Rejoice and be glad, for your reward in heaven is great; for in the same way they persecuted the prophets who were before you.*

This is quite the treasure hunt! We discovered 16 commands in this chapter; how many did you find? We don't have to get the exact same number, but it is important to find the LORD's commands and do as He says, like Peter, Andrew, James, and John immediately did (Matthew 4:18-22).

The first command we see in this chapter is to rejoice and be glad, even in the midst of persecution (vs. 10-12). Ugh, what a difficult command to wholeheartedly, immediately, and faithfully obey! "Rejoice and be glad." It is an easy command to fulfill on days when things are going right, but things in this world are usually not going right, so we must choose to rejoice and be glad in the LORD, remembering a day is coming when the things of this world will disappear, and we will be with Jesus face-to-face. Glory! What a great reward we have waiting for us!

Pray Matthew 5:10-12 over yourself and those for whom you stand guard as a faithful, prayerful watchman (Isaiah 62:6-7).

> *"LORD, You say _____ and I are blessed when we have been persecuted for the sake of righteousness, for ours is the kingdom of heaven. You say we are blessed when people insult us and persecute us and falsely say all kinds of evil against us because of You. We cling to Your promises, Jesus! We will rejoice and be glad, for our reward in heaven is great. Thank You for reminding us we are not alone, for in the same way they persecuted the prophets who were before us. We will rejoice and be glad! In Your name, Jesus, our great reward~"*

MARCH 25

Please read Matthew 6.

Meditate on these commands from verses 25 and 26.

Do not be worried. Look at the birds of the air.

Jesus takes His command to not worry seriously because He says it three times in this chapter (vs. 25, 31, 34). He knows worry is destructive to our spirit, soul, and body, and offensive to God, because when we worry, we admit we don't really trust Him.

In the middle of the "Do not worry" commands, Jesus commands us to "Look at the birds" (v. 26). How sweet of our LORD to want us to look up and out, away from our worries, at birds! And, He created plenty of them to watch, so it is an easy command to fulfill. New research suggests there are about 18,000 species of birds.[1] Amazing! "Oh, Jesus, change me from a worrier to a birdwatcher!"

As a faithful, prayerful watchman and birdwatcher, pray Matthew 6:25-28 and 31-33 over yourself and those for whom you stand guard as a faithful, prayerful watchman (Isaiah 62:6-7).

*"LORD, help _____ and me stop worrying about our life! Help us look at the birds of the air; they do not sow, nor reap, nor gather into barns, yet Father, You feed them. Are we not worth much more than they? By being worried, we cannot add a single hour to our life. Help us observe how the lilies of the field grow. They do not toil, nor do they spin. LORD, help us not worry, saying, 'What will we eat? What will we drink? What will we wear for clothing?' Heavenly Father, You know we need all these things. Help us seek first Your kingdom and Your righteousness, and all these things will be added to us.
In Your name, Jesus-"*

We discovered 19 commands in this chapter. How many do you see?

---

1. Retrieved from: www.amnh.org/explore/news-blogs/research-posts/study-doubles-estimate-of-world-bird-species

MARCH 26

Please read Matthew 7.

Meditate on the first command in verse 7.

Ask.

Jesus commands you to ask the Father for what you need. The word ask is repeated five times in verses 7-11. Ask is the Greek word *aiteo*, and it means "to beg, crave, call for, desire, and require."[1] The command comes with the promise that when you keep asking the Father, He gives you good gifts (vs. 7, 11). Ponder the gravity of this command, keeping it in the context of two more commands in verse 7: "Seek" and "Knock." As you read God's Word and talk to Him about the things He desires and requires, hear Jesus say to you:

If you abide in Me, and My words abide in you, ask whatever you wish, and it will be done for you.
—JOHN 15:7

Pray Matthew 7:7 and 11 as a faithful, prayerful watchman (Isaiah 62:6-7).

"LORD, You command me to ask, seek, and knock. You promise when I do, it will be given to me. I will find, and it will be opened to me. Thank You, Father, that You know much more than I, how to give good to me when I ask You. (Continue to beg the Father for the desires He places on your heart [Psalm 37:4].) In Your name, Jesus~"

We discovered 12 commands in this chapter. How many can you find? As you walk the rest of this day with Jesus, focus on obeying His last two commands in the chapter:

"Hear these words of Mine and act on them."
—MATTHEW 7:24

---

1. Retrieved from www.blueletterbible.org/lang/lexicon/lexicon.cfm?Strongs=G154&t=NASB

MARCH 27

Please read Matthew 8.

Meditate on verse 13.

> *And Jesus said to the centurion, "Go; it shall be done for you as you have believed." And the servant was healed that very moment.*

Jesus' repeated command in Matthew 8 is "Go" (vs. 4, 13, 32). It is the Greek word *hypago*, and it means "to depart, get thee hence, go away."[1] Notice the results from obeying Jesus' command to go. The leper asked Jesus to make him clean; the LORD immediately cleansed his leprosy and told him to go show himself to the priest as a testimony (vs. 2-4). Jesus told the centurion to go to his sick servant who was healed the very moment the centurion believed (v. 13). Jesus cast out demon spirits with a single word; that word was "Go" (vs. 16, 31-32). A leper, a Roman soldier, and demons, all obeyed Jesus' command to go. They obeyed immediately, and the results were miraculous.

What is your response when Jesus says, "Go"? Quickly obey, so you do not miss out on the miraculous in your life and the lives of those you love.

Pray Matthew 8:4, 13, and 22 over yourself and those for whom you stand guard as a faithful, prayerful watchman (Isaiah 62:6-7).

> *"LORD, when You say, 'Go,' let _____ and me obey quickly as a testimony to others. Let us hear You say, 'Go; it shall be done for you as you have believed.' Let it happen this very moment. We go, following You, allowing the dead to bury their own dead. In Your name, Jesus~"*

---

1. Retrieved from www.blueletterbible.org/lang/lexicon/lexicon.cfm?Strongs=G5217&t=NASB

MARCH 28

Please read Matthew 9.

Meditate on verse 13.

> *But go and learn what this means: "I DESIRE COMPASSION, AND NOT SACRIFICE," for I did not come to call the righteous, but sinners.*

Jesus gave the command to go and learn what God means when He says: "I desire compassion and not sacrifice" (Hosea 6:6). And for the remainder of the chapter, Jesus showed by example what it means to give mercy, rather than perform religious rituals like fasting to please God (vs. 13-15).

Jesus went with a synagogue ruler whose daughter had died (vs. 18-19). On His way, He gave compassion to a hemorrhaging woman, healing her; then, He raised the dead girl (vs. 20-25). As He left the girl's house, He showed mercy to two blind men, restoring their sight (vs. 27-30). As He went on from there, a mute, demon-possessed man was brought to Him; Jesus cast out the demon, and the man was able to speak (vs. 32-33). Four recorded miracles in a single day because Christ is compassionate.

Today, you obeyed the command to learn what "I desire compassion and not sacrifice" means. Can you imagine the miracles you will see as you obey God's command to show compassion?

Pray Matthew 9:13 and 36-38 over yourself and those for whom you stand guard as a faithful, prayerful watchman (Isaiah 62:6-7).

> *"LORD, thank You for teaching me what 'I desire compassion and not sacrifice' means.*
> *You came to call sinners. Thank You for calling me. When I see people, help me feel Your compassion for them because they are distressed and dispirited like sheep without a shepherd. The harvest is plentiful, but the workers are few. LORD of the harvest, I beg You to send out workers into Your harvest.*
> *_____ and I will be Your compassionate workers.*
> *In Your name, Jesus~"*

MARCH 29

Please read Matthew 10.

Meditate on verse 28.

> *Do not fear those who kill the body but are unable to kill the soul;*
> *but rather fear Him who is able to destroy both soul and body in hell.*

Just like Jesus commanded three times "Do not worry" in Matthew 6, He commanded three times "Do not fear" in Matthew 10 (vs. 26, 28, 31). Imagine the difference when you truly obey His commands to not worry and not be afraid.

Notice however, there is One whom Jesus commands us to fear, and He is God (v. 28). Many do the opposite, fearing everything except God. As you think about Jesus' command to fear God, consider these promises:

- The fear of the LORD is the beginning of knowledge and wisdom (Proverbs 1:7; 9:10).
- The fear of the LORD prolongs life (Proverbs 10:27).
- In the fear of the LORD, there is strong confidence (Proverbs 14:26).
- The fear of the LORD is a fountain of life (Proverbs 14:27).
- By the fear of the LORD, one keeps away from evil (Proverbs 16:6).
- The reward of the fear of the LORD is riches, honor, and life (Proverbs 22:4).

Pray Matthew 10:20 and 27-28 over yourself and those for whom you stand guard as a faithful, prayerful watchman (Isaiah 62:6-7).

> *"Father, let Your Spirit speak in _____ and me.*
> *What You tell us in the darkness, let us speak in the light and what*
> *we hear whispered in our ear, let us proclaim upon the housetops.*
> *We will not fear those who kill the body but are unable to kill the soul;*
> *but rather, we fear You, God, who is able to destroy*
> *both soul and body in hell. LORD, please let*
> *_____ fear You before it is too late.*
> *In Your name, Jesus~"*

MARCH 30

Please read Matthew 11.

Meditate on verse 15.

> *He who has ears to hear, let him hear.*

Jesus commands us to hear Him instead of the world's childish accusations and slanderous gossip (vs. 16-19). His words in this chapter snap us to reality because He says:

> *You have seen My miracles, yet you do not repent.*
> *The day of judgment is coming. Repent, or you will descend to Hades.*
> —MATTHEW 11:20-24

How much of your day is spent hearing God's Word instead of the world's words? When you obey Christ's command to hear, you hear Him say these amazing words:

> *Come to Me, all who are weary and heavy-*
> *laden, and I will give you rest.*
> *Take My yoke upon you and learn from Me, for*
> *I am gentle and humble in heart, and*
> *YOU WILL FIND REST FOR YOUR SOULS.*
> —MATTHEW 11:28-29

Obeying the command to come to Jesus, yoking yourself to Him, results in rest for your weary, heavy-laden soul (v. 28-29). "Thank You, Jesus!"

Pray Matthew 11:6, 15, and 27-29 over yourself and those for whom you stand guard as a faithful, prayerful watchman (Isaiah 62:6-7).

> *"LORD Jesus, I do not take offense at You.*
> *Please let _____ stop being offended at You.*
> *_____ and I have ears, so let us hear. Jesus, reveal the*
> *Father to us. We come to You weary and heavy-laden. Please give*
> *us Your rest. As we take Your yoke upon us, help us learn from You.*
> *Thank You for being gentle and humble in heart—make us like You.*
> *Thank You for giving rest to our souls.*
> *In Your name, Jesus~"*

MARCH 31

Please read Matthew 12.

Meditate on verse 13.

> *Then He (Jesus) said to the man, "Stretch out your hand!"*
> *He stretched it out, and it was restored to normal, like the other.*

Don't you know this man was thankful he obeyed Jesus! With one simple act of obedience, the man's hand was miraculously restored. What do you think would have happened had he refused?

What has Jesus commanded you to do, yet you refuse to obey? "Forgive the person who wronged you." "Stop worrying about this situation." "Do not be afraid to try."

Stretch out your hand, taking hold of Jesus' hand. Ask Him to help you obey. When you do, you, too, will experience His miraculous restoration.

Pray Matthew 12:13, 25, 32-36, and 50 over yourself and those for whom you stand guard as a faithful, prayerful watchman (Isaiah 62:6-7).

> *"LORD, help _____ and me stretch out in faithful obedience. Please restore us! Jesus, You know my thoughts. Let me never speak a word against You or the Holy Spirit. Please forgive me. Help me be a good tree, producing good fruit, for the tree is known by its fruit. Make my heart good, so my mouth speaks of that which fills my heart. May I bring out of my good treasure what is good. Let there be no evil treasure in my life. LORD, please forgive my every careless word. Help me stop speaking careless words. Jesus, I want to do the will of Your Father who is in heaven. In Your name, Jesus~"*

April

*On your walls, O Jerusalem,
I have appointed watchmen;
All day and all night they
will never keep silent.
You who remind the LORD,
take no rest for yourselves;
And give Him no rest until He establishes
And makes Jerusalem a
praise in the earth.*
Isaiah 62:6-7, NASB

APRIL 1

Please read Matthew 13.

Meditate on verse 9.

> *He who has ears, let him hear.*

This is the second time Jesus commands those with ears to listen (Matthew 11:15). And, in this chapter, He uses the word 'hear' sixteen times. Listening to Jesus, comprehending what He says, and obeying what He commands is a big deal!

Pray Matthew 13:9, 13-23, and 43 over yourself and those for whom you stand guard as a faithful, prayerful watchman (Isaiah 62:6-7).

"LORD, _____ and I have ears, let us hear! We want to see, hear, and understand what You speak, even the parables. LORD, do not let us be the fulfillment of Isaiah's prophecy. Let us keep on hearing and understand. Let us keep on seeing and perceive. Do not let our hearts become dull nor our ears scarcely hear. Do not let us close our eyes. Let us see with our eyes, hear with our ears, understand with our heart and return, so You will heal us. Let our eyes and ears be blessed because we see and hear. Thank You, Jesus, we get to see and hear things prophets and righteous men desired to see and hear. Help us hear the parable of the sower. When we hear the Word of the kingdom, help us understand it. Do not let the evil one come and snatch away what has been sown in our heart. Let us hear and immediately receive the Word with joy. Let it take firm root in us, so when affliction or persecution arises because of the Word, we do not fall away. When we hear the Word, do not let the worry of the world and the deceitfulness of wealth choke the Word, so it becomes unfruitful. Let us hear the Word and understand it. Let us indeed bear fruit and bring forth a hundredfold. Make us the righteous who shine forth as the sun in Your kingdom, Father. We have ears; let us hear! In Your name, Jesus~"

APRIL 2

Please read Matthew 14.

Meditate on Jesus' commands in verse 27.

Take courage, it is I; do not be afraid.

Do you ever feel like you just don't get a break? Jesus needed a break. His cousin had been executed, and Jesus wanted time alone to grieve his death (vs. 12-13). But a bunch of people followed him to his "secluded" spot. When Jesus saw them, instead of being upset about His disrupted quiet time, He felt compassion for them (v. 14). After feeding the whole group, He attempted again to have time alone, but He noticed His disciples were in a fix, out on an angry sea, so He again selflessly left His quiet place and walked out on the waves to quiet His beloved disciples (vs. 22-27).

Miraculously, Jesus constantly does the same for you; He comes to you in the midst of your choppiness and says, "Take courage, it is I; do not be afraid" (vs. 27). As you think about that command, consider His other commands in this chapter and how He wants you to obey them:

- You give them something to eat (v. 16).
- Bring them here to Me (v. 18).
- Sit down on the grass (v. 19).
- Get into the boat (v. 22).
- Come! (v. 29)

Pray Matthew 14:14, 16, 18-19, 22, 27, and 29 as a prayer of commitment as a faithful, prayerful watchman (Isaiah 62:6-7).

*"LORD, make me like You. Help me feel
compassion for people. Let me bring healing;
let me give them something to eat. I bring You what I have;
LORD, please use it! I want to sit down on the grass with You.
I want to get into the boat and go wherever You lead.
I take courage because I am with You; I will not be afraid.
LORD, I come to You in Your name, Jesus~"*

APRIL 3

Please read Matthew 15.

Meditate on verses 10-11.

> *After Jesus called the crowd to Him, He said to them, "Hear and understand. It is not what enters into the mouth that defiles the man, but what proceeds out of the mouth, this defiles the man."*

After reading what Jesus commanded us to hear and understand, do you feel like Peter, saying, "LORD, I don't get it" (v. 15)? "Oh, LORD, help me understand!"

The Pharisees came to Jesus all concerned about his disciples not washing their hands before eating. Jesus pointed out to these rule followers they should be more concerned about dishonoring words to their parents, such as, "Whatever I have that would help you has been given to God," than a few germs going into his disciples' bellies (v. 5). What goes into our mouths will eventually be eliminated; what comes out of our mouths is evidence of what is in our hearts and has eternal impacts. "Oh, LORD, cleanse my filthy heart and set a guard over my mouth!"

Hear and understand Jesus' words. Ask Him to reveal your heart issues, heal your heart, and make it a heart of compassion like His (v. 32).

Pray Matthew 15:10-11, 22, 25, and 32 over yourself and those for whom you stand guard as a faithful, prayerful watchman (Isaiah 62:6-7).

> *"LORD, help _____ and me hear and understand. Do not let anything come out of our mouths that would defile others and ourselves. Have mercy on us, LORD, Son of David! LORD, help us! Help us feel compassion for people like You do. In Your name, Jesus~"*

APRIL 4

Please read Matthew 16.

Meditate on verses 16 and 22-23.

> *Simon Peter answered, "You are the Christ,*
> *the Son of the living God."*
> *Peter took Him aside and began to rebuke Him, saying, "God forbid*
> *it, LORD! This shall never happen to You."*
> *But He turned and said to Peter,*
> *"Get behind Me, Satan! You are a stumbling block to Me; for*
> *you are not setting your mind on God's interests, but man's."*

Do you ever have Peter days? One moment you speak the very truths of God, and the next moment you say something regrettable. Peter declared, "Jesus is the Christ, the Son of the living God" (v. 16). But, when Jesus revealed His purpose as the Son of the Living God, Peter cried out, "God forbid!" (v. 22). Think about it. If Peter's prayer for God to forbid Jesus from suffering and dying on the cross had been answered the way Peter wanted, where would we be right now?

Read the meditation verses again. Are the things you say and the things you pray based on God's desires? If God answered your prayers the way you hope, would it cause you to stumble and not be in God's will? Check your heart's desires, making sure they are God's desires and not Satan's.

Pray Matthew 16:16 and 22-24 over yourself and those for whom you stand guard as a faithful, prayerful watchman (Isaiah 62:6-7).

> *"LORD, You are the Christ, the Son of the Living God.*
> *God, forbid me to follow You as a Satan, as a stumbling*
> *block to You. Help me set my mind on Your interests, not*
> *man's. Jesus, I wish to come after You, so I will obey Your*
> *command to deny myself, take up my cross, and follow*
> *You. Please help _____ do the same.*
> *In Your name, Jesus~"*

APRIL 5

Please read Matthew 17.

Meditate on verses 7-8 and 15-18.

> *And Jesus came to them and touched them and said, "Get up, and do not be afraid." And lifting up their eyes, they saw no one except Jesus Himself alone. When they came to the crowd, a man came up to Jesus, falling on his knees before Him and saying, "LORD, have mercy on my son, for he is a lunatic and is very ill; for he often falls into the fire and often into the water. I brought him to Your disciples, and they could not cure him." And Jesus answered and said, "You unbelieving and perverted generation, how long shall I be with you? How long shall I put up with you? Bring him here to Me." And Jesus rebuked him, and the demon came out of him, and the boy was cured at once.*

Notice the three commands in these verses and the results of obedience. "Get up. Do not be afraid. Bring him here to Me" (vs. 7, 17).

When Peter, James, and John got up, their fear was gone and all they could see was Jesus. When the distraught father brought his boy to Christ, Jesus told the demon to get out, and the boy was healed immediately.

We desperately need to obey these three commands. Get up. Do not be afraid. Bring your problems to Jesus. So many people lie on beds of depression, fearing and worrying. We need Jesus!

As a faithful, prayerful watchman (Isaiah 62:6-7), pray for yourself and those you love to obey Jesus' commands in Matthew 17:7-8 and 17-18.

> *"LORD, help _____ and me get up and not be afraid. As we do, give us eyes only for You, Jesus. I bring _____ to You. Rebuke our demons and cure us at once. In Your name, Jesus~"*

APRIL 6

Please read Matthew 18.

Meditate on Jesus' commands in verses 3-6 and 10.

> *Convert and become like children. Humble yourself as this child.*
> *Receive one such child in My name. Do not cause*
> *one of these little ones who believes in Me to stumble.*
> *Do not despise one of these little ones.*

Interestingly, Jesus gave these commands in answer to the disciples' question: "Who then is greatest in the kingdom of heaven?" (v. 1). These followers of Christ often concerned themselves with greatness (v. 1; Mark 9:33-37; Luke 9:46-48; 22:24). Jesus taught that humbling oneself as a little child, being last and a servant of all, was truly great in God's eyes (v. 4; Mark 9:35). And Jesus lived what He taught, receiving and teaching these grown men who were still so childlike in their understanding of God and His ways rather than despising them for their prideful selfishness. And, Jesus, the constant servant leader, washed their feet the night before He offered Himself in total humility as the sacrifice for their sins and ours (John 13:1-17).

When you are overcome with the desire for greatness, remember our LORD's commands, praying them over yourself and those for whom you stand guard as a faithful, prayerful watchman (Isaiah 62:6-7). Pray Matthew 18:3-6 and 10.

> "LORD, I had to convert and become like a child
> in order to enter the kingdom of heaven.
> *Please let* _____ convert and become like a child before
> it is too late. Help me humble myself as Your child. Help me receive
> Your children in Your name. Do not let me cause little ones who
> believe in You to stumble. Help me not despise any of Your little ones.
> For the sake of Your name, Jesus~"

APRIL 7

Please read Matthew 19.

Meditate on verse 6. Jesus is speaking.

> *"So, they are no longer two, but one flesh. What therefore God has joined together, let no man separate."*

Marriage was created by God, 6,000 years ago, with His blessing:

> *"For this reason, a man shall leave his father and his mother, and be joined to his wife; and they shall become one flesh."*
> —GENESIS 2:24

Marriage between one man and one woman unites them physically, spiritually, and emotionally. Marriage is a reminder of God's miracle of creating the first woman, Eve, from Adam's rib (Genesis 2:22). Marriage is the picture of Christ's unity with His church and His great love for her (Ephesians 5:31-32). Marriage is the picture of a Christian intimately knowing Jesus Christ (John 6:69). No wonder Satan loves divorce, and God hates it (Malachi 2:16). Divorce sends an unbelieving world a false picture of creation, Christianity, Christ, and His church.

Obey Christ's command not to separate a husband and wife. There is so much more at stake than one's "happiness." Your choice to stay in your marriage shows the world Jesus never leaves or forsakes those who know Him (John 14:1-3). God is faithful; trust Him with your marriage and the marriages of those for whom you stand guard as a faithful, prayerful watchman (Isaiah 62:6-7), by praying Matthew 19:4-6 and 8.

> *"LORD, from the beginning, You created us male and female. Because You created us male and female You said, 'For this reason a man shall leave his father and mother and be joined to his wife, and the two shall become one flesh.' So, God, _____ and I are no longer two, but one flesh. What therefore You have joined together, let no one separate— including me, LORD. Please remove our hardness of heart! For the sake of Your name, Jesus~"*

APRIL 8

Please read Matthew 20.

Meditate on verses 26b-28. Jesus is speaking.

> *"Whoever wishes to become great among you shall be your servant, and whoever wishes to be first among you shall be your slave; just as the Son of Man did not come to be served, but to serve, and to give His life a ransom for many."*

This chapter begins with a landowner hiring people to work his vineyard throughout the day. He ends up paying them all the same, whether they started early in the morning or late in the evening. There was a lot of complaining about unfair wages, but the workers were basically told to stop whining; the landowner had the right to pay whomever whatever he wanted. And then, Jesus speaks the sobering meditation verses, giving the command to serve others as a slave, just like He did, giving up His own life. Well, serving as a slave means we may not receive any compensation because slaves aren't wage earners. They belong to the master, and they do his bidding without expecting anything in return.

> *So, you too, when you do all the things*
> *which are commanded you, say,*
> *"We are unworthy slaves; we have done only*
> *that which we ought to have done."*
> —LUKE 17:10

Ponder what it really means to obey and serve Christ and pray Matthew 20:28, 30-31, and 33-34 over yourself and those for whom you stand guard as a faithful, prayerful watchman (Isaiah 62:6-7).

> *"LORD, You did not come to be served, but to serve, and to give Your life as a ransom for many. LORD, Son of David, have mercy on _____ and me!*
> *LORD, Son of David, have mercy on us!*
> *LORD, we want our eyes to be opened.*
> *Help us regain our sight for what it really means to follow You.*
> *Because we are Your servants, Jesus~"*

APRIL 9

Please read Matthew 21.

Meditate on verses 18-19 and 43. Jesus is speaking.

> *Now in the morning, when He was returning to the city, He became hungry. Seeing a lone fig tree by the road, He came to it and found nothing on it except leaves only; and He said to it, "No longer shall there ever be any fruit from you." And at once the fig tree withered. "Therefore, I say to you, the kingdom of God will be taken away from you and given to a people, producing the fruit of it."*

Jesus takes seriously His command to produce fruit. He had no patience with the fruitless fig tree nor the fruitless religious leaders. Hear His words about fruit bearing from the book of John:

> *"I am the true vine, and My Father is the vinedresser. Every branch in Me that does not bear fruit, He takes away; and every branch that bears fruit, He prunes it so that it may bear more fruit.*
> —JOHN 15:1-2

Matthew 21 ends with disobedient religious people, but it begins with an obedient donkey. Under the control of the Master, this unbroken colt maneuvered through crowded streets with people cheering and tossing cloaks and palm branches in front of its face (vs. 2-8). The Master does the same with us as we submit our lives to Him, obeying His slightest touch and bidding. Abide in Christ; let Him produce the miraculous fruit of His kingdom through you.

Pray Matthew 21:6 and 43 over yourself and those for whom you stand guard as a faithful, prayerful watchman (Isaiah 62:6-7).

> *"LORD, help _____ and me go and do just as You instruct us. You have given us the kingdom of God; help us produce the fruit of it. In Your name, Jesus~"*

APRIL 10

Please read Matthew 22.

Meditate on the command in verse 4.

Come to the wedding feast.

This most important command of Christ comes in the form of an invitation:

Come to the wedding feast of the Lamb

Dress:
The righteousness of Christ

God gives us a sneak peek into that glorious wedding feast:

> *"Hallelujah! For the LORD our God, the Almighty, reigns. Let us rejoice and be glad and give the glory to Him, for the marriage of the Lamb has come, and His bride has made herself ready." It was given to her to clothe herself in fine linen, bright and clean; for the fine linen is the righteous acts of the saints. Then he said to me, "Write, 'Blessed are those who are invited to the marriage supper of the Lamb.'"*
> —REVELATION 19:6B-9A

The wedding feast Jesus described in Matthew 22 is a reality, and you do not want to miss it, so accept His invitation to come and invite others to join you.

As a faithful, prayerful watchman (Isaiah 62:6-7), pray for people to hear and accept the LORD's invitation to "come to the wedding feast" (v. 4).

> *"LORD, I accept Your invitation
> to come to Your wedding feast.
> LORD, please let _____ come
> to the wedding feast with me.
> In Your name, Jesus~"*

APRIL 11

Please read Matthew 23.

Meditate on verses 8-10.

> *Do not be called Rabbi; for One is your*
> *Teacher, and you are all brothers.*
> *Do not call anyone on earth your father; for One*
> *is your Father, He who is in heaven.*
> *Do not be called leaders; for One is your Leader, that is, Christ.*

The context for Christ's commands not to be called, "Rabbi", "Father", or "Leader" is pride.

> *They love the place of honor at banquets and the chief*
> *seats in the synagogues, and respectful greetings in the*
> *marketplaces and being called Rabbi by men.*
> —MATTHEW 23:6-7

Jesus commands us not to be called Rabbi, Father, or Leader because it will go to our heads, so we think we are God over those we have the privilege to teach, parent, and lead. So, while you may be a rabbi (teacher), father, or a leader, do not lord that position over others. Refuse such titles as: Most Reverend, Lord Bishop, Very Holy Father. Jesus forbids titles and honors which exalt humans and exacerbate pride.

Perhaps this chapter is difficult for you and your church because of centuries-old traditions. Jesus calls us to die to traditions. We do not want Jesus saying, "Woe to you!" like He does the traditionalists in this chapter, referring to them as hypocrites, fools, sons of hell, blind guides, and serpents (vs. 13-33).

Pray Matthew 23:8-12 over yourself and those for whom you stand guard as a faithful, prayerful watchman (Isaiah 62:6-7).

> *"LORD, You are Rabbi. You are the One Teacher.*
> *Teach _____ and me.*
> *LORD, You are the One Father, who is in heaven.*
> *LORD, You are the One Leader, Jesus Christ. We are Your servants."*

APRIL 12

Please read Matthew 24.

Meditate on Jesus' commands in verses 4, 6, 20, 26, 33, and 44.

> *And Jesus answered and said to them, "See to it that no one misleads you. You will be hearing of wars and rumors of wars. See that you are not frightened, for those things must take place, but that is not yet the end. But pray that your flight will not be in the winter or on a Sabbath. So, if they say to you, 'Behold, He is in the wilderness,' do not go out, or, 'Behold, He is in the inner rooms,' do not believe them. So, you too, when you see all these things, recognize that He is near, right at the door. For this reason, you also must be ready; for the Son of Man is coming at an hour when you do not think He will."*

Wow! There are a lot of commands to obey in connection with Christ's return:

- Do not be misled.
- Do not be frightened.
- Pray.
- Do not go out and believe false prophets.
- Recognize Jesus is right at the door.
- Be ready!

God's Word has a lot to say about His return. This chapter is a treasure chest of those truths. Ask God to give you His insight for what is taking place in this chapter. Then, pray Matthew 24:4, 6, 44, and 46 over yourself and those for whom you stand guard as a faithful, prayerful watchman (Isaiah 62:6-7).

> *"LORD, do not let _____ and me be misled. Do not let us be frightened when we hear of wars and rumors of wars, for these things must take place. Make us ready for Your coming, Son of Man. Make us Your slaves whom You find so doing when You come. Because You are our Master, Jesus~"*

APRIL 13

Please read Matthew 25.

Meditate on verse 6.

> *But at midnight there was a shout, "Behold, the bridegroom! Come out to meet him."*

Here is a command you do not want to miss, and you certainly want to obey it.

> *"Come out to meet the bridegroom!"*

What a glorious day that will be for Christians! Dressed in robes of righteousness, lamps filled with oil, fully lit, and brilliantly shining for Jesus, we will meet our bridegroom, our LORD and Savior Jesus Christ—Glory!

Thankfully, Matthew recorded much of Jesus' teaching about these last days before His return to earth. In a few months, you will read and pray *Daniel* and *Revelation*, which will make you even more prepared for the days to come. Pray with urgency for those you know who are like the foolish in Matthew 25, with no oil in their lamps, those who need Jesus.

Pray Matthew 25:6, 13, 21, and 34 over yourself and those for whom you stand guard as a faithful, prayerful watchman (Isaiah 62:6-7).

> *"LORD, let _____ and me be ready for the shout:*
> *'Behold, the bridegroom! Come out to meet Him!'*
> *Keep us on the alert, for we do not know the day nor the hour. When You come, let us hear You say, 'Well done, good and faithful slave. You were faithful with a few things; I will put you in charge of many things. Enter into the joy of your Master.'*
> *King Jesus, we look forward to the day we hear Your command: 'Come, you who are blessed of My Father, inherit the kingdom prepared for you from the foundation of the world.'*
> *Bless _____ to hear that command.*
> *Save them, in Your name, Jesus~"*

APRIL 14

Please read Matthew 26.

Meditate on Jesus' command in verse 41.

> *Keep watching and praying that you may not enter into temptation; the spirit is willing, but the flesh is weak.*

Jesus' command to keep watching and praying came just as chaos was about to rain down on His disciples. As they watched one of their own betray their beloved Master with a kiss, a huge crowd, 600 Roman soldiers, plus officers and Pharisees from the temple, descended into their quiet prayer garden (John 18:1-3). Swords drawn; torches blazing; clubs ready for beating; an ear sliced—the disciples were in the fog of war, and they did not do well—they all left Jesus and fled (v. 56).

Heed Jesus' command to keep watching and praying, for the winds of life can quickly become a hurricane. Be prepared with God's Word, prayer, and the power of the Holy Spirit.

Pray Matthew 26:38-39 and 41-42 over desperate situations as a faithful, prayerful watchman (Isaiah 62:6-7).

> *"LORD, my soul is deeply grieved, to the point of death. I will remain here and keep watch with You, Jesus. As I fall on my face and pray, Father, if it is possible, let this cup pass from me, yet not as I will, but as You will. Help me keep watching and praying that I may not enter into temptation.*
> *LORD, my spirit is willing, but my flesh is weak.*
> *My Father, if this cannot pass away unless I drink it, Your will be done.*
> *In Your name, Jesus~"*

APRIL 15

Please read Matthew 27, observing Christ's profound silence. Meditate on verse 14.

> *And He did not answer him with regard to even a single charge, so the governor was quite amazed.*

Jesus is obediently quiet in this chapter. Contrast what Jesus does not say with what was said:

> *Pilate said to them, "Then what shall I do with Jesus who is called Christ?" They all said, "Crucify Him!" And he said, "Why, what evil has He done?" But they kept shouting all the more, saying, "Crucify Him!" And all the people said, "His blood shall be on us and on our children!" They knelt down before Him and mocked Him, saying, "Hail, King of the Jews!" And those passing by were hurling abuse at Him, wagging their heads. In the same way the chief priests also, along with the scribes and elders, were mocking Him. The robbers who had been crucified with Him were also insulting Him with the same words.*
> —MATTHEW 27:22-23, 25, 29B, 39, 41, 44

Can you imagine slanderous liars screaming for your death? Jesus had every right to defend Himself, yet He kept His mouth shut. His silence set the stage for His last breath's cry (v. 50). At that moment, the veil of the temple was torn in two; the earth shook, and rocks split (v. 51).

Jesus models for us silent obedience. When God says, "Keep your mouth shut," yet every fiber of your being screams, "But LORD, I have to say something," remember your Savior in Matthew 27. Hush! God will act according to His will; don't let hasty words ruin His performance.

Pray Matthew 27:14 over yourself and those for whom you stand guard as a faithful, prayerful watchman (Isaiah 62:6-7).

> *"LORD, let everyone be quite amazed when _____ and I do not answer even a single word. For the sake of Your name, Jesus~"*

APRIL 16

Please read Matthew 28.

Meditate on verse 10.

> *Then Jesus said to them, "Do not be afraid; go and take word to My brethren to leave for Galilee, and there they will see Me."*

Well, Matthew, ends the way it began, with the command to not be afraid (Matthew 1:20; 28:10). God really wants us to walk in obedience with Him, with no fear of humans, and only awe-filled, reverential fear of Him.

We hope you have been emboldened by your Savior on this 28-day journey. If you wrote out His commands from this amazing book, you probably found at least 120. Thankfully Jesus gives us a lifetime to practice obedience.

How does Jesus want you to obey His command to not be afraid and take Word to His brethren? Who does He want you to disciple, teaching them His Words? Pray about using these Matthew devotionals to disciple others to follow Jesus. Obey quickly, praying Matthew 28:17-20 over yourself and those for whom you stand guard as a faithful, prayerful watchman (Isaiah 62:6-7).

> *"LORD, _____ and I worship You! Do not let us be doubtful because all authority has been given to You in heaven and on earth. LORD, we want to go and make disciples of all the nations, baptizing them in the name of You, Father, Son, and Holy Spirit. Help us teach them to observe all that You commanded us. Thank You for being with us always, even to the end of the age. Because You are the Savior, Jesus~"*

APRIL 17

Please read Joshua 1.

Meditate on verses 1 and 5.

> *Now it came about after the death of Moses*
> *the servant of the LORD, that the*
> *LORD spoke to Joshua the son of Nun, Moses'*
> *servant, saying, "No man will be*
> *able to stand before you all the days of your*
> *life. Just as I have been with Moses,*
> *I will be with you; I will not fail you or forsake you."*

Moses was dead, and Joshua was to lead the people into the Promised Land. From his youth, Joshua was a faithful follower of the LORD and attendant of Moses (Numbers 11:28; 14:6-9). He loved being in God's presence, not wanting to leave the tabernacle (Exodus 33:11). The LORD commissioned him to replace Moses and filled him with the spirit of wisdom (Deuteronomy 31:14; 34:9). And, although Joshua was a faithful Godly man, the LORD knew he needed encouragement for the task at hand.

Thankfully, we have God's words to Joshua, for they are encouraging words for us as well when the LORD calls us to tasks, making us rely on His strength and courage. Pray Joshua 1:5 and 7-9 over yourself and those for whom you stand guard as a faithful, prayerful watchman (Isaiah 62:6-7).

> *"LORD, just as You were with Moses and Joshua, be*
> *wih _____ and me all the days of our lives; do not*
> *fail us or forsake us. Make us strong and very courageous. Let us be*
> *careful to do according to all Your Word; do not let us turn from it*
> *to the right or to the left, so we may have success wherever we go.*
> *Do not let this book of the law depart from our mouth, but*
> *let us meditate on it day and night, so we may be careful to*
> *do according to all that is written in it. Please make our way*
> *prosperous and let us have success. You command us to be*
> *strong and courageous! Do not let us tremble or be dismayed,*
> *for You, LORD our God, are with us wherever we go.*
> *Thank You, in Your name, Jesus-"*

APRIL 18

Please read Joshua 2.

Meditate on verses 11 and 21. Rahab is speaking:

> *"When we heard it, our hearts melted and no courage remained in any man any longer because of you, for the LORD your God, He is God in heaven above and on earth beneath." She said, "According to your words, so be it." So, she sent them away, and they departed, and she tied the scarlet cord in the window.*

Despite being a Canaanite, growing up in a culture which worshiped many idols, Rahab declared her faith in the one true God. She immediately put her faith into action, tying the scarlet cord in her window because it represented God's salvation for her and her family. Her active faith was rewarded, for she and her relatives were indeed spared (Joshua 6:17, 23, 25). She even married an Israelite named Salmon, making her the mother of Boaz and the grandmother of King David. This faith-filled woman is forever recorded in the lineage of Jesus Christ and the *Hebrews'* Hall of Faith (Matthew 1:5; Hebrews 11:31).

It is amazing what God does with a life that actively trusts and follows Him!

Pray for God to save those you love to faithfully follow Him, using the words from Joshua 2:11-13 as their faithful, prayerful watchman (Isaiah 62:6-7).

> *"LORD, You are God. You are God in heaven above and on earth beneath. Please deal kindly with _____ and their household and spare their father and their mother and their brothers and their sisters, with all who belong to them, and deliver their lives from death. Through salvation in Your name, Jesus~"*

APRIL 19

Please read Joshua 3.

Meditate on verses 3 and 8.

> *When you see the ark of the covenant of the LORD your God with the Levitical priests carrying it, then you shall set out from your place and go after it. You shall, moreover, command the priests who are carrying the ark of the covenant, saying, "When you come to the edge of the waters of the Jordan, you shall stand still in the Jordan."*

Imagine the faith it took to obey God's command to step into a flooded river and stand still. Imagine hundreds of thousands of Israelites, following the ark of the covenant, between the waters of that flooded Jordan River, steadily stepping in faith with God. What a picture God gave us for our walk of faith in this life!

- When God says, "Move," set out from your place, confidently following Him (v. 3).
- When God says, "Be still," stand firm in the midst of the flood, knowing He is your firm foundation (v. 8).
- When God says, "Trust Me," believe that His presence cuts off what wants to swallow you (v. 13).

Pray Joshua 3:3, 8, 11, and 17 over yourself and those for whom you stand guard as a faithful, prayerful watchman (Isaiah 62:6-7).

> *"LORD, when _____ and I see You move, let us set out from our place and go after You. When we come to the edge of a flooded situation, help us stand still in You. LORD of all the earth, You will cross over ahead of us wherever we go. Help us stand firm on dry ground.*
> *In Your name, Jesus~"*

APRIL 20

Please read Joshua 4.

Meditate on verses 21-22.

> *He (Joshua) said to the sons of Israel, "When your children ask their fathers in time to come, saying, 'What are these stones?' then you shall inform your children, saying, 'Israel crossed this Jordan on dry ground.'"*

What an amazing moment for the children of Israel—a moment worth remembering! God kept His word which He spoke through Moses:

> *It is the LORD your God who will cross ahead of you; He will destroy these nations before you, and you shall dispossess them. Joshua is the one who will cross ahead of you, just as the LORD has spoken.*
> —DEUTERONOMY 31:3

A memorial was erected, with the exhortation to tell the children about God's faithfulness.

What has the LORD done for you and those you love? How have you memorialized the events? Are you telling and retelling the stories, so others will know "the hand of the LORD is mighty" (v. 24)?

Pray Joshua 4:22-24 over yourself and those for whom you stand guard as a faithful, prayerful watchman (Isaiah 62:6-7).

> *"LORD, help _____ and me tell our children and their children what You have done, so all the peoples of the earth may know that Your hand is mighty that we may fear You, LORD our God forever.*
> *In Your name, Jesus~"*

APRIL 21

Please read Joshua 5.

Meditate on verse 13.

> *Now it came about when Joshua was by Jericho that he lifted up his eyes and looked, and behold, a man was standing opposite him with his sword drawn in his hand, and Joshua went to him and said to him, "Are you for us or for our adversaries?"*

Have you ever asked God that question? "LORD, whose side are You on—theirs or ours?" Or, do you even bother to ask God the question because of course He is on your side; why wouldn't He be?

Did the man's answer surprise you? "No, I don't pick sides; rather I am captain of the LORD's army." It certainly surprised Joshua because he fell on his face before this mighty warrior, wanting to hear a word from him.

Be mindful it is not for God to be on your side, but rather, for you to choose to be on God's side. When Joshua obeyed the captain of the LORD'S host, reverently removing his sandals, he became a warrior in God's army. Pray for those you love to do the same.

Pray Joshua 5:14-15 over yourself and those for whom you stand guard as a faithful, prayerful watchman (Isaiah 62:6-7).

> *"LORD of hosts, I bow down before You. What do You have to say to _____ and me, Your servants? As we join Your army, may the places we stand be holy. May we do as You say. In Your name, Jesus~"*

APRIL 22

Please read Joshua 6.

Meditate on verse 18.

> *But as for you, only keep yourselves from the things under the ban, so that you do not covet them and take some of the things under the ban and make the camp of Israel accursed and bring trouble on it.*

"Under the ban" is a repeated phrase in this chapter. It comes from the Hebrew word, *cherem*, which means: "a thing appointed to utter destruction."[1] God warned the Israelites not to be tempted to take things from Jericho which He banned because those things would bring trouble to Israel.

The world is filled with things banned to us as Christians, things that when brought into our lives and homes bring trouble to us and those we love. And, with electronic media, it is easy for banned things to enter. Take heed to God's Word and "set no worthless thing before your eyes" (Psalm 101:3). Purpose to utterly destroy and remove from your media libraries things the Holy Spirit bans.

Pray Joshua 6:18 over yourself and those for whom you stand guard as a faithful, prayerful watchman (Isaiah 62:6-7).

> *"LORD, may _____ and I keep ourselves from the things under the ban so that we do not covet them and take some of the things under the ban and make our home accursed and bring trouble on it. In Your name, Jesus~"*

---

1. Retrieved from www.blueletterbible.org/lang/lexicon/lexicon.cfm?Strongs=H2764&t=NASB

APRIL 23

Please read Joshua 7.

Meditate on verse 1.

> *But the sons of Israel acted unfaithfully in regard to the things under the ban, for Achan, the son of Carmi, the son of Zabdi, the son of Zerah, from the tribe of Judah, took some of the things under the ban, therefore the anger of the LORD burned against the sons of Israel.*

The repeated phrase, "under the ban," continues into chapter 7 of *Joshua*. Recall from yesterday's devotional, the phrase is translated from the Hebrew word *cherem*, meaning "a thing appointed to utter desctruction."[1] Tragically, rather than utterly destroy the things under the ban, Achan chose to keep some banned things for himself. The consequences were devastating.

> *Then Joshua and all Israel with him, took Achan the son of Zerah, the silver, the mantle, the bar of gold, his sons, his daughters, his oxen, his donkeys, his sheep, his tent and all that belonged to him; and they brought them up to the valley of Achor. Joshua said, "Why have you troubled us? The LORD will trouble you this day." And all Israel stoned them with stones; and they burned them with fire after they had stoned them with stones.*
> —JOSHUA 7:24-25

An entire family destroyed because a man could not control himself. Determine to protect yourself and those you love by obeying God and His Word. Pray Joshua 7:11 over yourself and those for whom you stand guard as a faithful, prayerful watchman (Isaiah 62:6-7).

> *"LORD, please keep _____ and me from sinning and transgressing Your covenant which You command. Do not let us take things under the ban. Do not let us steal and deceive. Do not let us put banned things among our own things. In Your name, Jesus~"*

---

1. Retrieved from www.blueletterbible.org/lang/lexicon/lexicon.cfm?Strongs=H2764&t=NASB

APRIL 24

Please read Joshua 8.

Meditate on verse 27.

> *Israel took only the cattle and the spoil of that city as plunder for themselves,* ***according to the word of the LORD*** *which He had commanded Joshua.*

The Israelites learned their lesson from the Achan debacle (Joshua 7). When they took Ai, they did it "according to the word of the LORD" rather than their own way (v. 27). What a difference God's way made for them and their families!

Ponder that phrase, "according to the word of the LORD." Is it a governing phrase in your life? Ask God to make it your heart's desire to do things according to His Word. Ask Him to give you a hunger for His Word, so you will know what it says and do accordingly.

Pray Joshua 8:27 and 34-35 over yourself and those for whom you stand guard as a faithful, prayerful watchman (Isaiah 62:6-7).

> *"LORD, please help _____ and me do according to Your Word. May we read all the words of Your law, the blessing and the curse, according to all that is written in Your Book. Let us read every word. LORD, let everyone in my family and in my church, even the little ones, hear, read, and know Your Word. In Your name, Jesus~"*

APRIL 25

Please read Joshua 9.

Meditate on verse 14.

> *So the men of Israel took some of their provisions,*
> *and did not ask for the counsel of the LORD.*

Joshua's God-given marching orders were to utterly destroy all the inhabitants of Canaan because they were godless idolaters who would lead the Israelites into paganism. One of those groups was the Gibeonites. They tricked the Israelites into believing they were not from Canaan, cutting a covenant with them. Duped by the Gibeonites, Israel had to keep their covenant vows and spare their lives (v. 19). The Gibeonites will be a thorn in Israel's side for years to come.

Oh, what complications we create when we act on our presumptions without seeking the counsel of God! Oh, what complications we create when we enter into a covenant relationship with the godless instead of acting on the counsel of the LORD!

> *Do not be bound together with unbelievers; for what*
> *partnership have righteousness and lawlessness, or*
> *what fellowship has light with darkness?*
> —2 CORINTHIANS 6:14

Pray to do the opposite of Joshua 9:14 over yourself and those for whom you stand guard as a faithful, prayerful watchman (Isaiah 62:6-7).

> *"LORD, please let _____ and me*
> *always ask for Your counsel and obey it.*
> *In Your name, Jesus~"*

APRIL 26

Please read Joshua 10.

Meditate on verses 12-14.

> *Then Joshua spoke to the LORD in the day when the LORD delivered up the Amorites before the sons of Israel, and he said in the sight of Israel, "O sun, stand still at Gibeon, And O moon in the valley of Aijalon." So the sun stood still, and the moon stopped, until the nation avenged themselves of their enemies. Is it not written in the book of Jashar? And the sun stopped in the middle of the sky and did not hasten to go down for about a whole day. There was no day like that before it or after it, when the LORD listened to the voice of a man; for the LORD fought for Israel.*

What an amazing chapter in Israel's history! God fought for the Israelites because Joshua obeyed Him, confidently trusting Him to do the impossible on behalf of His people.

There are situations in your life where you need God to do the impossible for the sake of those you love. There are people who need to be saved, people who need healing, people facing incredibly difficult situations. Ask the LORD to reveal unconfessed sin in your life. Repent, desiring to be faithful and pleasing to Him. Then, pray for God to do the impossible for yourself and those you love.

Pray Joshua 10:14 over yourself and those for whom you stand guard as a faithful, prayerful watchman (Isaiah 62:6-7).

> *"LORD, let this be a day like no other when You listen to my voice and fight for _____ and me.*
> *In Your name, Jesus~"*

APRIL 27

Please read Joshua 11.

Meditate on verses 4-6a.

> *They came out, they and all their armies with them, as many people as the sand that is on the seashore, with very many horses and chariots. So all of these kings having agreed to meet, came and encamped together at the waters of Merom, to fight against Israel. Then the LORD said to Joshua, "Do not be afraid because of them, for tomorrow at this time I will deliver all of them slain before Israel."*

Israel conquered the southern kingdoms of Canaan (Joshua 10), and the news prompted the northern kingdoms to combine forces in an effort to stop Israel from conquering them, too. Can you imagine so many kings with so many armies, as many as the sand on the seashore, coming with their horses and chariots to fight against you? How fearful Joshua must have felt! How comforting God's words must have been to him! "Do not be afraid, for tomorrow at this time, I will deliver all of them slain before Israel" (v. 6).

God promised to do the impossible on behalf of His people. He delivered these enemies of Israel into their hand, so they could defeat them (v. 8).

Are you and your loved ones facing overwhelming situations which war against you? Give these enemies to the LORD, asking Him to fight for you, praying Joshua 11:23 over yourself and those for whom you stand guard as a faithful, prayerful watchman (Isaiah 62:6-7).

> *"LORD, help _____ and me to do according to all that You have spoken. As we do, please give us rest from war. In Your name, Jesus~"*

APRIL 28

Please read Joshua 12.

Meditate on verse 1a.

Now these are the kings of the land whom the sons of Israel defeated.

There was to be no doubt God gave Israel all the land of Canaan, for He listed the conquered kings and kingdoms as a forever reminder of their inheritance from Him. And, He uses the word *one* after every kingdom named because every individual victory is important to God.

Recall God's faithfulness to you and those you love. Every sin He has conquered and every victory He has won is part of your forever inheritance from the LORD. Any one thing He does on your behalf is worth celebrating. List what God has done for you, like He listed the thirty-one conquered kings in Joshua 12:7-24, in a prayer of thanksgiving as a faithful, prayerful watchman (Isaiah 62;6-7).

"LORD, now these are areas
in _____ and my life that
You defeated and conquered, giving us victory:

_____, *one;*
_____, *one;*
_____, *one;*
_____, *one;*
_____, *one;*
_____, *one;*
_____, *one;*
_____, *one;*
_____, *one;*
_____, *one;*
_____, *one;*
_____, *one;*

_____, *one;*

_____, *one;*

_____, *one;*

_____, *one;*

_____, *one;*

_____, *one;*

_____, *one;*

_____, *one;*

_____, *one;*

_____, *one;*

_____, *one;*

_____, *one;*

_____, *one;*

_____, *one;*

_____, *one;*

_____, *one;*

_____, *one;*

_____, *one;*

_____, *one:*

In all, thirty-one victories for Your glory, Jesus~"

APRIL 29

Please read Joshua 13.

Meditate on verse 1.

> *Now Joshua was old and advanced in years*
> *when the LORD said to him,*
> *"You are old and advanced in years, and very*
> *much of the land remains to be possessed."*

Have you ever felt like Joshua—old—yet, with so very much of the LORD's work still to be done? It's refreshing to hear God acknowledge Joshua was old because we all have days (whether we are literally old or not) when we cry out, "LORD, do You realize how old and tired I am? LORD, help me!"

Observe how God takes control of the situation by saying:

> *"All the inhabitants of the hill country from*
> *Lebanon as far as Misrephoth-maim,*
> *all the Sidonians, I will drive them out from before the sons of Israel;*
> *only allot it to Israel for an inheritance as I have commanded you."*
> —JOSHUA 13:6

God promised to take possession of the land for His people; Joshua just had to divide it among the tribes as the LORD commanded.

Appeal to the LORD for His help by praying Joshua 13:1, 6, and 33 as His faithful, prayerful watchman (Isaiah 62:6-7).

> *"LORD, You know I am old and advanced in years; at least I*
> *feel that way, and there is very much of Your Kingdom on earth*
> *to be possessed. LORD, drive out Your enemies from before Your*
> *people and give us the inheritance as You have commanded.*
> *LORD God, thank You that You are our inheritance.*
> *In Your name, Jesus~"*

APRIL 30

Please read Joshua 14.

Meditate on verse 8. Caleb is speaking.

> *"Nevertheless, my brethren who went up with me made the heart of the people melt with fear, but I followed the LORD my God fully."*

Recall Caleb and Joshua were two of the twelve men sent to spy out the land of Canaan (Numbers 13). They returned with a good report about the land, encouraging the people, confident God would give them the land; the other ten spies put fear into the people's hearts, causing them to distrust the LORD and His provision (Numbers 14). The results were disastrous (Numbers 14:26-35). Forty-five years later, God rewarded Caleb for his faithfulness, giving him the land of Hebron and allowing him to be as strong at the age of 85 as he was at the age of 40 (vs. 10-14).

Read the meditation verse again. Which half of the verse best describes you? Are you a fearful person, imagining the worst, causing your heart and the hearts of others to melt with fear, or are you a person who follows the LORD your God fully, confidently knowing He protects you and those you love?

Ask the LORD to make you and those you love like Caleb by praying Joshua 14:8 and 10-11 as a faithful, prayerful watchman (Isaiah 62:6-7).

> *"LORD, do not let _____ and me cause the heart of people to melt with fear, but let us follow You, LORD our God, fully. Let us be as strong today as when You called us years ago. Even when we are 85, let our strength be for fighting for Your Kingdom. And for going out and coming in Your name, Jesus~"*

May

*On your walls, O Jerusalem,
I have appointed watchmen;
All day and all night they
will never keep silent.
You who remind the LORD,
take no rest for yourselves;
And give Him no rest until He establishes
And makes Jerusalem a
praise in the earth.*
ISAIAH 62:6-7, NASB

MAY 1

Please read Joshua 15.

Meditate on verses 16-19.

> *And Caleb said, "The one who attacks Kiriath-sepher and captures it, I will give him Achsah my daughter as a wife." Othniel the son of Kenaz, the brother of Caleb, captured it, so he gave him Achsah his daughter as a wife. It came about that when she came to him, she persuaded him to ask her father for a field. So, she alighted from the donkey, and Caleb said to her, "What do you want?" Then she said, "Give me a blessing; since you have given me the land of the Negev, give me also springs of water." So he gave her the upper springs and the lower springs.*

In the middle of a chapter filled with place names, is a beautiful story about Caleb and his daughter. Achsah must have been a daddy's girl because she not only inherited land from her father, but also his bold confidence. After persuading her husband to ask Caleb for a field, she herself approached her father, requesting a blessing—springs of water to accompany the land he had already given her. Caleb granted her request, giving her both the upper and the lower springs.

As a child of God, you have already inherited eternal life from the Father, and He has given you His confidence:

> *Such confidence we have through Christ toward God.*
> —2 CORINTHIANS 3:4

Confidently come to the Father asking Him for springs of living water for those who need salvation (John 4:10). Pray Joshua 15:19 as their faithful, prayerful watchman (Isaiah 62:6-7).

> *"LORD, give me a blessing. Please give Your springs of living water to _____ . Through Your name, Jesus~"*

MAY 2

Please read Joshua 16.

Meditate on verse 10.

> *But they did not drive out the Canaanites who lived in Gezer, so the Canaanites live in the midst of Ephraim to this day, and they became forced laborers.*

Why was complete removal of the Canaanites from the Promised Land so important to God? Canaan was divided into city-states and ruled by individual kings, but the people had a common religion characterized by the worship of many gods. These gods were seen as guardians of the universe and vital to nature and society. Their images were in Canaanite homes and temples, with priests supplying them with food and clothing, hoping they would provide abundant crops, fertile herds, and prosperity to the ruling king and his family.[1]

> *Hear, O Israel! The LORD is our God; the LORD is one! You shall love the LORD your God with all your heart and with all your soul and with all your might.*
> —DEUTERONOMY 6:4-5

The LORD knew His people's heart, soul, and might would easily turn to other gods if those gods and the people who worshiped them were allowed to remain in the land. The same is true for us today. We can be easily distracted by worldly things competing for our heart, soul, and might.

Seek the LORD and His strength to drive out the distractions in your life, using the words from Joshua 16:10 as a faithful, prayerful watchman (Isaiah 62:6-7).

> *"LORD, please help _____ and me drive out anything in our lives that is god instead of You. Do not let those things become forced laborers controlling our lives.*
> *In Your name, Jesus~"*

MAY 3

Please read Joshua 17.

Meditate on verses 14-15a.

> *Then the sons of Joseph spoke to Joshua, saying, "Why have you given me only one lot and one portion for an inheritance, since I am a numerous people whom the LORD has thus far blessed?" Joshua said to them, "If you are a numerous people, go up to the forest and clear a place for yourself."*

Ephraim and Manasseh were given an inheritance of land, but they did not drive out the Canaanites as God commanded (Joshua 16:10; 17:12). They came whining and complaining to Joshua that they needed more land. Joshua wisely told them to go and take what God had already given them. They had plenty of land; they needed to obey God and wipe out the inhabitants and possess the land. But the people were like baby birds, with mouths wide open, chirping "Give me; give me, God. Give me more, God!"

Can you relate to these descendants of Joseph wanting God to give easy blessings, yet ignoring His call for faithful obedience? Search your heart for Ephraim and Manasseh tendencies, replacing them with a heart like Caleb's (Joshua 14:11-12).

As a faithful, prayerful watchman (Isaiah 62:6-7), ask God to help you and those you love obey Joshua 17:18.

> "LORD, You have given _____ and me _____.* Now it is a forest, but help us clear it, and to its farthest borders let it be ours. Help us drive out everything hindering us, even though it appears they have chariots of iron and though they are strong. Because of Your strength, Jesus~"

---

*The blank could be filled with: your marriage, your family, your job, your church, etc

MAY 4

Please read Joshua 18.

Meditate on verses 2-3.

> *There remained among the sons of Israel seven tribes who had not divided their inheritance. So, Joshua said to the sons of Israel, "How long will you put off entering to take possession of the land which the LORD, the God of your fathers, has given you?"*

Surprisingly, over half the tribes of Israel had not taken possession of their land. Perhaps they were content with wandering; after all, it had been their life for 40 years. But now, the blessing was theirs for the taking; all they had to do was possess the land, dividing it among the sons of each tribe. The sin of procrastination kept them from their God-given destiny.

What are you waiting for? Is there a ministry God wants you part of? Is there a person God wants you to forgive? Is there a friend God wants you to call? Is there a Bible study to attend, a child to read a book to, a spouse to love well…? What are you waiting for? There are blessings in the obedience. No more dilly-dallying. Pray and do Joshua 18:3-4 as a faithful, prayerful watchman (Isaiah 62:6-7).

> *"LORD, I hear You asking me, 'How long will you put off taking possession of what I, the LORD God, have given you?'*
> *LORD, I will arise and walk through this day, writing a description of what You have for me. I will return to You ready to do as You say.*
> *In Your name, Jesus~"*

MAY 5

Please read Joshua 19.

Meditate on verse 1.

> *Then the second lot fell to Simeon, to the tribe of the sons of Simeon according to their families, and their inheritance was in the midst of the inheritance of the sons of Judah.*

Does it seem odd that of all the tribes of Israel, Simeon was given a land inheritance in the middle of Judah's land? Their inheritance was merely pieces of Judah's land because of prophecies made over 400 years earlier.

> *Simeon and Levi are brothers; their swords are implements of violence. Let my soul not enter into their council; let not my glory be united with their assembly; because in their anger they slew men, and in their self-will, they lamed oxen. Cursed be their anger, for it is fierce; and their wrath, for it is cruel. I will disperse them in Jacob and scatter them in Israel.*
> —GENESIS 49:5-7

The sons of Simeon did not receive their own section of land because their forefathers had anger issues. Let that soak in for a moment. An entire people group missed out on significant blessings from God because of their violent, self-willed, angry great-great...great-grandfathers.

"Oh, LORD, keep me from sinning, so my children, grandchildren, great-grandchildren, and great-great-grandchildren do not miss out on Your blessings!"

Pray for God not to have to do Joshua 19:9 to you and those for whom you stand guard as a faithful, prayerful watchman (Isaiah 62:6-7).

> *"LORD, do let the inheritance of _____ and me be taken from the portion of someone else because You curse our anger, self-will, and wrath. Let our inheritance be in the midst of Your blessings as we quickly repent and obey You. In Your name, Jesus~"*

MAY 6

Please read Joshua 20.

Meditate on verses 1-2.

> *Then the LORD spoke to Joshua, saying,*
> *"Speak to the sons of Israel, saying,*
> *'Designate the cities of refuge, of which I*
> *spoke to you through Moses.'"*

Six cities were designated in Israel as cities of refuge for a manslayer, one who unintentionally killed someone (v. 3). The city of refuge gave the manslayer a place of protection from the blood avenger, the one responsible for carrying out vengeance for the murder of a family member.

> *Do homage to the Son, that He not become angry,*
> *and you perish in the way, for His wrath may soon be*
> *kindled. How blessed are all who take refuge in Him!*
> —PSALM 2:12

For Christians, Jesus Christ is our city of refuge. You have the privilege to live in Him, eternally safe from the blood avenger. It is important for Jesus to be your city of refuge because a day will come when He returns to earth as the blood avenger, and all who are not in Him will perish in His wrath.

Pray for those you love to make Jesus their city of refuge. Use the words from Joshua 20:2-3 as their faithful, prayerful watchman (Isaiah 62:6-7).

> *"LORD, You are the City of Refuge.*
> *Please let _____ flee to You.*
> *Become their refuge, Jesus, so You are not*
> *the avenger of blood to them.*
> *In Your name, Jesus~"*

MAY 7

Please read Joshua 21.

Meditate on verse 41.

> *All the cities of the Levites in the midst of the possession of the sons of Israel were forty-eight cities with their pasture lands.*

Unlike the rest of the tribes, God scattered the Levites throughout Israel rather than giving them a portion of land for their inheritance. God's reason was two-fold: the Levites did not get an inheritance of land because the LORD was their inheritance (Joshua 13:33), and their ministry was to be a priestly presence among the people, rather than be cloistered in only one geographical section of Israel.

As a Christian, you have the same Levitical ministry.

> *You also, as living stones, are being built up as a spiritual house for a holy priesthood, to offer up spiritual sacrifices acceptable to God through Jesus Christ. But you are a chosen race, a royal priesthood, a holy nation, a people for God's own possession, so that you may proclaim the excellencies of Him who has called you out of darkness into His marvelous light.*
> —1 PETER 2:5, 9

You are a holy priest; the LORD is your inheritance, and you live where the LORD has placed you to share the good news of Jesus Christ with those around you.

What a high calling! Confidently fulfill it, praying Joshua 21:44-45 over yourself and those for whom you stand guard as a faithful, prayerful watchman (Isaiah 62:6-7).

> *"LORD, as Your priests, give _____ and me rest on every side. Let none of all our enemies stand before us. LORD, give all of our enemies into our hand. Not one of Your good promises which You made, LORD, will fail. All Your promises will come to pass. In Your name, Jesus~"*

MAY 8

Please read Joshua 22.

Meditate on verse 16.

> *Thus says the whole congregation of the LORD, "What is this unfaithful act which you have committed against the God of Israel, turning away from following the LORD this day, by building yourselves an altar, to rebel against the LORD this day?"*

When the tribes of Israel perceived Reuben, Gad, and the half-tribe of Manasseh had built an altar against God's commands, they addressed the issue, going to the offenders and asking, "What have you done?" They didn't want sin to enter a few of the tribes yet impact the entire nation. After discussing the situation with them, it was determined there was no offense. Thankfully, the issue was addressed rather than letting misperceptions simmer and sin run rampant.

Ask the LORD to give you, your family, and your church the courage to confront sin, so it doesn't permeate everyone. Be willing to question others' actions to understand what they are doing and to give Biblical counsel when necessary.

Pray Joshua 22:5 and 34 over yourself and those for whom you stand guard as a faithful, prayerful watchman (Isaiah 62:6-7).

> *"LORD, let _____ and me be very careful to observe the commandment and the law which Moses, Your servant, commanded us, to love You, LORD our God, and walk in all Your ways and keep Your commandments and hold fast to You and serve You with all our heart and with all our soul. LORD, let us be called, 'Witness,' for we will be a witness that You, LORD, are God.*
> *In Your name, Jesus~"*

MAY 9

Please read Joshua 23.

Meditate on verses 8 and 12-13. These are some of Joshua's final words.

> *"But you are to cling to the LORD your God, as you have done to this day. For if you ever go back and cling to the rest of these nations, these which remain among you, and intermarry with them, so that you associate with them and they with you, know with certainty that the LORD your God will not continue to drive these nations out from before you, but they will be a snare and a trap to you, and a whip on your sides and thorns in your eyes, until you perish from off this good land which the LORD your God has given you."*

Joshua knew the Israelites' tendency would be to turn from their faithful God and follow the ways of their idolatrous neighbors, so he encouraged them to cling to God, warning them of the consequences of clinging to anyone else. In the coming weeks, as you read and pray *1 & 2 Chronicles*, you will discover whether or not Joshua's warning was heeded.

It is important to heed God's Word. To whom or what do you cling? Cling to Christ and His Word.

Pray Joshua 23:6, 8, and 11 over yourself and those for whom you stand guard as a faithful, prayerful watchman (Isaiah 62:6-7).

> *"LORD, may _____ and I be very firm to keep and do all that is written in Your Book, so we may not turn aside from it to the right hand or to the left. May we cling to You, LORD our God. Let us take diligent heed to ourselves to love You, LORD our God. In Your name, Jesus~"*

MAY 10

Please read Joshua 24.

Meditate on verse 1a.

> *Then Joshua gathered all the tribes of Israel to Shechem.*

Just before he died, Joshua brought the Israelites back to the place where their story began. It was at Shechem, 600 years earlier, where God brought Abraham and first promised him the land of Canaan (Genesis 12:6-7). Now, Joshua is with Abraham's promised descendants in their promised land, and with his dying breath, Joshua reminds the people of God's faithfulness (Joshua 24:2-13):

> *"Thus says the LORD, the God of Israel, 'I took your father Abraham from beyond the River and led him through all the land of Cannan, and multiplied his descendants and gave him Isaac. To Isaac, I gave Jacob and Esau. I sent Moses and Aaron, and I plagued Egypt. I brought your fathers out of Egypt. I brought you into the land of the Amorites. I gave them into your hand; I destroyed them before you. I gave you a land on которых you had not labored.'"*

Recall God's faithfulness in your life. In a prayer of commitment, pray Joshua 24:14-18 as a faithful, prayerful watchman (Isaiah 62:6-7).

> *"LORD, may _____ and I fear and serve You in sincerity and truth. Let us put away the gods of this world and serve You, LORD. As for me and my house, we will serve You, LORD. Far be it from us that we should forsake You, LORD, to serve other gods, for You brought us out from the house of bondage. You did all these great things in our sight and preserved us through all the way in which we went and among all the peoples through whose midst we passed. We will serve You, LORD, for You are our God. In Your name, Jesus~"*

MAY 11

Please read 1 Chronicles 1.

Meditate on verse 10.

> *Cush became the father of Nimrod; he began
> to be a mighty one in the earth.*

God gave Israel the book of *Chronicles** after returning from the Babylonian exile because He knew how much they needed reassurance He had not abandoned them; He remembered them, and He keeps His promises. These are important truths for us to remember as well.

The first nine chapters of *Chronicles* contain genealogies. Imagine how important these were to the Jewish people who needed to be reminded of God's faithfulness. As you read those names, keep in mind that God also knows you and your loved ones by name. Use these next nine days to pray specifically, by name, for those who need:

1. to be mighty in the LORD (v. 10)
2. to stop being wicked (1 Chronicles 2:3)
3. more days to serve God (1 Chronicles 3:4)
4. to be honorable (1 Chronicles 4:9)
5. to trust God (1 Chronicles 5:20)
6. to serve God and His people (1 Chronicles 6:33)
7. to be mighty people of valor (1 Chronicles 7:40)
8. to get rid of their giants (1 Chronicles 8:13)
9. to be keepers of God's Truth (1 Chronicles 9:23)

Use the words from 1 Chronicles 1:10 to pray for yourself and those for whom you stand guard as a faithful, prayerful watchman (Isaiah 62:6-7).

> *"LORD, make _____ and me a
> mighty one in the earth for You.
> In Your name, Jesus"*

**1 & 2 Chronicles* was originally written as one book. www.blueletterbible.org/Comm/guzik_david/StudyGuide2017-1Ch/1Ch-1.cfm?a=339001

MAY 12

Please read 1 Chronicles 2.

Meditate on verses 3b and 7.

> *And Er, Judah's firstborn, was wicked in the sight*
> *of the LORD, so He put him to death.*
> *The son of Carmi was Achar, the troubler*
> *of Israel, who violated the ban.*

Just when you might be tempted to skip a chapter of God's Word, you discover a couple of treasure verses to keep in your arsenal of prayers for your loved ones. Next to 1 Chronicles 2:3 in your Bible, consider writing something like: "LORD, do not let my family be wicked in Your sight!" Write out family members' names in the margin. Next to verse 7 write a note to God asking Him to keep your family free from troublers by making you faithful followers of Him.

As you continue to read God's Word, take it personally, for it is certainly more than a history book; it is the Living Word that wants to penetrate your life and the lives of those you love.

Pray 1 Chronicles 2:3b and 7 over yourself and those for whom you stand guard as a faithful, prayerful watchman (Isaiah 62:6-7).

> *"O, LORD, do not let _____ and me*
> *be wicked in Your sight. Put to death any wickedness in*
> *us. Do not let us be troublers of others, who violate what*
> *You have banned. Keep troublers from our midst.*
> *In Your name, Jesus~"*

MAY 13

Please read 1 Chronicles 3.

Meditate on verses 1a and 4.

> *Now these were the sons of David who were born to him in Hebron:*
> *Six were born to him in Hebron, and there he*
> *reigned seven years and six months.*
> *And in Jerusalem he reigned thirty-three years.*

What an important genealogical chapter in God's Word! It is the royal line of King David, which will ultimately contain the name King Jesus. Christ's genealogy in Matthew 1 contains the same names in the same order as this one in 1 Chronicles 3 (vs. 9-17). The Matthew genealogy also contains the names of Jesus' ancestors from Abraham to David's father, Jesse (Matthew 1:1-6). And, Matthew contains Jesus' ancestors after the Babylonian exile starting with Shealtiel's descendants (Matthew 1:12-16). The accuracy of God's Word is amazing and increases our faith to trust His every Word for our lives.

How wonderful God allowed King David to reign for forty years and six months! I want God to do that for my family—allow us to serve Him for a really long time. It can be the cry of your heart, too, for your family to serve Jesus all the days of your lives.

Use the words from 1 Chronicles 3:4 to pray over yourself and those for whom you stand guard as a faithful, prayerful watchman (Isaiah 62:6-7).

> "LORD, You let King David reign seven
> years and six months in Hebron.
> And, You allowed Him to reign thirty-three years in Jerusalem.
> LORD, please let _____ and
> me serve You for at least that long.
> In Your name, Jesus-"

MAY 14

Please read 1 Chronicles 4.

Meditate on verse 9.

> *Jabez was more honorable than his brothers, and his mother named him Jabez saying, "Because I bore him with pain."*

Perhaps you have heard of the prayer of Jabez. It is a prayer tucked in the middle of 407 genealogy verses (1 Chronicles 1-9). God wanted the chronicler to include the prayer because a guy named Pain and Sorrow[1] was an honorable man (vs. 9-10). Incredible! It doesn't matter who your family is or what they say about you; you can be an honorable person, whom God hears and answers their prayers.

This chapter has at least five treasure verses to pray. Pray 1 Chronicles 4:9-10 and 38-40 as a faithful, prayerful watchman (Isaiah 62:6-7).

> *"LORD, make _____ and me more honorable. Oh God, please bless us indeed and enlarge our border. Let Your hand be with us and keep from harm that it might not pain us! God, please grant our requests. Make us leaders in our families and let our families' houses increase greatly. We seek pasture for our flocks. Please let us find rich and good pasture. May our land be broad and quiet and peaceful. In Your name, Jesus~"*

---

1. Retreived from www.blueletterbible.org/lang/lexicon/lexicon.cfm?Strongs=H3258&t=NASB

MAY 15

Please read 1 Chronicles 5.

Meditate on verses 20b and 22a.

> *They cried out to God in the battle, and He answered their prayers because they trusted in Him. For many fell slain, because the war was of God.*

There were 44,760 valiant warriors from the tribes of Reuben, Gad, and Manasseh, who needed God to fight their battle in order to win the war (vs. 18-22). These men, skilled with sword and bow, trusted Almighty God, crying out to Him. Miraculously, God answered their prayers.

What an encouraging story in the middle of a genealogy! God answers the prayers of those who trust Him.

So, this is your story. You are praying verses from Scripture because you are a warrior, a valiant prayer warrior on the wall for the sake of those you love. And, now you have another prayer for your arsenal. Cry out to God with 1 Chronicles 5:20 and 22 as a faithful, prayerful watchman (Isaiah 62:6-7).

> *"LORD God, I am crying out to You in the midst of this battle for _____ .*
> *I trust in You; please answer my prayers! This war is of You, God! For the sake of Your name, Jesus~"*

MAY 16

Please read 1 Chronicles 6.

Meditate on verse 33a.

These are those who served with their sons.

As you observe the genealogies in 1 Chronicles 1-9, you see things that are important to God. For example, all nations descended from Adam (1 Chronicles 1). The nation of Israel descended from Abraham through Isaac (1 Chronicles 1:34). King David descended from the tribe of Judah, and from his lineage will come King Jesus (1 Chronicles 2-4). God gave Reuben, Gad, and the half-tribe of Manasseh land on the east side of Jordan (1 Chronicles 5). The tribe of Levi has a special role among the 12 tribes of Israel (1 Chronicles 6). The Levites were set apart by God and scattered throughout Israel for the purpose of serving God and His people and teaching His Word.

As a spiritual Levite, your ministry is the same: serve Christ and His Church, proclaiming His excellencies (1 Peter 2:9-10). We love that the Kohathites served with their sons. From the time our children were preschoolers, they served in church: setting out signs, putting up chairs, and handing out bulletins. As they got older, they were part of the praise team: setting up sound equipment, playing instruments, and cleaning up after rehearsals. As they got even older, they started children's programs, led youth groups, and volunteered where the body of Christ needed help. Today, they and their spouses continue to serve Jesus, and their children are serving the church with their parents.

Ask the LORD to give your family, even your little ones, opportunities to serve in your church. Pray 1 Chronicles 6:33 and 48 as a faithful, prayerful watchman (Isaiah 62:6-7).

"LORD, let _____ and me
serve You with our children.
Appoint our family for all the service of Your Church, God.
In Your name, Jesus~"

MAY 17

Please read 1 Chronicles 7.

Meditate on verse 40a.

> *All these were the sons of Asher, heads of the fathers' houses, choice and mighty men of valor, heads of the princes.*

"Mighty men of valor" is repeated six times in 1 Chronicles 7 (vs. 2, 5, 7, 9, 11, 40). These were brave, strong, virtuous men—leaders of their families—ready to go to war if necessary (v. 11). What a great chapter to pray over men! Pray for God to make men valiant and courageous for Christ and their families. Pray for God to grow up boys to become mighty men, leading their families in Godliness.

Satan and the world want men to be weak and self-centered, instead of mighty men of God. As a faithful, prayerful watchman (Isaiah 62:6-7), pray 1 Chronicles 7:2, 3, 5, 7, 9, 11, 23, and 40 over men and families.

> *"LORD, make this male generation mighty men of valor. Make _____ and _____ chief men. (Leaders in their homes, churches, businesses, communities, etc.) Make the men in our family mighty men of valor. Make _____ the head of his household, a mighty man of valor. Make the men in this generation heads of their households, mighty men of valor. Make these heads of households, mighty men of valor who are ready to go out with the army to war. Make them men of valor who will spiritually go to war for the sake of their family. LORD, please do not let misfortune come upon _____ and my house. Make all our sons heads of their houses, choice and mighty men of valor, heads even of princes. In Your name, Jesus~"*

MAY 18

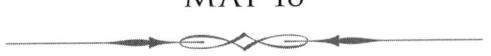

Please read 1 Chronicles 8.

Meditate on verse 13.

> *And Beriah and Shema, who were heads of fathers' households of the inhabitants of Aijalon, who put to flight the inhabitants of Gath.*

Think about Beriah and Shema. These two men are in a chapter containing more than 120 names; most have no more of a descriptor than a comma after their name. But, in the middle of the name comma name comma list, are Beriah and Shema, who will forever be remembered for "putting to flight the inhabitants of Gath" (v. 13).

Gath was one of five royal cities of the Philistines and the native city of the giant, Goliath (1 Samuel 17:4, 23). Beriah and Shema drove out those who dwelled in a city renowned for giants and idolatry (1 Samuel 6:17-18; 2 Samuel 21:20-22). Now their names are renowned by God because they did so.

Ask God to make you and your family like Beriah and Shema, not afraid of the giants. Drive out the giants, those things that keep you from walking whole-heartedly with God. With God's help, drive them out of your home, workplace, school, church, etc.

Pray 1 Chronicles 8:13 over yourself and those for whom you stand guard as a faithful, prayerful watchman (Isaiah 62:6-7).

> *"LORD, make _____ and me like Beriah and Shema, heads of our households who put to flight the inhabitants of what keep us from You. LORD, give us the courage to remove the giants. In Your all-powerful name, Jesus~"*

MAY 19

Please read 1 Chronicles 9.

Meditate on verse 23.

> *So, they and their sons had charge of the gates of the house of the LORD, even the house of the tent, as guards.*

What a privilege to be a Levite trusted to keep watch over the house of the LORD! Nothing was allowed into the temple that did not belong there. Anything and anyone who could defile God's house were faithfully kept out day and night.

The spiritual applications from this genealogy scream off the page. God wants you to guard yourself and those you love. Keep the trusted watch God has given you for your family, not allowing anyone or anything into your home, even via electronic media, that would defile you and your loved ones. Faithfully stand guard at the threshold of your church—do not allow false teaching to creep in that corrupts the body of Christ. Pray day and night for God to keep you and yours from evil (2 Thessalonians 3:3).

Use the words from 1 Chronicles 9:19, 21, 23 and 26-27 to pray over yourself and those for whom you stand guard as a faithful, prayerful watchman (Isaiah 62:6-7).

> *"LORD, _____ and I will be keepers of the thresholds of Your tent. Let us be over Your camp, LORD, keepers of the entrance. Make us gatekeepers of the entrance of the tent of meeting. Let us and our children have charge of the gates of Your house, LORD. Let us serve as guards of Your truth. Keep us faithful in this office of trust. We will spend the night around Your house, God, because the watch has been committed to us. We will be in charge of opening Your house morning by morning so others can know You.*
> *In Your name, Jesus~"*

MAY 20

Please read 1 Chronicles 10.

Meditate on verses 13-14.

> *So Saul died for his trespass which he committed against the LORD, because of the word of the LORD which he did not keep; and also because he asked counsel of a medium, making inquiry of it, and did not inquire of the LORD. Therefore, He killed him and turned the kingdom to David the son of Jesse.*

What a tragic chapter in Scripture! The king of Israel and his sons died in a single day, with King Saul's head ignobly paraded by idolatrous Philistines as a battle trophy then placed in the temple of Dagon (v. 10; 1 Samuel 5). The chapter probably made your stomach turn, especially the last two verses: God killed Saul for two reasons—He did not keep God's Word, and he consulted with a medium (vs. 13-14).

Do not be tempted to take lightly the consequences of disobeying God and His Word. Do not be attracted to teachers who focus on God's love and forgiveness but ignore His hatred of sin and the life-altering results of abiding in it. Learn from the entire Word of God, both Old and New Testaments, so you can live with Christ in a manner pleasing to Him.

Pray not to experience 1 Chronicles 10:13-14 over yourself and those for whom you stand guard as a faithful, prayerful watchman (Isaiah 62:6-7).

> *"LORD, do not let _____ and me die for trespasses which we commit against You. Let us keep Your Word, LORD, and let us never seek counsel from a medium. Let us always inquire of You. We do not want to be in a situation where You need to kill us. Thank You for Your salvation, Jesus~"*

MAY 21

Please read 1 Chronicles 11.

Meditate on verse 9.

> *David became greater and greater, for the*
> *LORD of hosts was with him.*

Observe God's hand on David in this chapter.

- ❧ Despite Saul being king of Israel, the people recognized David as their leader because God said he would be prince over His people (v. 2).
- ❧ The people made a covenant with David and anointed him king over Israel "according to the Word of the LORD" (v. 3).
- ❧ The inhabitants of Jerusalem said David was not allowed to enter; however, he captured the stronghold of Zion, and it became the city of David (vs. 4-5).
- ❧ David became greater and greater because the LORD was with him (v. 9).
- ❧ The heads of the mighty men, together with all Israel, gave David strong support according to the Word of the LORD (v. 10).
- ❧ David and the mighty men struck down the Philistines because the LORD saved them by a great victory (vs. 13-14).

Ask the LORD to do the same for you and those you love by praying 1 Chronicles 11:2-5, 9-10, and 14 as a faithful, prayerful watchman (Isaiah 62:6-7).

> *"LORD, speak over _____ and me. Despite*
> *circumstances, let it be according to Your Word, LORD.*
> *_____ has said we cannot enter here;*
> *nevertheless, let us capture the enemy's strongholds for the*
> *sake of Your Kingdom. LORD of hosts, let us become greater*
> *and greater because You are with us. May we have*
> *strong support according to Your Word.*
> *LORD, save us by a great victory.*
> *In Your name, Jesus~"*

MAY 22

Please read 1 Chronicles 12.

Meditate on verse 32a.

> *Of the sons of Issachar, men who understood the times, with knowledge of what Israel should do...*

Thankfully, David was surrounded by men who understood the times and had knowledge of what the people should do. Three-thousand-years later, we are still in desperate need of people like that. Thankfully, you can be one of them. As a Christian, you have God's Word and the Holy Spirit to let you see with God's eyes what is happening in our world and the knowledge of what to do.

There are lots of verses in this chapter for people of understanding to pray. Pray them now using the words from 1 Chronicles 12:8, 14, 18, 21-23, 32-33, 38, and 40 as a faithful, prayerful watchman (Isaiah 62:6-7).

*"LORD, make _____ and me, mighty people of valor, people trained for spiritual war, who can handle shield and spear, and whose faces are like the faces of lions, and who are as swift as the gazelles on the mountains. May the least among us be equal to a hundred people and the greatest equal to a thousand. Bring us people who have Your Spirit. Give us Your peace and give Your peace to those who help us. Indeed, God, You are the One who helps us! Make us mighty people of valor. Make us a great army like the army of God. Turn the kingdom of this world to Your Kingdom, according to Your Word, LORD. Make us people who understand the times with knowledge of what we should do. Give us undivided hearts. Give us a perfect heart and let us be of one mind. Let there be joy indeed in our land.
Because of You, Jesus~"*

MAY 23

Please read 1 Chronicles 13.

Meditate on this phrase from verse 2.

If it is from the LORD our God...

David and the people discerned correctly the LORD wanted them to assemble and bring the ark of God from Kiriath-jearim (vs. 2, 5). Their mistake was not bringing the ark back correctly. The ark should have never been placed on a cart; it should have been carried with poles on the shoulders of Levites and never touched by human hands (Exodus 25:10-16). David accurately perceived God wanted the ark returned, but he did not do it according to God's Word. Instead of taking time to search the Scriptures, or possibly ignoring God's command completely, David and the people moved forward with expedient convenience; the consequence was disastrous (vs. 7-10).

Take this chapter to heart as you discern God's will. Listen to the Holy Spirit AND read His Word, so you can walk with Jesus, pleasing Him every step of the way.

Pray 1 Chronicles 13:2, 6, and 14 over yourself and those for whom you stand guard as a faithful, prayerful watchman (Isaiah 62:6-7).

*"LORD our God, if it is from You,
let _____ and me do _____ .
LORD God, You are enthroned in our lives. As we call on Your
name, please bless our family with all that we have.
Because of Your name, Jesus-"*

MAY 24

Please read 1 Chronicles 14.

Meditate on verse 2.

> *And David realized that the LORD had established him as king over Israel, and that his kingdom was highly exalted, for the sake of His people Israel.*

What an important realization David made! The LORD arranged for David to be king, and He made his kingdom great for the sake of His (God's) people (v. 2). David's kingdom was all about God; therefore, David asked Him how to lead His people and how to fight His enemies (vs. 10, 14). God gave detailed instructions for surrounding the Philistines; then, God Himself fought on David's behalf (vs. 14-15).

The LORD establishes you for the sake of His Kingdom and His people. Do not be tempted to take credit for successes in your life or think accolades are for your glory. Seek the LORD and His way for doing things. Let Him fight battles that need to be fought.

Pray 1 Chronicles 14:2, 10-11, and 14-16 over yourself and those for whom you stand guard as a faithful, prayerful watchman (Isaiah 62:6-7).

> *"LORD, I realize You have established _____ and me. Please establish _____ in You. May Your Kingdom be highly exalted for the sake of Your people. God, I'm inquiring of You. Shall we go up against _____ ? Will You give them into our hands? God, break through our enemies by our hands, like the breakthrough of waters! God, give us Your specific instructions when we inquire of You. God, go before us to strike the army of the enemy. We will do just as You command.*
> *In Your name, Jesus~"*

MAY 25

Please read 1 Chronicles 15.

Meditate on verse 13.

> *Because you did not carry it at the first,*
> *the LORD our God made an outburst on us, for we*
> *did not seek Him according to the ordinance.*

David figured out what went wrong in 1 Chronicles 13 when God killed Uzza for steadying the ark on a cart. Carting the ark across the country was contrary to God's Word; it was to be carried with poles by Levites from the family of Kohath (Numbers 4:5-6, 15). Sadly, instead of consulting God's Law, David "consulted with the captains of the thousands and the hundreds, even with every leader, and the thing was right in the eyes of all the people" (1 Chronicles 13:1, 4). However, the thing was not right in the eyes of God. Seeking the opinion of thousands and failing to seek God's Word, resulted in an outburst from God (v. 13).

Let the application soak in—it is really important to God for His people to know and obey the Bible. He does not take lightly the ignorance and ignoring of His Word. As you determine what to do and how to do it, consult Christ and His Word every step of the way.

Pray 1 Chronicles 15:13 over yourself and those for whom you stand guard as a faithful, prayerful watchman (Isaiah 62:6-7).

> *"LORD our God, help _____ and*
> *me seek You according to Your ordinances. We*
> *want to carry this correctly the first time, so*
> *You do not make an outburst on us.*
> *For the sake of Your name, Jesus~"*

MAY 26

Please read 1 Chronicles 16.

Meditate on verse 11.

Seek the LORD and His strength; seek His face continually.

The ark of God represented God's presence, and in His presence, the Levites ministered by celebrating, thanking, and praising Him (v. 4). Ask the LORD to give you a joyful, grateful heart to serve in His presence.

Celebrate, thank, and praise the LORD with 1 Chronicles 16:8-12, 23-29, 31, and 34-36 as a faithful, prayerful watchman (Isaiah 62:6-7).

"Oh, thank You, LORD, I call upon Your name and make known Your deeds among the peoples. I sing to You, sing praises to You, and speak of all Your wonders. I glory in Your holy name. Let the heart of _____ , who seeks You, be glad. We seek You and Your strength. We seek Your face continually. We remember Your wonderful deeds which You have done, Your marvels and the judgments from Your mouth. Let all the earth sing to You, LORD! We proclaim good tidings of Your salvation from day to day. We tell of Your glory among the nations, Your wonderful deeds among all the peoples. For great are You, LORD, and greatly to be praised; You also are to be feared above all gods. For all the gods of the peoples are idols, but LORD, You made the heavens. Splendor and majesty are before You; strength and joy are in Your place. Glory and strength belong to You, LORD. We give glory to Your name and worship You. LORD, You reign! We give thanks to You, LORD, for You are good; for Your lovingkindness is everlasting. Save us, O God of our salvation, and gather us and deliver us to give thanks to Your holy name and glory in Your praise. Blessed be You, LORD, the God of Israel and the God of my family, from everlasting, even to everlasting. Amen."

MAY 27

Please read 1 Chronicles 17.

Meditate on verses 2-4.

> *Then Nathan said to David, "Do all that is
> in your heart, for God is with you."
> It came about the same night that the word of God came to
> Nathan, saying, "Go and tell David My servant, 'Thus says the
> LORD, "You shall not build a house for Me to dwell in."'"*

God quickly checked Nathan's advice for David to follow his heart. David's desire to build a house for God was not God's will. The prophet Nathan and King David presumed upon God's will without seeking His will.

Keep this story in mind when giving and seeking advice. Do not be quick to assume God's will without talking to Him and reading His Word. No matter who you are or what leadership position God has given you, constantly seek God's heart for His plans.

As a faithful, prayerful watchman (Isaiah 62:6-7), use the words from 1 Chronicles 17:16 and 23-27 to pray for God to establish you and your family in Him forever.

> *"Who am I, O LORD, and what is my family
> that You have brought us this far?
> Now, O LORD, let the word You speak concerning Your
> servant and concerning my family be established forever. Let
> Your name be established and magnified forever, saying, 'The
> LORD of hosts is the God of _____ . The family
> of _____ , Your servant, is established before You.'
> For You, O my God, have revealed to Your servant that You will
> build my family; therefore, Your servant has found courage to
> pray before You. Now, O LORD, You are God, and You have
> promised this good thing to Your servant. And now please bless the
> family of Your servant that we may continue forever before You;
> for You, O LORD, have blessed us, and we are blessed forever.
> Because of Your name, Jesus~"*

MAY 28

Please read 1 Chronicles 18.

Meditate on this repeated sentence from verses 6 and 13.

And the LORD helped David wherever he went.

"And the LORD helped David wherever he went" explains this entire chapter (vs. 6, 13). Defeating and subduing the Philistines, Israel's persistent enemies since the days of Isaac, happened because the LORD helped David (v. 1; Genesis 26:12-15). Establishing the border of Israel to the Euphrates River, as promised by God to Abraham, happened because the LORD helped David (v. 3; Genesis 15:18). Providing building materials to help his son build the temple happened because the LORD helped David (vs. 7-11; 1 Chronicles 17:11-12). God helped David and gave him the privilege of seeing the fulfillment of 1,000-year-old promises because David believed God and trusted Him to keep His Word.

> *Now, O LORD, let the word that You have spoken concerning Your servant and concerning his house be established forever and do as You have spoken. For You, O my God, have revealed to Your servant that You will build for him a house; therefore, Your servant has found courage to pray before You. Now, O LORD, You are God, and have promised this good thing to Your servant.*
> —1 CHRONICLES 17:23, 25-26

Pray those words David prayed, trusting God to fulfill His promises to you and those you love (1 Chronicles 17:23, 25-26). Then pray 1 Chronicles 18:6 and 13-14 over yourself and those for whom you stand guard as a faithful, prayerful watchman (Isaiah 62:6-7).

> "LORD, please help _____ and me wherever we go. LORD, help us wherever we go. Help us administer justice and righteousness for all Your people.
> In Your name, Jesus~"

MAY 29

Please read 1 Chronicles 19.

Meditate on verse 4.

> *So Hanun took David's servants and shaved them and cut off their garments in the middle as far as their hips and sent them away.*

Unbelievable! Can you imagine showing kindness to someone; then afterward, your thoughtful act being treated with humiliating contempt? If you are like us, you probably can. We all have memories of being misunderstood or having false motives assumed for deeds done out of love and a pure heart. Those times are gut-wrenching and feel like they just happened yesterday. When those moments come, seek the heart of Jesus for how to respond. "Father, forgive them, for they do not know what they are doing" (Luke 23:34). Then trust King Jesus to defend you like King David did his humiliated men.

Pray 1 Chronicles 19:13 over yourself and those for whom you stand guard as a faithful, prayerful watchman (Isaiah 62:6-7).

> *"LORD, help _____ and me be strong and let us show ourselves courageous for the sake of our people and for Your Kingdom, God. LORD, do what is good in Your sight. Because You are our defender, King Jesus~"*

MAY 30

Please read 1 Chronicles 20.

Meditate on verse 6.

> *Again, there was war at Gath, where there was a man of great stature who had twenty-four fingers and toes, six fingers on each hand and six toes on each foot, and he also was descended from the giants.*

1 Chronicles 20:4-8 records three victories over three giants: Sibbecai killed the giant named Sippai (v. 4). Elhanan killed Goliath's brother, Lahmi (v. 5). And, David's nephew, Jonathan, killed the 24 fingers and toes giant (vs. 6-7). It is encouraging to know these testimonies of giant slayings, for we all have times of being beset by giants.

The psalmist knew the value of such testimonies. We can take hope in them as well.

> *The wicked wait for me to destroy me; I shall diligently consider Your testimonies.*
> *You have removed all the wicked of the earth like dross; therefore, I love Your testimonies.*
> —PSALM 119:95, 119

Using the words from 1 Chronicles 20:4-8, pray for God to kill any giants wreaking havoc in your life and the lives of those for whom you stand guard as a faithful, prayerful watchman (Isaiah 62:6-7).

> *"LORD, war has broken out in the lives of _____ and me. Please kill the giant of _____ . Subdue this evil in our lives. LORD, there is spiritual warfare. Kill the sinful giant, the shaft of whose spear is like a weaver's beam. The giant we face is like one with 24 fingers and toes, six fingers on each hand and six toes on each foot. He taunts Your people, LORD. LORD, kill this situation. LORD, these are our giants. Let them fall by Your hand and by the hand of us, Your servants. In Your name, Jesus~"*

MAY 31

Please read 1 Chronicles 21.

Meditate on verse 1.

> *Then Satan stood up against Israel and*
> *moved David to number Israel.*

Taking a census may not seem sinful; however, God did not want David to take confidence in numbers to defeat his enemies. God could make David's army 100 times bigger in an instant in order to win a battle (v. 3). Knowing exactly how many human bodies he had for going to war would cause David to trust in his human army rather than God's army. So, Satan tempted David to take a census, and David fell for it. God was furious.

In order to appease God's wrath, the angel of the LORD told David to "build an altar to God on the threshing floor of Ornan the Jebusite" (v. 18). This place of sacrifice would become the location of God's temple where sacrifices would be made for the sins of the people; and where, 1,000 years later, Jesus died as the sacrifice for the sins of the world.

> *Then Solomon began to build the house of the LORD*
> *in Jerusalem on Mount Moriah, where the LORD had*
> *appeared to his father David, at the place that David had*
> *prepared on the threshing floor of Ornan the Jebusite.*
> —2 CHRONICLES 3:1

Use the words from 1 Chronicles 21:1 and 7-8 in confession and repentance as a faithful, prayerful watchman (Isaiah 62:6-7).

> *"LORD, please stop Satan from standing up against*
> *_____ and me and moving me to sin. God, You are*
> *displeased with this thing, and You have struck us. God, I have*
> *sinned greatly in that I have done this thing. But now, please take*
> *away the iniquity of Your servant, for I have done very foolishly.*
> *Because You are our Sacrifice and our Savior, Jesus~"*

June

*On your walls, O Jerusalem,
I have appointed watchmen;
All day and all night they
will never keep silent.
You who remind the LORD,
take no rest for yourselves;
And give Him no rest until He establishes
And makes Jerusalem a
praise in the earth.*
ISAIAH 62:6-7, NASB

JUNE 1

Please read 1 Chronicles 22.

Meditate on verse 13b.

Be strong and courageous; do not fear or be dismayed.

When David saw the LORD had accepted his sacrifice and answered him on the threshing floor of Ornan the Jebusite, he began making preparations for his son Solomon to build the temple on that location (1 Chronicles 21:28; 22:1-6). Realizing Solomon needed much strength and help from God for such a daunting task, David spoke encouraging words over his son. Pray those words from 1 Chronicles 22:11-13 and 18-19 over yourself and those for whom you stand guard as a faithful, prayerful watchman (Isaiah 62:6-7).

> *"LORD, please be with _____ and me that we may be successful and build Your church just as You have spoken. LORD, give us discretion and understanding and give us charge over those You place in our care, so that we may keep Your law, LORD our God. Let us prosper as we carefully observe Your statutes and ordinances. Make us strong and courageous; do not let us fear nor be dismayed. LORD God, You are with us. Give us rest on every side. Give the inhabitants of the land into our hand. Subdue the land before You and before Your people. Now, may we set our heart and our soul to seek You, LORD our God. Let us arise and build for the sake of Your Kingdom.*
> *In Your name, Jesus~"*

JUNE 2

Please read 1 Chronicles 23.

Meditate on verse 32.

> *Thus, they are to keep charge of the tent of meeting, and charge of the holy place, and charge of the sons of Aaron their relatives, for the service of the house of the LORD.*

As New Testament believers, whom Jesus made priests to His God and Father (Revelation 1:5-6), it is important to pay close attention to Old Testament instructions to the Levites because in the eyes of God, that is who you are. You are set apart and sanctified as most holy to minister to God and bless in His name forever (v. 13; 1 Corinthians 1:2; Colossians 3:12). You are called to thank and praise the LORD day and night (v. 30; 1 Thessalonians 5:16-18). You are to continually offer a sacrifice of praise before the LORD (v. 31; Hebrews 13:15). You are called to keep charge—guard and protect as a watchman and a sentry—Christ's church (v. 32; Acts 20:28).

Pray 1 Chronicles 23:13, 30, and 32 to be faithful to God's Levitical call over yourself and those for whom you stand guard as a faithful, prayerful watchman (Isaiah 62:6-7).

> *"LORD, set _____ and me apart to sanctify us as most holy forever, to minister to You and to bless in Your name forever. Let us stand every morning to thank and praise You, LORD, and likewise at evening. Let us keep charge of the holy place for the service of Your church, LORD.*
> *In Your name, Jesus~"*

JUNE 3

Please read 1 Chronicles 24.

Meditate on verse 2.

> *But Nadab and Abihu died before their father and had no sons. So Eleazar and Ithamar served as priests.*

It is important to remember the story of Aaron's sons, Nadab and Abihu:

> *Now Nadab and Abihu, the sons of Aaron, took their respective firepans, and after putting fire in them, placed incense on it and offered strange fire before the LORD, which He had not commanded them. And fire came out from the presence of the LORD and consumed them, and they died before the LORD.*
> —LEVITICUS 10:1-2

Nadab and Abihu made their own way for entering God's presence, and as priests, led others with them down their deadly path. When they tried to approach God with strange fire, He consumed them with His fire for blatant disregard of His Word.

God still takes seriously how one enters His presence—no one comes to the Father except through Jesus Christ (John 14:6). All other ways are like Nadab and Abihu's strange fire, leading to death.

As a Christian, and therefore a priest of God (1 Peter 2:9), know God's Word and teach correctly the way of salvation through Jesus Christ alone (Acts 4:8-12). As a faithful, prayerful watchman (Isaiah 62:6-7), use the words from 1 Chronicles 24:2 and 4 to pray for yourself and those you love to be faithful priests.

> *"LORD, make _____ and me Your faithful priests. Do not let us be a Nadab and Abihu, doing things leading to death. Make us Your choice ones, who lead according to Your Word. May more choice people be found to lead. For the sake of Your name, Jesus~"*

JUNE 4

Please read 1 Chronicles 25.

Meditate on these phrases from verses 1 and 3.

Who were to prophesy with lyres, harps, and cymbals ...
Who prophesied in giving thanks and praising the LORD ...

Have you thought about worship leaders and church musicians as prophets? King David set apart musicians to prophesy with their instruments and voices.

This is an important chapter for us as worshipers and leaders of worship. Think about the songs you hear, play, and sing. Do the music and lyrics correctly declare Truth about God? Analyze the songs, making certain they are Biblical, for God hates false prophecy.

An appalling and horrible thing has happened in the
land: The prophets prophesy falsely, and the priests rule
on their own authority; and My people love it so!
But what will you do at the end of it? Beware of the false prophets,
who come to you in sheep's clothing, but inwardly are ravenous wolves.
—JEREMIAH 5:30-31; MATTHEW 7:15

Worship leaders, you are Bible teachers, and God holds you accountable for the words being sung, making sure they are Scripturally sound. Worshipers, test the prophets, making sure the words you sing are not contrary to God's Word (1 John 4:1).

Use the words from 1 Chronicles 25:1 and 3 to pray over yourself and those for whom you stand guard as a faithful, prayerful watchman (Isaiah 62:6-7).

"LORD, set apart _____ and me to
prophesy according to Your Word and for Your service
with our instruments—lyres, harps, cymbals, etc.
Let us prophesy in giving thanks and praising You, LORD.
In Your name, Jesus~"

JUNE 5

Please read 1 Chronicles 26.

Meditate on this phrase from verse 31.

Men of outstanding capability were found among them.

Israel's gatekeepers, treasurers, officers, and judges had to be people of integrity. They are described as valiant, able, and strong—capable to oversee all the affairs of God and the king (vs. 7, 8, 32). What an incredible description of Godliness! And, what a great chapter to pray over those you love.

Treasure hunt this chapter for specific verses God wants you to pray. Here are some of the ones we found; pray 1 Chronicles 26:6-9, 12, 14, 20, 22, 24, 26, 28, and 30-32 over yourself and those for whom you stand guard as a faithful, prayerful watchman (Isaiah 62:6-7).

> *"LORD, make _____ and me mighty people of valor. Make us valiant and able, with strength for the service You call us to do. Make our men valiant men. Give us duties to minister in Your house, LORD. Make us counselors with insight. Make us people of integrity who can have charge of the treasures of Your house, God, and of the treasures of Your dedicated gifts. Make us capable of being officers over the treasures. If it is Your will, let us have charge of all the treasures of the dedicated gifts. Let everyone who has dedicated anything be able to trust it to our care. Make us capable to be given charge of the affairs of Your people. Make us people of outstanding capability. Make our men capable heads of their households. Make us capable overseers concerning all the affairs of God and the king. In Your name, King Jesus~"*

JUNE 6

Please read 1 Chronicles 27.

Meditate on verse 33.

> *Ahithophel was counselor to the king, and Hushai the Archite was the king's friend.*

1 Chronicles 27 describes the military divisions in Israel. The Israeli army was divided into 12 divisions, each with 24,000 men (v. 1). The commander of each division was a capable man, the head of his household, ready and able to serve the king in all the affairs of his military division (v. 1).[1]

What a great chapter to pray over the men in your family! "LORD, make our men capable heads of their families, ready and able commanders of Your army, serving You, King Jesus, in all the affairs of Your Kingdom!"

Pray 1 Chronicles 27:32-33 over yourself and those for whom you stand guard as a faithful, prayerful watchman (Isaiah 62:6-7).

> "LORD, make _____ and me
> a counselor, a person of understanding,
> and a scribe—one who recounts accurately the things of God.[1]
> May we be a counselor to the king and the king's friend.
> For the sake of Your name, Jesus~"

---

1. Retrieved from www.blueletterbible.org/lang/lexicon/lexicon.cfm?Strongs=H5608&t=NASB

JUNE 7

Please read 1 Chronicles 28.

Meditate on verse 6.

> *He (God) said to me, "Your son Solomon is the one who shall build My house and My courts; for I have chosen him to be a son to Me, and I will be a father to him."*

In front of his royal court, military commanders, overseers, and mighty men, King David entrusted his son, Solomon, with the plans for building God's temple (vs. 1, 11-12). God chose Solomon to build the temple instead of David, so rather than being jealous of his son or upset with God for not choosing him, David did all he could to ensure Solomon's success.

What a great chapter for parents—both physical and spiritual—to help us propel others to do great things for God. Think about those God gives you to mentor. What are you doing to ensure their success? Do you pray daily for them? Do you spend time with them, teaching them things of the LORD? Do you provide resources for their walk with Christ? Do you cheer them in God's will for their lives?

Use the words from 1 Chronicles 28:7-10 to pray over those for whom you stand guard as a faithful, prayerful watchman (Isaiah 62:6-7).

> *"LORD, establish _____ in You, forever. May they resolutely perform Your commandments and ordinances. Let them observe and seek after all Your commandments, so they may possess the good and bequeath it to their children after them forever. Let them know You, God, and serve You with a whole heart and a willing mind, for LORD, You search all hearts and understand every intent of the thoughts. Let them seek You and find You. Let them never forsake You! Choose them to build Your church. Let them be courageous and act. In Your name, Jesus~"*

JUNE 8

Please read 1 Chronicles 29.

Meditate on verse 5b.

Who then is willing to consecrate himself this day to the LORD?

This chapter contains a great prayer for faithful, prayerful watchmen (Isaiah 62:6-7). Pray 1 Chronicles 29:10-19 over yourself and those you love.

"Blessed are You, O LORD God of _____ and me, forever and ever. Yours, O LORD, is the greatness and the power and the glory and the victory and the majesty, indeed everything that is in the heavens and the earth; Yours is the dominion, O LORD, and You exalt Yourself as head over all. Both riches and honor come from You, and You rule over all, and in Your hand is power and might, and it lies in Your hand to make great and to strengthen everyone. Now therefore, our God, we thank You and praise Your glorious name. But, who are we that we should be able to offer as generously as this? For all things come from You, and from Your hand, we have given to You. For we are sojourners before You, and tenants, as all our fathers were; our days on the earth are like a shadow, and our hope is in You, Jesus. O LORD our God, all this abundance, it is from Your hand, and all is Yours. We are Yours—build us into a house for Your holy name. Since we know, O our God, that You try the heart and delight in uprightness, we, in the integrity of our hearts, willingly offer ourselves; so now with joy, may Your people make the offering of their lives willingly to You. O LORD, the God of my family, preserve this forever in the intentions of the heart of Your people and direct our heart to You and give us a perfect heart to keep Your commandments, Your testimonies and Your statutes, and to do them all, and to build our lives, for which You have made provision—
For the glory of Your name, Jesus~"

JUNE 9

Please read 2 Chronicles 1.

Meditate on verse 7.

> *In that night God appeared to Solomon and said to him, "Ask what I shall give you."*

Amazingly, Almighty God, Ruler of All, said to an earthly king, "Ask Me for what I will give you." Incredibly, He says the same thing to you:

> *Ask, and it will be given to you; seek, and you will find; knock, and it will be opened to you.*
> —MATTHEW 7:7

> *If you abide in Me, and My words abide in you, ask whatever you wish, and it will be done for you.*
> —JOHN 15:7

> *This is the confidence which we have before Him, that, if we ask anything according to His will, He hears us.*
> —1 JOHN 5:14

Observe in these verses a relationship with God is required in order to make this kind of request. "LORD, what will You give me? That is what I seek. Your Word says ... That is what I wish You to do for me. LORD, Your will be done. Please hear my prayer."

With confident humility, pray 2 Chronicles 1:1, 8, and 10 over yourself and those for whom you stand guard as a faithful, prayerful watchman (Isaiah 62:6-7).

> *"LORD, please establish _____ and me securely over the kingdoms and ministries You give us. LORD, be with us and exalt us greatly. Deal with us with great lovingkindness. Give us wisdom and knowledge that we may go out and come in before the people You place in our care. For the sake of Your Kingdom, Jesus~"*

JUNE 10

Please read 2 Chronicles 2.

Meditate on verses 4a and 5.

> *Behold, I am about to build a house for the name of the LORD my God, dedicating it to Him, to burn fragrant incense before Him. The house which I am about to build will be great, for greater is our God than all the gods.*

As you ponder the enormity of building a house for God, think about what the LORD is building in your life because the temple is actually a picture of you—the dwelling place of God's Spirit.

> *Do you not know that you are a temple of God and that the Spirit of God dwells in you? You are being built up as a spiritual house for a holy priesthood, to offer up spiritual sacrifices acceptable to God through Jesus Christ because greater is He who is in you than he who is in the world.*
> —1 CORINTHIANS 3:16; 1 PETER 2:5; 1 JOHN 4:4B

As you continue to learn about the temple, ask the Holy Spirit to reveal how you are His temple.

> *Therefore, I urge you, brethren, by the mercies of God, to present your bodies a living and holy sacrifice, acceptable to God, which is your spiritual service of worship.*
> —ROMANS 12:1

Pray 2 Chronicles 2:12 over yourself and those for whom you stand guard as a faithful prayerful watchman (Isaiah 62:6-7).

> "Blessed are You, LORD, the God of _____ and me, who has made heaven and earth and who makes us wise. Endow us with discretion and understanding. Build us into Your house, LORD. For the sake of Your name, Jesus~"

JUNE 11

Please read 2 Chronicles 3.

Meditate on verse 1.

> *Then Solomon began to build the house of the LORD in Jerusalem on Mount Moriah, where the LORD had appeared to his father David, at the place that David had prepared on the threshing floor of Ornan the Jebusite.*

This is not the first time Mount Moriah is mentioned in the Bible. The first was 1,000 years earlier:

> *Now it came about after these things, that God tested Abraham, and said to him, "Abraham!" And he said, "Here I am." He said, "Take now your son, your only son, whom you love, Isaac, and go to the land of Moriah and offer him there as a burnt offering on one of the mountains of which I will tell you."*
> —GENESIS 22:1-2

The temple of the LORD, the place where sacrifices were made for sins, was built on Mount Moriah, the mountain where God provided a substitutionary ram in place of Isaac (Genesis 22:13). One thousand years after the temple was built, God provided Himself as the substitutionary Lamb on Mount Moriah, taking away the sin of the world (Genesis 22:8; John 1:29).

As you ponder the enormity of the sacrifice of Jesus Christ for sins, use the words from 2 Chronicles 3:1 to pray for those who need to accept His sacrifice for their sins as their faithful, prayerful watchman (Isaiah 62:6-7).

> *"LORD, You appeared to David and Abraham on Mount Moriah. LORD, please appear to _____ . Let them accept Your sacrifice on Mount Moriah, so You can begin to build them into Your house, LORD. For the sake of Your name, Jesus~"*

JUNE 12

Please read 2 Chronicles 4.

Meditate on verses 2a and 6b.

> *Also, he made the cast metal sea.*
> *The sea was for the priests to wash in.*

Picture the giant sea, a huge bronze tub holding approximately 12,000 gallons of water elevated on the backs of twelve bronze oxen.[1] Its purpose was for cleansing the priests so they could perform their priestly duties in the presence of God, offering sacrifices on behalf of the people and caring for the temple.

In the book of *Revelation*, John describes a new heaven and a new earth, where "there is no longer any sea" (Revelation 21:1). Perhaps, John meant this temple sea that was required for coming into God's presence. Think about these verses:

> *These are the ones who come out of the great tribulation,*
> *and they have washed their robes and made them white in the blood*
> *of the Lamb. For this reason, they are before the throne of God;*
> *and they serve Him day and night in His temple.*
> *Blessed are those who wash their robes, so that they may have the*
> *right to the tree of life and may enter by the gates into the city.*
> —REVELATION 7:14B-15A; 22:14

As a Christian, you are made clean by the blood of Christ. You are constantly in God's presence because of Jesus. There is no longer any sea because Jesus cleanses you of all unrighteousness (1 John 1:9).

As a faithful, prayerful watchman (Isaiah 62:6-7), use the words from 2 Chronicles 4:6 to pray for those who need to be cleansed by Jesus.

> *"LORD, please be the sea for _____ to wash*
> *in and become one of Your priests (Revelation 1:6).*
> *In Your name, Jesus~"*

---

[1] Retrieved from King Solomon's Molten Sea by Albert Zuidhof, The Biblical Archaeologist @1982 The University of Chicago Press

JUNE 13

Please read 2 Chronicles 5.

Meditate on verse 14b.

> *The glory of the LORD filled the house of God.*

Imagine how thrilling that day was when the glory of the LORD filled the house of the LORD! Even more thrilling is the fact that as a Christian you are now the house of the LORD, and the Spirit—the glory of the LORD—fills you (1 Corinthians 3:16)! Live with that truth governing you:

> *Or do you not know that your body is a temple of the Holy Spirit who is in you, whom you have from God, and that you are not your own? For you have been bought with a price; therefore, glorify God in your body. But we all, with unveiled face, beholding as in a mirror the glory of the LORD, are being transformed into the same image from glory to glory, just as from the LORD, the Spirit. God has chosen you from the beginning for salvation through sanctification by the Spirit and faith in the truth. It was for this He called you through our gospel, that you may gain the glory of our LORD Jesus Christ.*
> —1 Corinthians 6:19-20; 2 Corinthians 3:18;
> 2 Thessalonians 2:13b-14

Glory! In praise and commitment for all the LORD has done for you, glorify Him with 2 Chronicles 5:13-14 as a His faithful, prayerful watchman (Isaiah 62:6-7).

> *"LORD, I praise and glorify You! You indeed are good, for Your lovingkindness is everlasting. LORD, let me stand and minister for You because Your glory fills me.*
> *By Your Spirit, Jesus~"*

JUNE 14

Please read 2 Chronicles 6.

Meditate on verse 19.

> *Yet have regard to the prayer of Your servant and to his supplication, O LORD my God, to listen to the cry and to the prayer which Your servant prays before You.*

Thankfully, Solomon's prayer of dedication of God's temple is recorded in 2 Chronicles 6. It is a prayer of adoration, confession, and supplication—a great prayer to keep in your arsenal. Pray 2 Chronicles 6:14, 19, 24-27, 29-31, 33, and 42 over yourself and those for whom you stand guard as a faithful, prayerful watchman (Isaiah 62:6-7).

> *"O LORD, the God of _____ and me, there is no god like You in heaven or on earth, keeping covenant and showing lovingkindness to Your servants who walk before You with all their heart. Please have regard to the prayer of Your servant and to my supplication, O LORD my God, to listen to the cry and the prayer which Your servant prays before You. When Your people are defeated before an enemy because we have sinned against You, and we return to You and confess Your name and pray and make supplication before You, then hear from heaven and forgive the sin of Your people and bring us back. I have sinned against You. LORD, I confess Your name and turn from my sin. Please hear from heaven and forgive my sin. Teach me the good way in which I should walk. LORD, You know the pain of _____ . Let them spread their hands toward You; then, hear from heaven and forgive and render to them according to all their ways, whose heart You know, for You alone know the hearts of people. Let us fear You to walk in Your ways as long as we live. LORD, please let all the people of the earth know Your name. O, LORD God, remember Your lovingkindness. For the sake of Your name, Jesus~"*

JUNE 15

Please read 2 Chronicles 7.

Meditate on verse 12a.

> *Then the LORD appeared to Solomon at night and said to him, "I have heard your prayer."*

What a comfort to discover verses in the Bible reassuring us God hears prayer! After Solomon prayed, dedicating the temple to the LORD, God heard his prayer and filled the temple with His glory (2 Chronicles 6:14-7:2). Pray for God to fill you and those you love with His glory. Then pray the many treasure verses found in this chapter as a faithful, prayerful watchman (Isaiah 62:6-7). Pray 2 Chronicles 7:2-3, 10-12, and 14-17.

> *"LORD, please fill _____ and me with Your glory! We worship and give praise to You. Truly You are good; truly Your lovingkindness is everlasting. Let us rejoice and be happy of heart because of the goodness You have shown to us. Let us successfully complete all that You have planned for us to do. LORD, hear our prayer. We are called by Your name. We humble ourselves and pray and seek Your face and turn from our wicked ways. LORD, please hear from heaven, forgive our sin, and heal our land. Let Your eyes be open and Your ears attentive to our prayers. LORD, choose and consecrate _____ that Your name may be in them forever, so Your eyes and Your heart will be with them perpetually. Let us walk before You to do according to all that You have commanded. In Your name, LORD our God, Jesus~"*

June 16

Please read 2 Chronicles 8.

Meditate on verse 16.

> *Thus, all the work of Solomon was carried out from the day of the foundation of the house of the LORD, and until it was finished. So, the house of the LORD was completed.*

As you meditate on 2 Chronicles 8:16, think about these verses:

> *According to the grace of God which was given to me, like a wise master builder I laid a foundation, and another is building on it. But each man must be careful how he builds on it. For no man can lay a foundation other than the one which is laid, which is Jesus Christ. Now if any man builds on the foundation with gold, silver, precious stones, wood, hay, straw, each man's work will become evident; for the day will show it because it is to be revealed with fire, and the fire itself will test the quality of each man's work. If any man's work which he has built on it remains, he will receive a reward. If any man's work is burned up, he will suffer loss; but he himself will be saved, yet so as through fire. Do you not know that you are a temple of God and that the Spirit of God dwells in you?*
> —1 Corinthians 3:10-16

With God's Spirit inside of you and Jesus Christ as the firm foundation, the LORD is building you and fellow believers into His holy temple. You are a participant in this building process as you walk in the good works God has prepared for you (Ephesians 2:10). Solomon's temple is a beautiful picture of what God is doing in your life and the lives of those you love. Pray for God to complete the work, using the words from 2 Chronicles 8:16 as a faithful, prayerful watchman (Isaiah 62:6-7).

> *"LORD, let all Your work be carried out in _____ and me to be Your house, from the day You lay the foundation until all Your work is finished. Complete us in Your name, Jesus~"*

JUNE 17

Please read 2 Chronicles 9.

Meditate on verse 4b.

She was breathless.

Why was Queen Sheba breathless in the presence of King Solomon? It wasn't his livestock, gold, and precious stones; she had plenty of that (v. 1). What left Sheba breathless was Solomon's incredible wisdom.

> *Then she said to the king, "It was a true report which I heard in my own land about your words and your wisdom. Nevertheless, I did not believe their reports until I came and my eyes had seen it. And behold, the half of the greatness of your wisdom was not told me. You surpass the report that I heard. How blessed are your men, how blessed are these your servants who stand before you continually and hear your wisdom."*
> —2 CHRONICLES 9:5-7

Recall God gave Solomon His wisdom (2 Chronicles 1:10), and in Jesus, you have His wisdom, too:

> *By His doing, you are in Christ Jesus, who became to us wisdom from God. We have the mind of Christ.*
> —1 CORINTHIANS 1:30A; 2:16B

Because of Jesus Christ, you are as wise as King Solomon. Let that truth leave you breathless as you pray 2 Chronicles 9:2-3 and 5-8 over yourself and those for whom you stand guard as a faithful, prayerful watchman (Isaiah 62:6-7).

> *"LORD, please let nothing be hidden from _____ and me as we explain Your truths. May others see Your wisdom in us. Let people hear about Your Words and Your wisdom. Let them come and see with their own eyes the greatness of Your wisdom. May they be blessed as they continually hear Your wisdom. LORD our God, delight in us, love us, and establish us forever to do justice and righteousness. Because You are our wisdom, Jesus~"*

JUNE 18

Please read 2 Chronicles 10.

Meditate on verse 15.

> *So, the king did not listen to the people, for it was a turn of events from God that the LORD might establish His word, which He spoke through Ahijah the Shilonite to Jeroboam the son of Nebat.*

What was this word that God established? It is recorded in 1 Kings 11.

> *It came about at that time, when Jeroboam went out of Jerusalem, that the prophet Ahijah the Shilonite found him on the road. Now Ahijah had clothed himself with a new cloak; and both of them were alone in the field. Then Ahijah took hold of the new cloak which was on him and tore it into twelve pieces. He said to Jeroboam, "Take for yourself ten pieces; for thus says the LORD, the God of Israel, 'Behold, I will tear the kingdom out of the hand of Solomon and give you ten tribes (but he will have one tribe, for the sake of My servant David and for the sake of Jerusalem, the city which I have chosen from all the tribes of Israel), because they have forsaken Me, and have worshiped Ashtoreth the goddess of the Sidonians, Chemosh the god of Moab, and Milcom the god of the sons of Ammon; and they have not walked in My ways, doing what is right in My sight and observing My statutes and My ordinances, as his father David did.'"*
> —1 KINGS 11:29-33

How tragic! Israel became a divided kingdom because of disobedience and idolatry.

Ask the LORD to make you aware of idols in your life because they will divide your allegiance to Him. As a faithful, prayerful watchman (Isaiah 62:6-7), use the words from 2 Chronicles 10:19 to pray for yourself and those you love not to rebel against God.

> "LORD, help _____ and me not be in rebellion against You. In Your name, Jesus~"

June 19

Please read 2 Chronicles 11.

Meditate on verses 14-16.

> *For the Levites left their pasture lands and their property and came to Judah and Jerusalem, for Jeroboam and his sons had excluded them from serving as priests to the LORD. He set up priests of his own for the high places, for the satyrs and for the calves which he had made. Those from all the tribes of Israel who set their hearts on seeking the LORD God of Israel followed them to Jerusalem, to sacrifice to the LORD God of their fathers.*

God made Solomon's servant, Jeroboam, king of the 10 northern tribes of Israel because of Solomon's idolatrous rebellion (1 Kings 11:4-11). Jeroboam should have learned from the mistakes of his master and devoted himself to the LORD who had elevated him from servant to king. However, Jeroboam proved himself foolish, building high places, satyrs, and calves for the people to worship. He forbade the Levites from serving as priests, instead appointing his own priests to serve in his high places. Jeroboam's sinful choices put the northern kingdom of Israel on a path of destruction; all of Israel's kings were evil, and the nation was destroyed by the Assyrians in 722 B.C.

Allow God's Word to search your heart for Jeroboam tendencies. When the LORD elevates you, do not get full of yourself and succumb to self-reliant idolatry. Set your heart to seek the LORD and walk in His ways.

Pray 2 Chronicles 11:16-17 over yourself and those for whom you stand guard as a faithful, prayerful watchman (Isaiah 62:6-7).

> *"LORD, let _____ and me set our hearts on seeking You, God. We will follow You and sacrifice to You, LORD our God. Let us work to strengthen Your Kingdom and to support those who serve You. Let us walk in Your ways and Your name, LORD Jesus~"*

JUNE 20

Please read 2 Chronicles 12.

Meditate on verse 1.

> *When the kingdom of Rehoboam*
> *was established and strong, he and all Israel*
> *with him forsook the law of the LORD.*

Ugh, as soon as I read 2 Chronicles 12:1, I wrote, "No, LORD!!!!!" in my Bible next to the verse in bright red ink with bright red stars at the beginning and end of the verse. "Oh, LORD, why is it our sinful, prideful tendency to forsake You when things start going well? LORD, help us!"

Well, the life lessons in this chapter are obvious, and the text is full of verses to pray, so let's get started. Use the words from 2 Chronicles 12:1-2, 5-9, and 12-14 to pray over yourself and those for whom you stand guard as a faithful, prayerful watchman (Isaiah 62:6-7).

> *"LORD, when You establish and make _____ and*
> *me strong, do not allow us to forsake You and Your law.*
> *Do not let us be unfaithful to You. Do not let us forsake*
> *You, so that You forsake us to our enemies. LORD, we*
> *humble ourselves and say, 'LORD, You are righteous.'*
> *LORD, keep us humble so You do not have to destroy us. Grant us*
> *deliverance and do not pour out Your wrath on us. Let us learn,*
> *without having to become slaves to the world, the difference between*
> *Your service and the service of the kingdoms of the countries.*
> *LORD, please do not take Your shield of protection*
> *from us. As we humble ourselves,*
> *let Your anger be turned away from us, so as not to*
> *destroy us completely. Please let conditions be good in our*
> *family. We will strengthen ourselves in You, LORD.*
> *Do not let us do evil. Let us set our hearts to seek You, LORD.*
> *In Your name, Jesus~"*

JUNE 21

Please read 2 Chronicles 13.

Meditate on verses 13-15.

> *But Jeroboam had set an ambush to come from the rear, so that Israel was in front of Judah and the ambush was behind them. When Judah turned around, behold, they were attacked both front and rear, so they cried to the LORD, and the priests blew the trumpets. Then the men of Judah raised a war cry, and when the men of Judah raised the war cry, then it was that God routed Jeroboam and all Israel before Abijah and Judah.*

Picture the scene: the armies of Judah surrounded by the armies of Israel. Being attacked from behind and before, the priests blasted their trumpets and the men shouted to God with a war-cry. When God heard their cry, He struck King Jeroboam and his army, thus conquering Judah's enemies.

What and who is surrounding you and your loved ones, hoping to destroy you? Cry out to the LORD using the words from 2 Chronicles 13:10-12, 15, 18, and 20 as a faithful, prayerful watchman (Isaiah 62:6-7).

> *"LORD, You are _____ and my God, and we have not forsaken You. We are ministering to You, LORD, attending to Your work. We are keeping Your charge; we have not forsaken You. God, You are with us. Make _____ stop fighting against You, LORD God, for they will not succeed. We raise a war cry! God, route Your enemies! Subdue Your enemies! Let us conquer because we trust in You, LORD our God! Let those who fight against You never again recover strength. Strike them in Your name, Jesus~"*

JUNE 22

Please read 2 Chronicles 14.

Meditate on verses 2-4.

> *Asa did good and right in the sight of the LORD his*
> *God, for he removed the foreign altars and high places,*
> *tore down the sacred pillars, cut down the Asherim, and*
> *commanded Judah to seek the LORD God of their fathers*
> *and to observe the law and the commandment.*

What a relief to read a chapter in God's Word about a man who wanted to please the LORD! As you seek God, wanting to do what is good and right in His sight, learn from King Asa. Ask the LORD to reveal any idols in your life, so you can remove them.

This is a powerful chapter and nearly every verse can become a prayer. In fact, verse 11 is a prayer. Pray 2 Chronicles 14:1-7 and 11-14 over yourself and those for whom you stand guard as a faithful, prayerful watchman (Isaiah 62:6-7).

> *"LORD, please let _____ and me live in the land*
> *undisturbed. Help us do good and right in Your sight, LORD our*
> *God. Remove our prideful high places; tear down and cut down*
> *our idols. Let us seek You, LORD God, and observe Your law and*
> *commandments. As we do, let us be undisturbed with no one at war*
> *with us because You, LORD, have given us rest. LORD, we seek*
> *You; please, give us rest on every side; let us build and prosper.*
> *LORD, there is no one besides You to help in the battle between*
> *the powerful and those who have no strength, so help us, O*
> *LORD our God, for we trust in You, and in Your name,*
> *have come against this multitude of troubles.*
> *O LORD, You are our God; let not man prevail against You!*
> *LORD, route Your enemies and make them flee.*
> *Shatter them before You and before Your army.*
> *Let the dread of You, LORD, fall upon Your enemies.*
> *In Your name, Jesus~"*

JUNE 23

Please read 2 Chronicles 15.

Meditate on verse 1.

> *Now the Spirit of God came on*
> *Azariah the son of Oded.*

I love a good sermon, and this chapter has a great one! It was first preached to King Asa and the people of Judah and Benjamin, and thankfully, today, it is preached to us (vs. 1-7). It is a three-point sermon with Israel as the sermon illustration. The northern kingdom of Israel had no peace because they were living without God and His law (vs. 3, 5). They were crushed because "God troubled them with every kind of distress" (v. 6). The sermon points are:

- Seek God; He will let you find Him (v. 2)
- Do not forsake the LORD; you do not want Him to forsake you (v. 2)
- Be strong and courageous; there is reward for your work (v. 7)

Thankfully, King Asa took the sermon to heart, removing idols throughout the land and restoring the altar of the LORD (v. 8).

How does the sermon impact you? Let it move you to take Godly action. Pray 2 Chronicles 15:3-4, 7-9, and 12 over yourself and those for whom you stand guard as a faithful, prayerful watchman (Isaiah 62:6-7).

"LORD, _____ and I need You, our true God.
We need a teaching pastor and Your law.
We turn to You and seek You.
Thank You for letting us find You. Help us be strong
and not lose courage, for we know there is reward for
our work. Give us courage to remove the abominable
idols from the land and restore places of worship.
Let people see that You are with us, God. Let them want to enter into
the covenant to seek You, LORD God, with all their heart and soul.
In Your name, Jesus~"

JUNE 24

Please read 2 Chronicles 16.

Meditate on verses 7-9, God's message to King Asa.

> *At that time Hanani the seer came to Asa king of Judah and said to him, "Because you have relied on the king of Aram and have not relied on the LORD your God; therefore, the army of the king of Aram has escaped out of your hand. Were not the Ethiopians and the Lubim an immense army with very many chariots and horsemen? Yet because you relied on the LORD, He delivered them into your hand. For the eyes of the LORD move to and fro throughout the earth that He may strongly support those whose heart is completely His. You have acted foolishly in this. Indeed, from now on you will surely have wars."*

Sadly, after trusting God for the first 35 years of his reign, Asa succumbed to fear and relied on people to deliver him from his enemies. God sent Hanani to tell King Asa of His displeasure. Rather than hear and heed the LORD's message, Asa was furious and imprisoned Hanani for speaking God's truth (v. 10). So, instead of being remembered as a king who trusted God, Asa is remembered as a king with severely diseased feet (v. 12; 1 Kings 15:23).

How do you want to be remembered? I hope it is for unapologetically trusting Jesus, and if there is any mention of feet, I pray it is: "How lovely are the feet of them who bring good news, who announce salvation and say, 'Our God reigns!'" (Isaiah 52:7).

Pray 2 Chronicles 16:9 over yourself and those for whom you stand guard as a faithful, prayerful watchman (Isaiah 62:6-7).

> *"LORD, Your eyes move to and fro throughout the earth that You may strongly support those whose heart is completely Yours. LORD, here are _____ and I! Do not let us act foolishly toward You. In Your name, Jesus~"*

June 25

Please read 2 Chronicles 17.

Meditate on verse 6.

> *He (Jehoshaphat) took great pride in the ways of the LORD and again removed the high places and the Asherim from Judah.*

What a great verse to ponder! "He took great pride in the ways of the LORD" (v. 6). Think about God's ways. Here are some verses to get you started:

> *Yet, God does not take away life but plans ways so that the banished one will not be cast out from him.*
> —2 SAMUEL 14:14B

> *"For My thoughts are not your thoughts, nor are your ways My ways," declares the LORD.*
> —ISAIAH 55:8

> *"Yet you say, 'The way of the LORD is not right.' Hear now, O house of Israel! Is My way not right? Is it not your ways that are not right?"*
> —EZEKIEL 18:25

As you walk with the LORD today, be aware of what He is doing in your life and the lives of those you love. Rather than question His ways, look for ways He restores, heals, and works for His glory. Rather than take pride in yourself, take pride in God and His sovereign ways.

Pray 2 Chronicles 17:3-6 over yourself and those for whom you stand guard as a faithful, prayerful watchman (Isaiah 62:6-7).

> *"LORD, please be with _____ and me as we follow Your example, not seeking the idols of this world. As we seek You, God, and follow Your commandments, establish us in Your control. Let us take great pride in Your ways, LORD. Remove our idolatrous high places.*
> *In Your name, Jesus~"*

JUNE 26

Please read 2 Chronicles 18.

Meditate on verse 7.

> *The king of Israel said to Jehoshaphat, "There is yet one man by whom we may inquire of the LORD, but I hate him, for he never prophesies good concerning me but always evil. He is Micaiah, son of Imla." But Jehoshaphat said, "Let not the king say so."*

King Ahab surrounded himself with 400 false prophets who told him what he wanted to hear (v. 5). King Jehoshaphat questioned the wisdom in that and asked to hear from a prophet of the LORD (v. 6). Reluctantly, Ahab called for Micaiah, a prophet who unapologetically spoke God's Word, proclaiming disaster from God against King Ahab (vs. 13-22). Ahab imprisoned Micaiah for his bold sermon, and despite crazy moves to save his own life, King Ahab was killed in battle, just as God prophesied through Micaiah (vs. 25-34).

With what kind of teaching do you surround yourself? If it is what you want to hear and what makes you feel good, consider finding Biblical pastors and teachers who are not afraid to unapologetically teach all of God's Word. Ask God to make you a Micaiah who says, "As the LORD lives, what my God says, that I will speak" (v. 13).

Pray 2 Chronicles 18:13 over yourself and those for whom you stand guard as a faithful, prayerful watchman (Isaiah 62:6-7).

> *"LORD, as You live, what You say, that I will speak!*
> *LORD, give _____ the courage to do the same.*
> *In Your name, Jesus~"*

JUNE 27

Please read 2 Chronicles 19.

Meditate on verses 6-7.

> *He said to the judges, "Consider what you are doing, for you do not judge for man but for the LORD who is with you when you render judgment. Now then let the fear of the LORD be upon you; be very careful what you do, for the LORD our God will have no part in unrighteousness or partiality or the taking of a bribe."*

I wish every judge in the land knew about this exhortation from the LORD (vs. 6-7). Thankfully, you have now unearthed this treasure chest of verses for judges. Keep them in your arsenal to share with those in judicial positions and to pray over them. Consider also King Jehoshaphat appointed Levites, priests, and heads of households to render God's judgments and settle disputes, so these verses can be applied to all of us.

Pray 2 Chronicles 19:6-11 over yourself and those for whom you stand guard as a faithful, prayerful watchman (Isaiah 62:6-7).

> *"LORD, help our judges consider what they are doing, for they do not judge for man, but for You. Make them realize You are with them when they render judgment. Let the fear of You, LORD, be upon them. May they be very careful what they do, for You, LORD our God, will have no part in unrighteousness or partiality or the taking of a bribe.*
> *As You appoint _____ and me for administering Your judgment and judging disputes among our people, let us do it in the fear of You, LORD, faithfully and wholeheartedly. Whenever any dispute comes to us from those who live among us, help us warn them, so they will not be guilty before You, LORD, so wrath may not come on us and our families. Help us act resolutely. LORD, be with the upright.*
> *In Your name, Jesus~"*

JUNE 28

Please read 2 Chronicles 20.

Meditate on verse 3.

> *Jehoshaphat was afraid and turned his attention to seek the LORD and proclaimed a fast throughout all Judah.*

When Jehoshaphat heard a multitude was coming to war against him, he focused on God instead of the problem marching his way (vs. 1-3). Fasting and praying, He acknowledged the LORD, reminding Him of His faithfulness (vs. 3-8). He cried to God in his distress, begging for deliverance from evil (vs. 9-12). God responded with words to reassure and calm the king's heart (vs. 15-17).

What do you do when you receive news that makes your heart pound with fear? Turn your attention to the LORD and pray 2 Chronicles 20:3, 6-7, 9, 12, and 17-18 over fearful situations as a faithful, prayerful watchman (Isaiah 62:6-7).

> *"LORD, I am afraid, so I turn my attention to seek You. O LORD, the God of _____ and me, are You not God in the heavens? And are You not ruler over all the kingdoms of the nations? Power and might are in Your hand so that no one can stand against You. O, our God, You have driven out our enemies in the past. Should evil come upon us, the sword, or judgment, or pestilence, or famine, we will stand before You and cry to You in our distress, and You will hear and deliver us. O our God, will You not judge for us? For we are powerless before this great multitude of problems coming against us, nor do we know what to do, but our eyes are on You. LORD, please fight for us in this battle. We will stand and see Your salvation on our behalf. We will not fear or be dismayed because You are with us, LORD. We bow with our face to the ground before You, Worshiping in Your name, Jesus~"*

JUNE 29

Please read 2 Chronicles 21.

Meditate on verses 6-7.

> *He (Jehoram) walked in the way of the kings of Israel, just as the house of Ahab did (for Ahab's daughter was his wife), and he did evil in the sight of the LORD. Yet the LORD was not willing to destroy the house of David because of the covenant which He had made with David, and since He had promised to give a lamp to him and his sons forever.*

What a sobering chapter from God's Word! Contrast the evil of King Jehoram with the faithfulness of God. Although Jehoram killed his six brothers and enticed Judah into adulterous idolatry, God did not totally wipe out his royal family because of His covenant promises to David (vs. 4, 7, 11). God keeps His covenant promises, but do not mistake His faithfulness to mean He turns a blind eye to sin. Jehoram's flagrant evil brought God's calamity on his family and a horrible bowel disease on himself (vs. 12-15).

Does this chapter convict you of areas where you take God's covenant of salvation lightly, forgetting the price Christ paid for sins? As you confess your sins to the LORD, use the words from 2 Chronicles 21:7 and 13-14 as a faithful, prayerful watchman (Isaiah 62:6-7).

> *"LORD, thank You for not being willing to eternally destroy me because of the covenant You made with me. Let Your lamp shine on _____ and me forever. Please forgive me for walking in the way of the world, causing others to play the harlot against You, killing them by not telling them about You. LORD, please help me walk with You, so You do not need to strike me, my people, my family, and all my possessions with great calamity.*
> *In Your name, Jesus~*

JUNE 30

Please read 2 Chronicles 22.

Meditate on verses 3-5a, noticing the words counsel and counselor.

> *He (Ahaziah) also walked in the ways of the house of Ahab, for his mother was his counselor to do wickedly. He did evil in the sight of the LORD like the house of Ahab, for they were his counselors after the death of his father, to his destruction. He also walked according to their counsel.*

This is such a tragic chapter—a mother counseling her son to do wickedly and the son walking in the destructive advice of evil counselors leading to his death (vs. 3-5, 9).

Contrast the meditation verses with these counseling verses.

> *I will bless the LORD who has counseled me; indeed, my mind instructs me in the night.*
> —Psalm 16:7

> *I (the LORD) will instruct you and teach you in the way which you should go; I will counsel you with My eye upon you.*
> —Psalm 32:8

> *Your testimonies also are my delight; they are my counselors.*
> —Psalm 119:24

Set your heart to seek the LORD's advice, getting your guidance from the Holy Spirit and His Word. Pray the opposite of 2 Chronicles 22:3-5 over yourself and those for whom you stand guard as a faithful, prayerful watchman (Isaiah 62:6-7).

> *"LORD, do not let _____ and me counsel others to do wickedly. Do not let us do evil in Your sight, nor seek the counsel of evildoers, leading to destruction. Let us walk according to Your counsel. In Your name, Jesus~"*

July

*On your walls, O Jerusalem,
I have appointed watchmen;
All day and all night they
will never keep silent.
You who remind the LORD,
take no rest for yourselves;
And give Him no rest until He establishes
And makes Jerusalem a
praise in the earth.*
Isaiah 62:6-7, NASB

JULY 1

Please read 2 Chronicles 23.

Meditate on verses 4-5.

> *This is the thing which you shall do: one third of you, of the priests and Levites who come in on the sabbath, shall be gatekeepers, and one third shall be at the king's house, and a third at the Gate of the Foundation; and all the people shall be in the courts of the house of the LORD.*

Jehoiada armed the priests and Levites and made them gatekeepers. Their job was to keep evil out of the palace and the temple, so 7-year-old, Joash, could be crowned king, and his wicked grandmother, Athaliah, deposed. Recall baby Joash was hidden in the temple for six years from his murdering grandmother (2 Chronicles 22:10-12). Athaliah was killed, and the people of Judah were freed from evil to devote themselves to God (vs. 12-16).

Notice these Levitical gatekeepers were stationed at the palace, the temple, and the Foundation Gate, thereby protecting the seat of government, worship, and the foundation of society from evil attack. God has placed you in the same position of gatekeeper, arming you with His Word, so you can protect your government, church, and the foundation of your family and society from evil as you proclaim the truth of God's Word.

Pray for God to make you a courageous gatekeeper using the words from 2 Chronicles 23:4-6 as a faithful, prayerful watchman (Isaiah 62:6-7).

> *"LORD, as Your spiritual priests and Levites (1 Peter 2:9), _____ and I will be Your gatekeepers. Help us be faithful at the king's house, at the Gate of the Foundation, and in the courts of Your house, LORD. May all the people be in the courts of Your house. Make us holy and help us keep Your charge. According to Your Word and because of Your name, Jesus~"*

JULY 2

Please read 2 Chronicles 24.

Meditate on verse 2.

> *Joash did what was right in the sight of the LORD all the days of Jehoiada the priest.*

What a profoundly foreshadowing verse! You could probably guess what was going to happen to King Joash after his mentor Jehoiada died before even reading the text. But, you were probably shocked by how horribly he behaved as you read the entire chapter. Joash, whose life was saved by his Aunt Jehoshabeath and mentored by her husband, Jehoiada, murdered their son, Zechariah (2 Chronicles 22:10-12; 24:20-22). How can one go from doing what is right in the sight of the LORD to committing murder? Joash's relationship with God was really more of a relationship with Jehoiada. He was a follower of his priest instead of a follower of the LORD. Then, when his priest and mentor died, Joash was easily persuaded to abandon God with disastrous results (vs. 17-18).

Beware of becoming a follower of a human instead of a follower of Christ, for when that person dies or loses our esteem, our foundation is rocked because it was not built on Christ and His Word. Spend time searching your soul to see if you are anchored to Christ or if you are anchored to a pastor, teacher, mentor, relative, etc. People come and go; they rise and fall; they are not God. Pray to do what is right in the sight of the LORD all the days of your life because Jesus is your "great high priest" forever (Hebrews 4:14; 7:24).

Pray 2 Chronicles 24:2 over yourself and those for whom you stand guard as a faithful, prayerful watchman (Isaiah 62:6-7).

> *"LORD, please help _____ and me do what is right in Your sight all the days of our lives. Because You are our priest, Jesus~"*

JULY 3

Please read 2 Chronicles 25.

Meditate on verse 2.

*He did right in the sight of the LORD,
yet not with a whole heart.*

Well, from the meditation verse, you could probably guess the course of King Amaziah's life. Pride and idolatry result from not walking wholeheartedly with the LORD, and King Amaziah was no exception. He started well, heeding God's word not to use the Israelite army to help battle the sons of Seir, but after God gave Amaziah the victory, he brought their idols back to Jerusalem and worshiped them (vs. 7-14). Of course, God was furious, and Amaziah did not repent, so God did not relent from bringing calamity to Amaziah and the people of Judah (vs. 15-28). Tragic!

Take the story of King Amaziah to heart, for this chapter is filled with practical spiritual applications for our lives. For example, if you have already committed money to do something you know is out of God's will, do not worry about the money; do what is right, for the LORD has much more to give you than that money can buy (v. 9). Determine to do what pleases God with a whole heart. Ask Him to help you not become full of yourself and fall into a pride trap like Amaziah did (vs. 10-14).

Use the words from 2 Chronicles 25:2 and 19 to pray over yourself and those for whom you stand guard as a faithful, prayerful watchman (Isaiah 62:6-7).

*"LORD, please let _____ and
me do right in Your sight with a whole heart.
Do not let our hearts become proud in boasting. Do not let us do
anything that would provoke trouble, causing us and others to fall.
For the sake of Your name, Jesus~"*

JULY 4

Please read 2 Chronicles 26.

Meditate on verses 5 and 16.

> *He (King Uzziah) continued to seek God in the days of Zechariah, who had understanding through the vision of God; and as long as he sought the LORD, God prospered him. But when he became strong, his heart was so proud that he acted corruptly, and he was unfaithful to the LORD his God, for he entered the temple of the LORD to burn incense on the altar of incense.*

Once again, the handwriting was on the wall for how the story would end for this next king of Judah. After his God-given success, King Uzziah was full of himself, presumptuously doing things contrary to God's will with tragic consequences. God afflicted him with leprosy until the day he died (vs. 20-21).

God still hates pride and the sin that results. Amazingly, the LORD humbled Himself to the point of death on the cross to save us from our prideful sin (Philippians 2:8). As that truth sinks in, determine to humbly and wholeheartedly walk with the LORD all the days of your life.

Use the words from 2 Chronicles 26:4-5, 16, and 20 to pray over yourself and those for whom you stand guard as a faithful, prayerful watchman (Isaiah 62:6-7).

> *"LORD, please help _____ and me do right in Your sight, according to all that You want us to do. Let us continue to seek You all the days of our lives. Give us understanding through Your vision, God, and prosper us as long as we seek You. When You make us strong, do not let our hearts be proud; do not let us act corruptly; do not let us be unfaithful to You, LORD our God. LORD Jesus, You were smitten for our transgressions (Isaiah 53:4). We remain humbly Yours, Jesus~"*

JULY 5

Please read 2 Chronicles 27.

Meditate on verse 2.

> *He did right in the sight of the LORD, according to all that his father Uzziah had done; however, he did not enter the temple of the LORD. But the people continued acting corruptly.*

King Jotham did not make the same mistake as his father Uzziah, who presumptuously entered the holy place of the temple to burn incense (2 Chronicles 26:16-18). Uzziah was furious when rebuked by God and refused to repent. God punished his rebellion by inflicting him with leprosy for the rest of his life (2 Chronicles 26:19-21). Just imagine the impact this had on young Jotham, who probably was not allowed to go near his diseased father. I wonder if Jotham feared even being close to the temple because of what happened to his father. What a different ending the story of Uzziah and Jotham might have if Uzziah had yielded to God instead of his proud heart (2 Chronicles 26:16)!

Prayerfully consider your actions and their impact on others. What do your children, grandchildren, other family members, and friends learn from your attitudes and behaviors toward Christ and His church? Think about the eternal consequences and pray 2 Chronicles 27:2 and 6 over yourself and those for whom you stand guard as a faithful, prayerful watchman (Isaiah 62:6-7).

> *"LORD, please help _____ and me do right in Your sight, according to all You desire. LORD, we will enter to worship with Your church. Please let Your people not act corruptly. Let us become mighty because we order our ways before You, LORD our God. In Your name, Jesus~"*

JULY 6

Please read 2 Chronicles 28.

Meditate on verse 19.

> *For the LORD humbled Judah because of Ahaz king of Israel, for he had brought about a lack of restraint in Judah and was very unfaithful to the LORD.*

What a sobering meditation verse! The LORD humbled an entire nation because of the lack of restraint brought about by an unfaithful leader.

The Hebrew word translated as "lack of restraint" is also used in these verses:[1]

> *Now when Moses saw that the people were out of control—for Aaron had let them get out of control…*
> —EXODUS 32:25A

> *Poverty and shame will come to him who neglects discipline.*
> —PROVERBS 13:18A

> *Where there is no vision, the people are unrestrained, but happy is he who keeps the law.*
> —PROVERBS 29:18

We live in a world lacking restraint. False teachers encourage others to run the Bible through a sieve, filtering out parts which they feel no longer apply. Such unfaithfulness to God and His Word is abhorrent. Examine your life for areas lacking restraint and pray 2 Chronicles 28:11, 19, and 22 over yourself and those for whom you stand guard as a faithful, prayerful watchman (Isaiah 62:6-7).

> "LORD, _____ and I do not want Your burning anger to be against us. You have humbled us because of our lack of restraint and being very unfaithful to You. In this time of our distress, do not let us become even more unfaithful. Forgive us, LORD. Restrain us by Your Spirit and Your Word. Make us faithful.
> In Your name, Jesus-"

---

1. Retrieved from www.blueletterbible.org/lang/lexicon/lexicon.cfm?Strongs=H6544&t=NASB

JULY 7

Please read 2 Chronicles 29.

Meditate on verses 35b-36.

> *Thus, the service of the house of the LORD was established again. Then Hezekiah and all the people rejoiced over what God had prepared for the people, because the thing came about suddenly.*

The temple was a neglected mess. With doors shut and lights out, no incense or burnt offerings were offered in the holy place, and God was furious (vs. 7-8). Perhaps no one dared go back into the holy place after King Uzziah was smitten there with leprosy over 32 years before (2 Chronicles 26:16-21). Thankfully, King Hezekiah realized he and his people needed to get back on track with God, so he called for a clean-up campaign, and in 16 days, the job was done. Sacrifices and worship were once again offered in God's temple (vs. 10-29).

Think about your life and the life of your church. Are you part of the body of Christ or did something happen a long time ago that made you stop meeting with other Christians? What about your church? Is unbiblical teaching corrupting the flock of God?

This chapter is rich with practicality for walking with Jesus. Let the LORD clean and establish you in Him. Then be ready because He will suddenly reveal what He has prepared for you and your church (v. 36). Exciting!

Pray 2 Chronicles 29:5, 24, 30, and 36 over yourself and those for whom you stand guard as a faithful, prayerful watchman (Isaiah 62:6-7).

> *"LORD, consecrate _____ and me; consecrate Your church. Help us carry the uncleanness out of Your holy place. Purge us by Your blood, Jesus, to atone for all our sins. We sing praises with joy and bow down and worship You. We rejoice over what You have prepared for us. Make us ready because Your thing will come about suddenly. In Your name, Jesus~"*

JULY 8

Please read 2 Chronicles 30.

Meditate on verse 26.

> *So, there was great joy in Jerusalem, because there was nothing like this in Jerusalem since the days of Solomon the son of David, king of Israel.*

Over 200 years passed since the Passover was celebrated, so King Hezekiah sent out an invitation to all the people of Israel, and it read:

> *O sons of Israel, return to the LORD God of Abraham, Isaac and Israel, that He may return to those of you who escaped and are left from the hand of the kings of Assyria. Do not be like your fathers and your brothers, who were unfaithful to the LORD God of their fathers, so that He made them a horror, as you see. Now do not stiffen your neck like your fathers but yield to the LORD and enter His sanctuary which He has consecrated forever, and serve the LORD your God, that His burning anger may turn away from you. For if you return to the LORD, your brothers and your sons will find compassion before those who led them captive and will return to this land. For the LORD your God is gracious and compassionate and will not turn His face away from you if you return to Him.*
> —2 CHRONICLES 30:6B-9

Sadly, most laughed at the invitation, mocking the messengers who delivered it; however, a few humbly accepted God's offer to return to Him (vs. 10-11). For those who received, the result was pardon, healing, and joy (vs. 18-20, 26). God's still extends the invitation. Most scornfully reject it; however, some humbly accept. Do not grow weary in extending the invitation and praying for those who need God's pardon, healing, and joy.

Ask God to hear your prayer like He did Hezekiah's. Start your prayer time with 2 Chronicles 30:20 as a faithful, prayerful watchman (Isaiah 62:6-7),

> *"LORD, please hear my prayer and heal _____.*
> *In Your name, Jesus~"*

JULY 9

Please read 2 Chronicles 31, remembering what you read yesterday in 2 Chronicles 30.

Meditate on verse 1.

> *Now when all this was finished, all Israel who were present went out to the cities of Judah, broke the pillars in pieces, cut down the Asherim, and pulled down the high places and the altars throughout all Judah and Benjamin, as well as in Ephraim and Manasseh, until they had destroyed them all. Then all the sons of Israel returned to their cities, each to his possession.*

Wow! Observing the Passover made a huge impact on the people. God's forgiveness resulted in them destroying the idols in their land. Once the evil was purged, these devoted ones eagerly gave to the LORD and His work (vs. 6-8).

What a beautiful picture of our lives once we are forgiven, made clean, and devoted to Christ our Passover (1 Corinthians 5:7)! There is an urgency to cut down and destroy things turning our attention and devotion from God. We generously give time, talent, and resources to serve Christ and His church. It is obvious when we belong to the LORD.

Ask God to make Himself and His work obvious in your life and the lives of those you love by praying 2 Chronicles 31:20-21 over yourself and those for whom you stand guard as a faithful, prayerful watchman (Isaiah 62:6-7).

> *"LORD our God, let _____ and me do throughout the land what is good, right, and true before You. Let every work we begin in the service of Your house be done according to Your law and commandment. As we work with all our heart, seeking You, God, please let us prosper. In Your name, Jesus~"*

JULY 10

Please read 2 Chronicles 32.

Meditate on verses 1a, 2, and 5a.

> *After these acts of faithfulness, Sennacherib king of Assyria came and invaded Judah. Now when Hezekiah saw that Sennacherib had come and that he intended to make war on Jerusalem, he took courage and rebuilt all the wall that had been broken down.*

After celebrating the Passover and removing the idols throughout the land, the enemy attacked King Hezekiah and his people. Thankfully Hezekiah didn't retreat, feeling sorry for himself or mad at God for allowing the attack. Instead, he rebuilt the 600 feet of wall that had been torn down 75 years earlier, and he strengthened himself and his people for battle (2 Chronicles 25:23; 32:5).

Do not believe the false teaching that faithfulness to God means an easy life. God's Word promises the testing of our faith for the purpose of building endurance (James 1:2-4). 2 Chronicles 32 teaches us how to handle these times of testing:

- Shore up areas of spiritual weakness (vs. 5-6).
- Trust in the LORD to help you and to fight your battles (vs. 7-8).
- Pray and cry to God when you are bullied, threatened, and taunted by the enemy. God will deal with your enemies (vs. 9-21).
- When God gives you victory, give Him the glory, taking no credit for yourself. Humble the pride of your heart (vs. 23-26).

Pray 2 Chronicles 32:7-8 over yourself and those for whom you stand guard as a faithful, prayerful watchman (Isaiah 62:6-7).

> *"LORD, help _____ and me be strong and courageous. Do not let us fear or be dismayed because of _____ and the horde that is with him, for the One with us is greater than the one with him. With him is only an arm of flesh, but with us is You, LORD our God, to help us and to fight our battles. Thank You, in Your name, Jesus~"*

JULY 11

Please read 2 Chronicles 33.

Meditate on verses 12-13.

> *When he was in distress, he entreated the LORD his God and humbled himself greatly before the God of his fathers. When he prayed to Him, He was moved by his entreaty and heard his supplication and brought him again to Jerusalem to his kingdom. Then Manasseh knew that the LORD was God.*

What does it take for God to get your attention? For evil King Manasseh, who practiced witchcraft, sacrificed his children, and worshiped Baal, God used the Assyrians (vs. 2-11). They captured Manasseh, bound him with chains, and led him by a hook in his nose to Babylon (v. 11). Ouch! Afterwards, he humbled himself and worshiped God (vs. 16, 19).

Allow God to use this chapter to convict you of sin. What high prideful places need to be removed (v. 3)? Do you sacrifice your family for the sake of career, hobbies, or friends (v. 6)? Are you interested in things of the occult: witchcraft, sorcery, mediums, and spiritists (v. 6)?

As a Christian, God put His name on you forever (v. 7). Determine to live to honor His name. Pray 2 Chronicles 33:7, 9-10, 12-13, and 23 over yourself and those for whom you stand guard as a faithful, prayerful watchman (Isaiah 62:6-7).

> *"LORD, let _____ and me never put an idol in our lives, in the place where You have put Your name forever. Do not let us mislead others to do evil. LORD, when You speak, let us pay attention. LORD, I am in distress. I humble myself greatly before You, God, and entreat You. Please be moved by my entreaty and hear my supplication and bring me back to You. LORD, I know You are God! LORD, I want to stay humble before You. Do not let me multiply guilt.*
> *In Your name, Jesus~"*

JULY 12

Please read 2 Chronicles 34.

Meditate on verse 3.

> *For in the eighth year of his (King Josiah's) reign while he was still a youth, he began to seek the God of his father David; and in the twelfth year he began to purge Judah and Jerusalem of the high places, the Asherim, the carved images and the molten images.*

The more you seek God and read His Word the easier it is to discern good and evil, purging things which displease Him. Notice King Josiah pulverized those things, completely destroying them (vs 4-5). When his grandfather, King Manasseh, removed the idols from the temple, he did not demolish them; rather, he threw them outside the city walls where others could still find them, perhaps taking a piece home as a souvenir (2 Chronicles 33:15). As God convicts you of sin, destroy it completely; do not leave bits and pieces lying around for others to pick up and toy with.

Pray 2 Chronicles 34:27, 31, and 33 over yourself and those for whom you stand guard as a faithful, prayerful watchman (Isaiah 62:6-7).

> *"LORD, my heart is tender as I humble myself before You. I have heard Your Words against this place and against its inhabitants. Please hear me, LORD, as I weep before You. I make a covenant before You, LORD, to walk after You and keep Your commandments and Your testimonies and Your statutes with all my heart and all my soul, to perform the Words of the covenant written in this Book. LORD, please help _____ and me remove all the abominations from all the land. May Your people serve You, LORD God. Throughout our lifetime, do not let us turn from following You, LORD God. In Your name, Jesus~"*

JULY 13

Please read 2 Chronicles 35.

Meditate on verses 2-3.

> *He (King Josiah) set the priests in their offices and encouraged them in the service of the house of the LORD. He also said to the Levites who taught all Israel and who were holy to the LORD, "Put the holy ark in the house which Solomon the son of David king of Israel built; it will be a burden on your shoulders no longer. Now serve the LORD your God and His people Israel."*

These verses are like a sigh of relief. Hear God say them as He encourages you in your service to Him and others:

> *"Give me the holy task you carry; it will be a burden on your shoulders no longer. I AM the LORD your God. Now serve Me and My people."*

What are you doing for the cause of Christ that weighs you down? Caring for children, tending an ill loved one, teaching Bible study, finishing school, going to work every day...

> *Blessed be the LORD, who daily bears our burden, the God who is our salvation. God is to us a God of deliverances.*
> —PSALM 68:19-20A

Give your burdens to the LORD as you pray 2 Chronicles 35:2-3 over yourself and those for whom you stand guard as a faithful, prayerful watchman (Isaiah 62:6-7).

> *"LORD, _____ and I need to be encouraged in the service of Your house. We are Your Levites; we teach those who are holy to You, LORD. We give this holy task to You; let it be a burden on our shoulders no longer. Help us serve You, LORD God, and Your people. In Your strength, Jesus~"*

JULY 14

Please read 2 Chronicles 36.

Meditate on verses 15-16.

> *The LORD, the God of their fathers, sent word to them again and again by His messengers because He had compassion on His people and on His dwelling place, but they continually mocked the messengers of God, despised His words and scoffed at His prophets, until the wrath of the LORD arose against His people, until there was no remedy.*

What a dismal chapter in God's Word! People living more than 2,500 years ago described in terms characterizing our world today: evil, defiled, unfaithful, stiff-necked, and hardhearted (vs. 12-14). Thankfully, the chapter has a surprise ending:

> *Now in the first year of Cyrus king of Persia—in order to fulfill the word of the LORD by the mouth of Jeremiah—the LORD stirred up the spirit of Cyrus king of Persia, so that he sent a proclamation throughout his kingdom, and also put it in writing, saying, "Thus says Cyrus king of Persia, 'The LORD, the God of heaven, has given me all the kingdoms of the earth, and He has appointed me to build Him a house in Jerusalem, which is in Judah. Whoever there is among you of all His people, may the LORD his God be with him, and let him go up!'"*
> —2 CHRONICLES 36:22-23

God ends *Chronicles* with hope. He will rebuild the burned-down temple in Jerusalem, and He wants to rebuild and restore our lives to Him.

Perhaps you feel hopeless. Use the words from 2 Chronicles 36:13b and 23b to confess and pray as a faithful, prayerful watchman (Isaiah 62:6-7).

> *"LORD, please forgive me for my stiff neck and*
> *hard heart against turning to You.*
> *LORD, I bend my neck in prayer and humble my heart toward You.*
> *LORD my God, please be with _____ and*
> *me! Let us go up and build!*
> *For the sake of Your Kingdom, Jesus~"*

JULY 15

Please read Acts 1.

Meditate on verse 8a.

> *But you will receive power when the Holy Spirit has come upon you.*

Acts is often referred to as "The Acts of the Apostles"; however, a better name might be "The Acts of the Holy Spirit." As you read and pray *Acts*, notice the Holy Spirit's work.

Jesus presented Himself alive for 40 days following His resurrection, and He gave Spirit-driven orders to His apostles, commanding them to remain in Jerusalem to be baptized by what the Father promised (vs. 2-5). The Holy Spirit is the Father's promise:

> *"I will ask the Father, and He will give you another Helper, that He may be with you forever; that is the Spirit of truth."*
> —JOHN 14:16-17A

After Jesus ascended into heaven, the disciples gathered in the upper room with 120 others, including Jesus' mother, Mary, and His brothers (vs. 12-15). The Holy Spirit foretold Judas' betrayal by the mouth of King David (v. 16); now, the same Holy Spirit inspired the eleven remaining disciples to select Matthias to take Judas' place (vs. 21-26).

Commanding, baptizing, empowering, inspiring—the work of the Holy Spirit will be seen in remarkable ways over the next four weeks. Ask God to enlighten your reading and fill you with admiration for what the Holy Spirit has done and for what He is doing in your life and the lives of those you love.

Pray Acts 1:8 over yourself and those for whom you stand guard as a faithful, prayerful watchman (Isaiah 62:6-7).

> *"Father, thank You that _____ and I receive power because Your Holy Spirit has come upon us. Make us Your witnesses in Jerusalem and in all Judea and Samaria, and even to the remotest part of the earth. For the sake of Your name, Jesus~"*

JULY 16

Please read Acts 2.

Meditate on verses 4, 7a, and 8.

> *And they were all filled with the Holy Spirit and began to speak with other tongues, as the Spirit was giving them utterance. They were amazed and astonished, saying, "And how is it that we each hear them in our own language to which we were born?"*

Ten days following His ascension, Jesus fulfilled His promise that His followers would be immersed by the Holy Spirit (Acts 1:4-5; 2:1-4). Filled with the Spirit, they miraculously spoke in other languages, so the thousands of people in Jerusalem from all over the known world could hear about Christ, His death, and His resurrection in their own native tongues (vs. 6-36). As they heard, 3,000 people believed in Jesus Christ (v. 41). The miracle of salvation and the miracle of hearing in tongues—you can be confident the Holy Spirit knows how to speak to you and those you love in a way you can understand.

So, Jesus started His Church by making the first Christians at Pentecost, gifting them with the Holy Spirit as promised by the Father (Acts 1:7-8; 2:38-39). What an amazing gift of Himself—His Life-giving Spirit!

Thank God for giving you His Spirit and pray for those who need the Holy Spirit in their lives, using the words from Acts 2:38 as their faithful, prayerful watchman (Isaiah 62:6-7).

> *"LORD, please let _____ repent and be baptized in Your name, Jesus Christ, for the forgiveness of their sins, so they can receive the gift of Your Holy Spirit. Thank You for giving me Your Holy Spirit! In Your name, Jesus~"*

JULY 17

Please read Acts 3.

Meditate on verses 19-20.

> *Therefore, repent and return, so that your sins may be wiped away, in order that times of refreshing may come from the presence of the LORD; and that He may send Jesus, the Christ appointed for you.*

Peter is again preaching in the temple. His sermon follows an amazing miracle, resulting in a man over 40-years-old, who had never walked, being healed (Acts 3:2; 4:22). Immediately, he was walking and leaping and praising God (v. 8)!

God's healing of this man is similar to His creation of Adam. He wired this man's brain, defective legs, and atrophied muscles to work as if they had never not worked. This was a mature miracle. The man is jumping! Just like God created a mature world where Adam and Eve were able to walk and talk and jump and praise the moment He made them. You, too, are a mature miracle, for when you became a Christian, you were recreated new, a completed child of God because of Christ in you (Colossians 1:27-28).

God's miraculous power makes our souls jump. The Holy Spirit provides us the presence of the LORD every moment of every day, giving us a life of refreshing as we walk with Jesus in step with His Spirit (v. 19; Galatians 5:16, 25).

Pray Acts 3:19-20 over yourself and those for whom you stand guard as a faithful, prayerful watchman (Isaiah 62:6-7).

> *"LORD, I repent and return, so that my sins may be wiped away, in order that times of refreshing may come from You. Father, thank You for sending Jesus, the Christ appointed for me. Please let _____ repent, return, and receive You, Jesus, the Christ appointed for them. For the sake of Your name, Jesus~"*

JULY 18

Please read Acts 4.

Meditate on verses 7-8.

> *When they had placed them in the center, they began to inquire, "By what power, or in what name, have you done this?" Then Peter, filled with the Holy Spirit, said to them, "Rulers and elders of the people,..."*

The leadership of the Jewish community was very concerned because the disciples boldly declared the healing of the man born lame came by the name of the resurrected Jesus Christ (v. 10). Five thousand more believed because the disciples taught: in Jesus there is resurrection from the dead (vs. 2, 4). Think about how Jesus provided physical fish and bread for the 5,000 and is now providing the Bread of Life in Himself as spiritual food for all who believe (John 6:1-14, 35).

Hear Peter's bold, Holy Spirit-filled response to the religious leaders' accusations (Acts 4:8-10):

> *"Rulers and elders of the people, if we are on trial today for a benefit done to a sick man, as to how this man has been made well, let it be known to all of you and to all the people of Israel, that by the name of Jesus Christ the Nazarene, whom you crucified, whom God raised from the dead—by this name this man stands here before you in good health."*

For 2,000 years, this testimony by Peter and John has encouraged millions of believers to share their faith. Let it encourage you in your stand for Christ today.

Pray Acts 4:29 and 31 over yourself and those for whom you stand guard as a faithful, prayerful watchman (Isaiah 62:6-7).

> *"LORD, grant that _____ and I, Your bond-servants, may speak Your Word with all confidence. Filled with the Holy Spirit, let us speak the Word of God with boldness. In Your name, Jesus~"*

JULY 19

Please read Acts 5.

Meditate on verses 1-3.

> *But a man named Ananias, with his wife Sapphira, sold a piece of property, and kept back some of the price for himself, with his wife's full knowledge, and bringing a portion of it, he laid it at the apostles' feet. But Peter said, "Ananias, why has Satan filled your heart to lie to the Holy Spirit and to keep back some of the price of the land?"*

Ananias and Sapphira were following many people's example by selling their property and giving the money to the poor. For some reason, they decided to keep part of the money. No foul yet, but then they acted like they gave all of the selling price to the church.

Peter tells Ananias he lied to the Holy Spirit which is lying to God (v. 4). To Sapphira he says she and her husband have conspired to put the Spirit of the LORD to the test (v. 9). Both died in this event by God's power (vs. 9-10).

Ask the Holy Spirit to search your life for places where you are lying or testing Him. Also, ask Him to show you areas of your personal life you no longer treat as sacred. In fearful respect of God, confess those sins, asking the LORD to help you live holy to Him.

Pray Acts 5:3-4 and 9 over yourself and those for whom you stand guard as a faithful, prayerful watchman (Isaiah 62:6-7).

> *"Holy Spirit, _____ and I do not want to lie to You. God, we do not want to lie to You. Holy Spirit, we do not want to put You to the test. Please forgive us and help us not to do it again.*
> *In Your name, Jesus ~"*

JULY 20

Please read Acts 6.

Meditate on verses 3, 8, and 10.

> *Therefore, brethren, select from among you seven men of good reputation, full of the Spirit and of wisdom, whom we may put in charge of this task. And Stephen, full of grace and power, was performing great wonders and signs among the people. But they were unable to cope with the wisdom and the Spirit with which he was speaking.*

The church had a management issue with the daily food distribution among non-Hebrew widows (v. 1). The responsibility to take charge of providing that food was given to seven reputable, wise, Spirit-filled men (v. 3). Those chosen were brought to the apostles who laid hands on them, commissioning them to do the work (v. 6).

Do these three traits identify you? As a Christian, would your friends and family say you have a good reputation? Are you full of the Holy Spirit? Are you a wise person?

These are traits we can all grow in as we journey with Jesus.

Pray Acts 6:3, 5, 8, and 10 over yourself and those for whom you stand guard as a faithful, prayerful watchman (Isaiah 62:6-7).

> *"LORD, make _____ and me people of good reputation, full of the Spirit and wisdom, whom You can put in charge of tasks. Make us full of faith and the Holy Spirit. Fill us with Your grace and power for performing great wonders and signs among the people. Make them unable to cope with the wisdom and the Spirit with which we speak; rather let them humbly come to You. In Your name, Jesus~"*

JULY 21

Please read Acts 7.

Meditate on verses 51 and 55.

> *You men who are stiff-necked and uncircumcised in heart and ears are always resisting the Holy Spirit; you are doing just as your fathers did.*

> *But being full of the Holy Spirit, he gazed intently into heaven and saw the glory of God, and Jesus standing at the right hand of God.*

One of the men selected for distributing food in Acts 6 was Stephen. After out-debating his oppressors, Stephen was falsely accused, arrested, and allowed to tell his side of the story to the High Priest and religious leaders (Acts 6:8-7:1). After recounting the history of Israel from Abraham through Solomon, he concludes by accusing the religious leaders of resisting the Holy Spirit, killing the prophets, and killing the Righteous One (vs. 2-53). Filled with rage, these leaders take Stephen outside Jerusalem to kill him (vs. 54, 58).

Contrast the glorious vision of Stephen with the murderous vision of his accusers. Stephen, full of the Holy Spirit, sees Jesus at the right hand of God; the religious leaders are blind to Who God truly is (vs. 55-57).

A Spirit-filled Stephen prays the same as His Spirit-filled Savior, "LORD, do not hold this sin against them!" (vs. 60; Luke 23:34).

Is the Holy Spirit dynamically active in your life? Do others see the Spirit working in you?

Pray Acts 7:51 and 55 over yourself and those for whom you stand guard as a faithful, prayerful watchman (Isaiah 62:6-7).

> *"LORD, do not let _____ and me be stiff-necked and uncircumcised in heart and ears, always resisting the Holy Spirit. Let us be full of the Holy Spirit, gazing intently into heaven, seeing Your glory, God, and Jesus standing at Your right hand. In Whose name, I pray~"*

JULY 22

Please read Acts 8.

Meditate on verse 29.

> *Then the Spirit said to Philip, "Go up and join this chariot."*

What an exciting chapter in God's Word! As Saul goes house-by-house in Jerusalem persecuting the Christians, many flee, preaching the Word as they go (vs. 3-4). Recall Jesus' last command in Acts 1:8:

> *"You will receive power when the Holy Spirit has come upon you, and you shall be My witnesses both in Jerusalem (where the church began), and in in all Judea (the territory around Jerusalem) and Samaria (where people not fully of the Jewish bloodline lived), and even to the remotest part of the earth."*

In this chapter, all four areas of ministry are active, with God using persecution to accomplish His will.

Observe the Holy Spirit's movement: He comes upon the Samaritans (vs. 14-17), then moves Phillip to explain Jesus to an Ethiopian eunuch (vs. 26-35). The Ethiopian believes and returns to his home where he is credited with starting one of the oldest Christian communities in the world.

The Holy Spirit transports Phillip to Azotus to make his way to Caesarea, telling people about Jesus every place he goes (v. 40).

God quickly covers a lot of ground. Does this excite you? Are you a "Send me anywhere Holy Spirit!" kind of believer? I think no matter your answer, this question should prompt a wonderful conversation with the LORD.

Pray Acts 8:29, 35, and 37 over yourself and those for whom you stand guard as a faithful, prayerful watchman (Isaiah 62:6-7).

> *"Holy Spirit, I hear you say, 'Go up and join this chariot.' Open my mouth with Scripture to preach Jesus to _____. Let them believe with all their heart that You, Jesus Christ, are the Son of God. For the sake of Your name~"*

JULY 23

Please read Acts 9.

Meditate on verse 31.

> *So, the church throughout all Judea and Galilee and Samaria enjoyed peace, being built up, and going on in the fear of the LORD and in the comfort of the Holy Spirit, it continued to increase.*

One of the great miracles of being a Christian is you are part of an international family. If you have the opportunity to host Christians from other backgrounds or visit them while traveling, you will be pleasantly surprised because authentic Christians are the same in Spirit and love of Jesus. It is amazing! Combined, we have been in 56 countries and find this to be true.

In our church in Qatar, 70 nationalities were present—one church, one Spirit—it was like being in heaven. The result of the Holy Spirit's work in your life and in your church is miraculous.

Observe these Holy Spirit-driven church characteristics from the meditation verse:

- Enjoying peace
- Being built up
- Going on in the fear of the LORD
- Going on in the comfort of the Holy Spirit
- Continuing to increase

Wow! What a great set of outcomes! Pray Acts 9:31 over yourself and those for whom you stand guard as a faithful, prayerful watchman (Isaiah 62:6-7).

> *"LORD, please let my church and the churches throughout the world enjoy peace and be built up. Let us go on in the fear of You, LORD. In the comfort of the Holy Spirit, let us continue to increase. In Your name, Jesus~"*

JULY 24

Please read Acts 10.

Meditate on verse 45b.

> *The gift of the Holy Spirit had been poured out on the Gentiles also.*

Cornelius, an officer in the Italian army, was based at Caesarea on the Mediterranean Sea (v. 1). Not only a dedicated soldier, he was a devout man who feared God and led his family and those in his household to do the same (v. 2). Until Cornelius, the apostles were not aware that Gentiles (non-Jews) could become Christians. Acts 10 describes God bringing Jews and Gentiles together into one body of Christ. As you ponder that fact, think of this chapter of the Bible, Acts 10, as one of the greatest chapters in history!

As Peter shares the Gospel, notice what God does to Cornelius and his family and friends (v. 24):

> *While Peter was still speaking these words, the Holy Spirit fell upon all those who were listening to the message.*
> —ACTS 10:44

Wow! With the power of the Word of God and the Holy Spirit, Jesus made it obvious He is the Savior for all mankind. Thankfully both Cornelius and Peter listened to God. What a glorious impact their obedience had on our entire world! Ask the LORD to make you obedient to Christ and His Word, speaking His Words to everyone, everywhere you go. Verses 34-43 of this chapter are great verses to mark in your Bible because the Gospel is clearly written out for you to share with others.

As a faithful, prayerful watchman (Isaiah 62:6-7), pray Acts 10:43-44 over those who need the Holy Spirit.

> *"LORD Jesus, through Your name,*
> *please let _____ believe in*
> *You to receive forgiveness of sins. Holy Spirit, fall*
> *upon them as they listen to Your Word.*
> *In Your name, Jesus~"*

JULY 25

Please read Acts 11.

Meditate on verses 23-24.

> *Then when he (Barnabas) arrived and witnessed the grace of God, he rejoiced and began to encourage them all with resolute heart to remain true to the LORD, for he was a good man, and full of the Holy Spirit and of faith. And considerable numbers were brought to the LORD.*

Barnabas went to Antioch, the third largest city in the Roman Empire, to meet with new believers. Only Rome and Alexandria were larger, and Antioch was a vital military and trade route in what is now present-day Turkey. It was here followers of Jesus were first called "Christians" (v. 26).

What a vital city for preaching the Gospel! Thankfully, good people like Barnabas, full of the Holy Spirit and faith, obeyed God's command to go because the LORD had many souls ready to believe in Antioch.

> *But there were some of them, men of Cyprus and Cyrene, who came to Antioch and began speaking to the Greeks also, preaching the LORD Jesus. And the hand of the LORD was with them, and a large number who believed turned to the LORD.*
> —ACTS 11:20-21

Do you want to be a "Barnabas"? As a faithful, prayerful watchman (Isaiah 62:6-7), pray for the LORD to make you and those you love like that faithful man, using the words from Acts 11:23-24.

> *"LORD, give _____ and me a resolute heart. Help us remain true to You, LORD, encouraging others to do the same. Make us good people, full of the Holy Spirit and faith. Use us to bring considerable numbers of people to You. For the sake of Your name, Jesus~"*

JULY 26

Please read Acts 12.

Meditate on verse 5.

> *So Peter was kept in the prison, but prayer for him*
> *was being made fervently by the church to God.*

The Holy Spirit is in the middle of every authentic prayer. Note the role of the Holy Spirit when you pray:

> *In the same way, the Spirit also helps our weakness; for we do*
> *not know how to pray as we should, but the Spirit Himself*
> *intercedes for us with groanings too deep for words, and He who*
> *searches the hearts knows what the mind of the Spirit is,*
> *because He intercedes for the saints according to the will of God.*
> —ROMANS 8:26-27

The Holy Spirit calls you to pray and helps you pray for God's will. He encouraged the church in Jerusalem to pray for Peter (v. 5). Soon Peter was no longer in prison but standing at the gate of the house where they were praying (v. 12). Miraculous! Young Rhoda didn't let him in because she was so overwhelmed to see him (vs. 13-16)!

Encourage your church to be led by the Holy Spirit and networked in fervent prayer. There are many media tools to instantly engage people in prayer. The Holy Spirit has networked believers around the world for centuries without texts and the internet, but the LORD inspired these tools to be made and used for good. There is great value in praying together as a church physically and with others electronically.

Pray Acts 12:5 over yourself and those for whom you stand guard as a faithful, prayerful watchman (Isaiah 62:6-7).

> "LORD God, keep _____ and Your church
> and me fervently praying by the power of Your Spirit.
> In Your name, Jesus~"

JULY 27

Please read Acts 13.

Meditate on verses 2 and 4.

> *While they were ministering to the LORD and fasting, the Holy Spirit said, "Set apart for Me Barnabas and Saul for the work to which I have called them." So, being sent out by the Holy Spirit, they went down to Seleucia and from there they sailed to Cyprus.*

Saul and Barnabas' first missionary journey was launched by the Holy Spirit, with God clearly orchestrating His timing for going to Cyprus, an island southwest of Antioch in the Mediterranean Sea. While in Cyprus, Saul encountered Elymas, a magician, discouraging their missionary work (v. 8). Be aware it is common for God's work to encounter opposition. In your own life or church, is there an "Elymas," who is unsaved or a false teacher, trying to hurt the work of the Kingdom? Observe Saul, who is also known as Paul (v. 9), confront Elymas:

> *Paul, filled with the Holy Spirit, fixed his gaze on him, and said, "You who are full of all deceit and fraud, you son of the devil, you enemy of all righteousness, will you not cease to make crooked the straight ways of the LORD?"*
> —ACTS 13:9B-10

This spiritually blind man became physically blind as a result of discouraging faith in others. The Holy Spirit prompted the mission trip and the rebuke. Being led by the Spirit is a great way to walk each day.

Pray Acts 13:2 and 4 over yourself and those for whom you stand guard as a faithful, prayerful watchman (Isaiah 62:6-7).

> *"Holy Spirit, set apart _____ and me for the work to which You have called us. Send us out, Holy Spirit, where You want us to go. In Your name, Jesus~"*

JULY 28

Please read Acts 13:52-14:28.

Meditate on verses 13:52 and 14:3a.

> *And the disciples were continually filled with joy and with the Holy Spirit. Therefore, they spent a long time there speaking boldly with reliance upon the LORD.*

Paul and Barnabas' proclamation of the Gospel often had similar outcomes. Many believed, but many opposed the message, persecuting Paul and his traveling companions. However, filled with joy and the Holy Spirit, they shared the Gospel everywhere they went (Acts 13:52; 14:7).

On one such adventure, Paul and the team fled for their lives to Lystra where they healed a man lame from birth (vs. 8-10). The locals thought Paul and Barnabas were Greek gods and wanted to offer sacrifices to them (vs. 12-13). Paul adamantly stopped them, telling them to turn from their vain things to the living God, Jesus Christ (vs. 14-15). Many believed, but then some Jews incited the people to stone Paul (v. 19). Left for dead, Paul revived and went right back into Lystra (v. 20). The following day, he was off to Derbe to preach the Gospel (v. 20). So changed by Jesus, nothing and no one stopped Paul from preaching the glorious news of his Savior.

Despite persecution, filled with joy and the Holy Spirit, relying on the LORD, sharing the Gospel with everyone—what an encouragement as we walk with Jesus!

Pray Acts 13:52 and 14:3 over yourself and those for whom you stand guard as a faithful, prayerful watchman (Isaiah 62:6-7).

> *"LORD, continually fill _____ and me with joy and the Holy Spirit. Let us speak boldly with reliance upon You as You testify to the Word of Your grace. LORD, grant that signs and wonders be done by our hands. For the sake of Your name, Jesus~"*

JULY 29

Please read Acts 15.

Meditate on verses 28-29.

> *For it seemed good to the Holy Spirit and to us to lay upon you no greater burden than these essentials: that you abstain from things sacrificed to idols and from blood and from things strangled and from fornication; if you keep yourselves free from such things, you will do well. Farewell.*

It is important to not add requirements for salvation, nor add unnecessary social or religious behaviors for holiness. It is also important to know well what is needed for salvation and Christian living.

Paul and Barnabas spoke to leadership in Jerusalem asking whether circumcision was necessary for salvation. While it is a visible reminder of the Old Covenant for a Jewish man, it is not a requirement for salvation in the New Covenant of Jesus. This New Covenant requires a spiritual circumcision of the heart (Romans 2:29). This circumcision is accomplished by the Holy Spirit and takes place when you become a Christian. One does not have to become Jewish to become Christian (vs. 8-9).

> *We are saved through the grace of the LORD Jesus.*
> —ACTS 15:11

Thankfully, Peter, Paul, Barnabas, and other church leaders listened to the Holy Spirit to answer their difficult questions. The same Spirit lives inside you. Listen carefully to Him; He answers your questions, too.

Pray Acts 15:28 over yourself and those for whom you stand guard as a faithful, prayerful watchman (Isaiah 62:6-7).

> *"Holy Spirit, what seems good to You?*
> *Let _____ and me do Your will,*
> *not laying upon ourselves or others any greater burden than what is essential for following You.*
> *In Your name, Jesus~"*

JULY 30

Please read Acts 16.

Meditate on verses 6-9.

> *They passed through the Phrygian and Galatian region, having been forbidden by the Holy Spirit to speak the word in Asia, and after they came to Mysia, they were trying to go into Bithynia, and the Spirit of Jesus did not permit them; and passing by Mysia, they came down to Troas. A vision appeared to Paul in the night: a man of Macedonia was standing and appealing to him, and saying, "Come over to Macedonia and help us."*

Paul and the team were working in present-day central Turkey. They wanted to go further west into a region called Asia. The Holy Spirit said, "No!" They moved north toward Bithynia on the Black Sea in northern Turkey. The Holy Spirit said, "No!" They end up in Troas on the northern part of the Aegean Sea near modern-day Istanbul.

There Paul had a vision from God of a man from Macedonia begging them to come and help. Macedonia is the northern part of present-day Greece. The team discerned this was God's will, so they moved quickly to Macedonia.

Sometimes God's call is like an emergency, and you go immediately. Sometimes you say, "yes" immediately, and God reveals the timing. Say "yes" when God calls, asking Him to lead you.

Pray Acts 16:6-7 and 10 over yourself and those for whom you stand guard as a faithful, prayerful watchman (Isaiah 62:6-7).

> *"LORD Jesus, help _____ and me obey when the Holy Spirit forbids us to speak. Help us obey when Your Spirit does not permit us to go. Let us go immediately, God, when You call us to preach the Gospel. In Your name, Jesus~"*

JULY 31

Please read Acts 17.

Meditate on verse 16.

> *Now while Paul was waiting for them in Athens, his spirit was being provoked within him as he was observing the city full of idols.*

As he waited in Athens for Silas and Timothy, Paul's spirit was troubled by the wickedness and sadness of this city filled with idols—thousands of idols. Here in Athens, the wisest and smartest people in the Roman Empire lived and taught. Paul was troubled because despite all they knew, they did not know the true God. He remembered being much like they were, really intelligent, but not knowing God, until the day he met Jesus—that miraculous day when God physically blinded him, so his spiritual blinders could be removed (Acts 9:1-20). Paul desperately wanted the Athenians to know Jesus and have their spiritual blinders taken away, so he introduced them to God, the LORD of heaven and earth, the Giver of life and breath, the Divine Nature which cannot be captured in gold, silver, or stone (vs. 24-25, 29).

Do you have a heart like Paul for those who do not know Jesus? Is your spirit provoked when you see people stumbling in their spiritual blindness? Pray for God to give you a heart like His and for others to know Him, using the words from Acts 17:16-17 and 27-28 as a faithful, prayerful watchman (Isaiah 62:6-7).

> *"Holy Spirit, provoke my spirit when I see a city full of idols. Help me reason in the synagogues and marketplaces every day, with those who happen to be present. God, may _____ grope for You and find You, for You are not far from each of us. Let them live and move and exist as Your children. In Your name, Jesus~"*

August

> On your walls, O Jerusalem,
> I have appointed watchmen;
> All day and all night they
> will never keep silent.
> You who remind the LORD,
> take no rest for yourselves;
> And give Him no rest until He establishes
> And makes Jerusalem a
> praise in the earth.
> ISAIAH 62:6-7, NASB

AUGUST 1

Please read Acts 18.

Meditate on verses 24-25.

> *Now a Jew named Apollos, an Alexandrian by birth, an eloquent man, came to Ephesus, and he was mighty in the Scriptures. This man had been instructed in the way of the LORD, and being fervent in spirit, he was speaking and teaching accurately the things concerning Jesus, being acquainted only with the baptism of John.*

Does Apollos describe you? You may have nodded your head without thinking this one through. He had all of the gifts and talents one could imagine. He was from Alexandria, Egypt and well-trained. With his training, came boldness and confidence in his abilities. He was fervent in spirit, yet, like all of us, he needed discipling. Thankfully, the Holy Spirit led Priscilla and Aquilla to go with Paul to Ephesus. When Paul left the city, they remained, and God used them to establish Apollos in the Christian life.

You may need a life coach, mentor, or shepherd to disciple you. Ask the Holy Spirit to lead you to the right person.

You may need to ask the Holy Spirit who you should disciple. Maybe you already know who that person is.

Pray Acts 18:24b-26 over yourself and those for whom you stand guard as a faithful, prayerful watchman (Isaiah 62:6-7).

> "LORD, make _____ and me mighty in the Scriptures. Instruct us in Your way, LORD. Make us fervent in spirit, speaking and teaching accurately the things concerning Jesus. Before we speak out boldly, let us be taken aside, so Your way can be explained to us more accurately. Then, let us accurately explain Your way to others. For the sake of Your name, Jesus~"

AUGUST 2

Please read Acts 19.

Meditate on verses 2-3.

> *He said to them, "Did you receive the Holy Spirit when you believed?"*
> *And they said to him, "No, we have not even*
> *heard whether there is a Holy Spirit."*
> *And he said, "Into what then were you baptized?"*
> *And they said, "Into John's baptism."*

Paul met twelve disciples of John the Baptist in Ephesus, and he wisely built on their beliefs and experiences. Paul used the start of their faith to finish their faith. Consider Paul's witnessing approach when you share Christ with others.

People sincerely believe they are right in their religiosity, not needing anything else for salvation. Many religions think works make you worthy; Jesus was a great prophet, merely a good man who was not resurrected from the dead. These beliefs seem reasonable; however, Jesus is God, the crucified Christ, and the risen Savior. Faith in Jesus makes us holy and good.

In addition, Jesus is with you, journeying with you for the rest of your life. Bonus Round—you have the Holy Spirit inside of you. Super Bonus Round—because of Jesus and through the Holy Spirit, you can come into the presence of the Creator of the universe all the time, saying, "Abba! Father!" (Galatians 4:6). The men at Ephesus were religious, but when they heard the rest of the story and believed, they received the Holy Spirit, making them children of God.

Pray Acts 19:4-6 and 20 over those for whom you stand guard as a faithful, prayerful watchman (Isaiah 62:6-7).

> *"LORD, let _____ repent and believe*
> *in You, Jesus. Let them be baptized in Your name,*
> *LORD Jesus, and receive Your Holy Spirit. Let*
> *Your Word grow mightily and prevail.*
> *Because of Your name, Jesus~"*

AUGUST 3

Please read Acts 20.

Meditate on verse 28.

> *Be on guard for yourselves and for all the flock, among which the Holy Spirit has made you overseers, to shepherd the church of God which He purchased with His own blood.*

Such a powerful command from God to everyone who serves in a faith community!

Be on guard; be on the alert (vs. 28, 31). Be on guard for yourself, staying strong in the LORD, not surrendering to false teaching, so you can protect the flock from savage wolves, false teachers, speaking perverse things contrary to the Word of God (vs. 29-30).

Be on guard for ALL the flock (v. 28). There is no exception for "all." Everyone in the flock needs to be protected.

"Among which the Holy Spirit has made you overseers" (v. 28)—this is a vital phrase for church life—the Holy Spirit gifts people, choosing who serves in which positions within a congregation. Therefore, a congregation must pray, asking the Holy Spirit who He wants serving in His ministries.

The purpose of an overseer is to "shepherd the church of God which He purchased with His own blood" (v. 28). The LORD invests in us the great responsibility of caring for His treasure, the church. Thankfully, He does not make us do this on our own. The Father, Son, and Holy Spirit participate with us in the family business of caring for the flock.

Pray Acts 3:28 over yourself and those for whom you stand guard as a faithful, prayerful watchman (Isaiah 62:6-7).

> *"LORD, help _____ and me be on guard for ourselves and for all the flock. Thank You, Holy Spirit, for making us overseers. Help us shepherd the church of God, which You purchased with Your own blood. In Your name, Jesus~"*

AUGUST 4

Please read Acts 21.

Meditate on verses 11 and 13b.

> *And coming to us, he took Paul's belt and bound his own feet and hands, and said, "This is what the Holy Spirit says: 'In this way the Jews at Jerusalem will bind the man who owns this belt and deliver him into the hands of the Gentiles.'" Then Paul answered, "I am ready not only to be bound, but even to die at Jerusalem for the name of the LORD Jesus."*

Paul and his missionary team moved quickly to Jerusalem. Excited to tell the elders about the new churches and thousands of new Christians throughout Greece and Asia, Paul wanted to be there by Pentecost (Acts 20:16).

The Holy Spirit gave him exciting travel plans, telling him he would go to Rome, but first he must go to Jerusalem (Acts 19:21). The Spirit warned Paul the trip would be tough (Acts 20:22-23). Everywhere Paul went on the way to Jerusalem, the Holy Spirit confirmed His message, telling local believers Paul would have trouble (vs. 4, 11-12). So, why did the Holy Spirit do this?

The larger purpose was to show churches they could discern God's will, and following His will was paramount regardless of the circumstances. The Holy Spirit's precise revelation of where Paul would go and the difficulties he would face, gave him the fortitude to endure the trials and the church clear reasons to pray with greater fervor for Paul.

Pray Acts 21:13b over yourself and those for whom you stand guard as a faithful, prayerful watchman (Isaiah 62:6-7).

> *"LORD, help _____ and me be ready not only to be bound, but even to do die for Your name, Jesus~"*

AUGUST 5

Please read Acts 22.

Meditate on verses 14-15.

> *And he (Ananias) said, "The God of our fathers has appointed you to know His will and to see the Righteous One and to hear an utterance from His mouth. For you will be a witness for Him to all men of what you have seen and heard."*

As foretold by the Holy Spirit, Paul's journey to Jerusalem resulted in mistreatment and being turned over to the Gentiles (Acts 21:11). Seven days after his arrival, he was hauled out of the temple to be killed by the Jews (Acts 21:27). As the Roman military rescued Paul, he paused to tell the crowd about his life before Christ and his conversion (Acts 21:31-40; 22:1-21).

As Paul recounts his story, we learn even more about the role Ananias played in Paul quickly going from villain to victory (Acts 9:10-19; 22:12-16). The LORD used him to work with the Holy Spirit in Paul's conversion to Christianity, giving Paul God's call to tell everyone about Who he saw on that road and what he heard that Righteous One say (vs. 14-16). As the Holy Spirit draws others to follow Him, be ready to be an "Ananias," telling them what you have seen and heard concerning the Righteous One.

Pray Acts 22:14-15 over yourself and those for whom you stand guard as a faithful, prayerful watchman (Isaiah 62:6-7).

> *"God of our fathers, appoint _____ and me to know Your will, to see You, the Righteous One, and hear an utterance from Your mouth. We want to be witnesses for You to everyone of what we have seen and heard. In Your name, Jesus~"*

AUGUST 6

Please read Acts 23.

Meditate on verses 11 and 16.

> *But on the night immediately following, the LORD stood at his side and said, "Take courage, for as you have solemnly witnessed to My cause at Jerusalem, so you must witness at Rome also." But the son of Paul's sister heard of their ambush, and he came and entered the barracks and told Paul.*

For his own protection, Paul was in jail after meeting with the Jewish Council (vs. 1-10). Unbeknown to Paul and the Roman leadership, the Council conspired to ambush Paul the following day on his way to more Council meetings (vs. 12-15). Paul's nephew overheard the plot, reporting it to Paul and the Roman commander. But prior to the plot being hatched, Jesus told Paul he would go to Rome (vs. 11-12). Can you imagine Paul's confidence he would not die because he heard from his LORD?

What confidence do Christ's Words bring to you? Hear what He says to you in John 14:27:

> *"Peace I leave with you; My peace I give to you; not as the world gives, do I give to you. Do not let your heart be troubled, nor let it be fearful."*

The Holy Spirit brings peace and self-control in our times of fear. Just imagine the courage He gave Paul's nephew to talk to the Romans! The more you walk with the Spirit, the more confidence you have when He urges you to do something. Be courageous. You are not alone on the journey.

Pray Acts 23:11 over yourself and those for whom you stand guard as a faithful, prayerful watchman (Isaiah 62:6-7).

> *"LORD Jesus, stand at _____ and my side. Give us courage to solemnly witness to Your cause every place we go. In Your name, Jesus~"*

AUGUST 7

Please read Acts 24.

Meditate on verses 24-25.

> *But some days later Felix arrived with Drusilla, his wife who was a Jewess, and sent for Paul and heard him speak about faith in Christ Jesus. But as he was discussing righteousness, self-control, and the judgment to come, Felix became frightened and said, "Go away for the present, and when I find time, I will summon you."*

Felix did meet with Paul many times over the next few years (vs. 26-27). His heart was troubled as Paul explained Jesus and God's Word to him. All of us should be sensitive to the Holy Spirit convicting us of truth for salvation and growth as believers. The Holy Spirit also convicts us in these ways:

> *And He (the Holy Spirit), when He comes, will convict the world concerning sin and righteousness and judgment.*
> — JOHN 16:8

> *But when He, the Spirit of truth, comes, He will guide you into all the truth.*
> —JOHN 16:13A

> *With all prayer and petition, pray at all times in the Spirit.*
> — EPHESIANS 6:18A

> *The sword of the Spirit, which is the Word of God, is living and active and sharper than any two-edged sword ... and able to judge the thoughts and intentions of the heart.*
> —EPHESIANS 6:17B; HEBREWS 4:12

God goes to great effort to help us know Him and grow in our faith. Pray Acts 24:24-25 over yourself and those for whom you stand guard as a faithful, prayerful watchman (Isaiah 62:6-7).

> *"LORD, help me speak about faith in Christ Jesus with _____ . As we discuss righteousness, self-control, and the judgment to come, do not let them be frightened and delay following You. In Your name, Jesus-"*

AUGUST 8

Please read Acts 25.

Meditate on verses 18-19.

> *When the accusers stood up, they began bringing charges against him not of such crimes as I was expecting, but they simply had some points of disagreement with him about their own religion and about a dead man, Jesus, whom Paul asserted to be alive.*

Imprisoned at Caesarea by the Sea for two years was not wasted time for Paul (Acts 24:27). The Holy Spirit gave him many opportunities to share his faith in this vital port city, and He gave Luke, who was with Paul, time to interview eyewitnesses of Jesus as he penned the *Gospel of Luke* and the book of *Acts* (Luke 1:1-4; Acts 1:1-2). God's timing is perfect.

The LORD often uses circumstances greater than we can fathom to move us and help us grow. Paul relied on the Holy Spirit for what to say and do in his circumstances. And after he did indeed go to Rome to appeal to Caesar, Paul penned these words to the Ephesian Christians:

> *So then do not be foolish but understand what the will of the LORD is. And do not get drunk with wine, for that is dissipation, but be filled with the Spirit.*
> —EPHESIANS 5:17-18

Paul lived those words in his passionate plea to the Roman Governor Festus to appear before Caesar (vs. 10-12). A Texas evangelist once said, "If you are drunk with wine, you say and do things you would not normally do. If you are filled with the Spirit, you say and do things you would not normally do." As the Holy Spirit controls you, you miraculously do and say things you never thought possible for God's glory.

Pray Acts 25:19 over yourself and those for whom you stand guard as a faithful, prayerful watchman (Isaiah 62:6-7).

> "LORD, make _____ and me like Paul, always ready to declare You are alive, Jesus!"

AUGUST 9

Please read Acts 26.

Meditate on verse 1.

> *Agrippa said to Paul, "You are permitted to speak for yourself." Then Paul stretched out his hand and proceeded to make his defense.*

In the book of *Acts*, you see heroes of faith speak to Roman and Jewish leaders, Athenian scholars, royal households, and angry mobs. They rise to the occasion and say the things God uses to change lives. What makes them successful is they are prompted by the Holy Spirit to say what God wants the listeners to hear.

Speaking to people of power and those who hate God, results in nervous times for most people. Jesus said to all of His followers:

> *"When they bring you before the synagogues and the rulers and the authorities, do not worry about how or what you are to speak in your defense, or what you are to say, for the Holy Spirit will teach you in that very hour what you ought to say. When they arrest you and hand you over, do not worry beforehand about what you are to say, but say whatever is given you in that hour, for it is not you who speak, but it is the Holy Spirit."*
> —LUKE 12:11-12; MARK 13:11

God wants you to trust Him. He enables you to speak about and live out your faith in front of others.

Note Agrippa's response after Paul finished speaking: "In a short time, you will persuade me to become a Christian" (v. 28).

Pray Acts 26:29 over those for whom you stand guard as a faithful, prayerful watchman (Isaiah 62:6-7).

> *"I wish to God that whether in a short or long time, _____ and all who hear me might become as I am, a follower of the LORD Jesus Christ. For the sake of Your name, Jesus~"*

AUGUST 10

Please read Acts 27.

Meditate on verses 22-25. Paul is speaking.

> *"Yet now I urge you to keep up your courage, for there will be no loss of life among you, but only of the ship. For this very night an angel of the God to whom I belong and whom I serve stood before me, saying, 'Do not be afraid, Paul; you must stand before Caesar; and behold, God has granted you all those who are sailing with you.' Therefore, keep up your courage, men, for I believe God that it will turn out exactly as I have been told."*

The LORD continued revealing His secrets to Paul as he was sent from Caesarea by the Sea to Rome. In the meditation passage, the people onboard ship were in dire circumstances and losing hope. Paul encouraged them he would see Caesar, and all 276 of them would survive the journey (v. 37).

As the ship breaks apart, some of the Roman soldiers wanted to kill the prisoners to ensure they did not escape (v. 42). "But the centurion, wanting to bring Paul safely through, kept them from their intention" (v. 43).

The centurion and the shipwreck are an example of the Holy Spirit working through people and events to fulfill God's purposes.

Pray Acts 27:23-25 over yourself and those for whom you stand guard as a faithful, prayerful watchman (Isaiah 62:6-7).

> *"LORD God, _____ and I belong to and serve You. Do not let us be afraid to do what You say we will do. Spare those who are with us. Help us keep up our courage, for we believe You, God, that it will turn out exactly as You have told us. For the sake of Your name, Jesus~"*

AUGUST 11

Please read Acts 28.

Meditate on verse 14b.

> *Thus we came to Rome.*

Wow! What a journey (Acts 23:11-28:14)! Paul finally made it to Rome where he had many day-long conversations with prominent Jews about Jesus (v. 23). Some believed; some did not (v. 24). To those who refused to believe, Paul said:

> *"The Holy Spirit rightly spoke through Isaiah the prophet to your fathers, saying, 'Go to this people and say, "You will keep on hearing, but will not understand, and you will keep on seeing, but will not perceive, for the heart of this people has become dull, and with their ears, they scarcely hear, and they have closed their eyes; otherwise they might see with their eyes and hear with their ears, and understand with their heart and return, and I would heal them."'"*
> —ACTS 28:25B-27

There are three wonderful truths in this last chapter of *Acts*:
1. The Holy Spirit wrote the Bible (v. 25).
2. The good news for those who do not yet perceive their situation is that God is working and wants all people to hear and repent so Jesus can come into their lives (vs. 26-28).
3. And finally, Paul arrived in Rome, just like the Holy Spirit said (Acts 19:21).

> *And he stayed two full years in his own rented quarters and was welcoming all who came to him, preaching the kingdom of God and teaching concerning the LORD Jesus Christ with all openness, unhindered.*
> —ACTS 28:30-31

Pray Acts 28:30-31 over yourself and those for whom you stand guard as a faithful, prayerful watchman (Isaiah 62:6-7).

> *"LORD, let _____ and me welcome all who come to us, preaching the kingdom of God and teaching concerning the LORD Jesus Christ with all openness, unhindered. For the sake of Your name, Jesus~"*

AUGUST 12

Please read Job 1.

Meditate on verse 20.

> *Then Job arose and tore his robe and shaved his head, and he fell to the ground and worshiped.*

The day we began writing the *Job* devotionals we received two pieces of difficult news concerning our family within a couple of hours. Our hearts were broken and sad, and we questioned what God was doing in the midst of these situations. So, it is no accident that God wanted us to write prayer devotionals from a book addressing the fact that bad things happen to us and to those around us. How do we as Christians respond when we are the afflicted ones, and how do we respond to others in the midst of their affliction? Thankfully God gave us the book of *Job*. As you read these first two chapters, observe God, Job, and Satan. Let God's Word teach you how to walk with the LORD.

Ponder Job's response to receiving the horrific news that all of his children are dead. He worshiped God. Amazing! Ask the LORD to make you a worshiper, so that worship is your first response to Him no matter what is happening in your life.

Pray Job 1:1 and 20-22 as the LORD's faithful, prayerful watchman (Isaiah 62:6-7).

> *"LORD, please make _____ and me like Job—blameless, upright, fearing You, and turning away from evil. May we always fall to the ground and worship You. LORD, naked we came from our mother's womb and naked we shall return there. You give and You take away. Blessed be Your name, LORD! Through it all, do not let us sin or blame You, God.*
> *In Your name, Jesus~"*

AUGUST 13

Please read Job 2.

Meditate on verse 3.

> *The LORD said to Satan, "Have you considered My servant Job? For there is no one like him on the earth, a blameless and upright man fearing God and turning away from evil. And he still holds fast his integrity, although you incited Me against him to ruin him without cause."*

Satan's reason for attacking Job, a God-fearing, honorable man, was to get him to lose his integrity. Yet, despite the death of his ten children, servants, 11,500 head of livestock, and being diseased with boils from his head to his toes, "Job did not sin with his lips" (Job 1:2-3, 13-19; 2:10). Incredible! Be mindful of Satan's schemes when you are attacked; his goal is to incite you to sin and lose your integrity. The psalmist David was often attacked by the enemy; hear what he said to God about his integrity:

> *Let integrity and uprightness preserve me, for I wait for You.*
> —PSALM 25:21

> *As for me, You uphold me in my integrity, and You set me in Your presence forever.*
> —PSALM 41:12

No matter what is happening in your life, wait for God to deliver you. As a Christian, you abide in His presence forever; He will uphold you.

Pray Job 2:3 and 10 over yourself and others in difficult situations as a faithful, prayerful watchman (Isaiah 62:6-7).

> *"LORD, keep _____ and me blameless, upright, fearing You, and turning away from evil. Let us still hold fast our integrity, although it feels like You are against us to ruin us without cause. God, shall we indeed accept good from You and not accept adversity? Do not let us sin with our lips. In Your name, Jesus~"*

AUGUST 14

Please read Job 3. Job is pouring out his anguish.

Meditate on verses 25-26.

> *For what I fear comes upon me, and what I dread befalls me. I am not at ease, nor am I quiet, and I am not at rest, but turmoil comes.*

For the next 36 days, you have the privilege of listening in on the conversation between Job, Eliphaz, Bildad, Zophar, and Elihu. You may want to note in your Bible which one of the five is speaking. At the end of their discourse, God reveals His thoughts. Before you read any further, you need to know what God thinks about Job and his friends:

> *It came about after the LORD had spoken these words to Job, that the LORD said to Eliphaz the Temanite, "My wrath is kindled against you and against your two friends, because you have not spoken of Me what is right as My servant Job has. Now therefore, take for yourselves seven bulls and seven rams, and go to My servant Job, and offer up a burnt offering for yourselves, and My servant Job will pray for you. For I will accept him so that I may not do with you according to your folly, because you have not spoken of Me what is right, as My servant Job has."*
> —JOB 42:7-8

Keeping God's Words in mind, learn from Job's friends what not to say when someone is hurting and learn from Job how to handle difficulty.

Pour out your heart to the LORD with Job 3:25-26 as a faithful, prayerful watchman (Isaiah 62:6-7).

> *"LORD, what I fear comes upon me, and what I dread befalls me. I am not at ease, nor am I quiet, and I am not at rest, but turmoil comes. Thank You that I can pour out my heart to You, Jesus~"*

AUGUST 15

Please read Job 4. Eliphaz is speaking.

Meditate on verses 7-9.

> *Remember now, whoever perished being innocent? Or where were the upright destroyed? According to what I have seen, those who plow iniquity and those who sow trouble harvest it. By the breath of God they perish, and by the blast of His anger they come to an end.*

Job's friend Eliphaz assumes God is punishing Job because of sin in his life, reminding Job he admonished others in the past, and now he is the one who needs admonishing (vs. 3-5). Eliphaz's words are as cutting as the potsherd Job used to scrape his painful boils (Job 2:8). He even has the audacity to relate his demonic vision to Job as if it is a word from the LORD (vs. 12-21).

What have you been taught and what do you believe about pain and suffering? Thankfully, we have the book of Job to refine our thoughts. Let God's Word temper your words when you speak to others in their pain. Test everything you hear and say with God's Word, making sure it is the Spirit of God speaking and not the spirit of the demonic.

Use the words from Job 4:1-4, asking God to make you a Godly counselor and a faithful, prayerful watchman (Isaiah 62:6-7).

> *"LORD, help me refrain from speaking until You want me to speak. When You tell me to admonish, let it be received with patience. Help me strengthen weak hands. May my words help the tottering to stand. Let me strengthen feeble knees. In Your name, Jesus~"*

AUGUST 16

Please read Job 5. Eliphaz continues to counsel Job.

Meditate on verses 3 and 8.

> *"I have seen the foolish taking root, and I cursed his abode immediately. But as for me, I would seek God, and I would place my cause before God."*

"Oh, self-righteous, arrogant Eliphaz, how much I sound like you! LORD, forgive me!" We are only in chapter five, and the LORD is really using this book—I've been avoiding—to show me how much I need to grow in Him. We hope you are taking it personally as well.

Eliphaz speaks from his experiences, and in a back-handed way, calls Job a fool (v. 3). He even has the audacity to infer Job's children were not kept safe and delivered because of their foolish father (v. 4). Eliphaz assumes Job does not seek God because he tells Job that's what he would do in this situation (v. 8). Finally, Eliphaz prophesies prosperity over Job (vs. 17-27). Perhaps he thinks his cutting words can be softened by self-willed declarations that everything will be fine in the end.

It is easy to be an Eliphaz, thinking we have God figured-out and telling others what we presume about the LORD. Pray for God to keep you from saying foolish things, using the words from Job 5:3-4 as a faithful, prayerful watchman (Isaiah 62:6-7).

> *"LORD, please give me Your heart and eyes for those in whom foolishness is taking root. May I never curse anyone's abode. Let no one's children be far from safety or oppressed in the gate. LORD, we all need a deliverer! Deliver us in Your name, Jesus~"*

AUGUST 17

Please read Job 6. Job is speaking.

Meditate on verse 14.

> *For the despairing man there should be kindness from his friend; so that he does not forsake the fear of the Almighty.*

Job responds to Eliphaz with, "Be kind!" Kindness goes a long way and keeps you from doing and saying the regrettable. It is easy to look at a person, assess their situation, and eagerly tell them what they need to do to fix it. The holier-than-thou Eliphaz approach is usually met with rebellious disdain. But, observing others with kindness, infuses your thoughts, words, and actions with Christ, making all the difference.

> *Seeing the people, He (Jesus) felt compassion for them, because they were distressed and dispirited like sheep without a shepherd.*
> —MATTHEW 9:36

Ask the LORD to let His kindness govern you, giving you His heart, the heart of a good shepherd, who sincerely loves and cares about others.

> *Do not let kindness and truth leave you; bind them around your neck; write them on the tablet of your heart.*
> —PROVERBS 3:3

Pray Job 6:10 and 14 over yourself and those for whom you stand guard as a faithful, prayerful watchman (Isaiah 62:6-7).

> *"Holy One, even in unsparing pain, let it be my consolation that I never deny Your Words. When _____ and I see a despairing person, let there be kindness from us, so they do not forsake the fear of You, the Almighty. When we are in despair, give us people who are kind, so we do not forsake the fear of You. Because You are the Almighty and Holy One, Jesus~"*

AUGUST 18

Please read Job 7. Job is speaking.

Meditate on verse 4.

> *When I lie down, I say, "When shall I arise?" But the night continues, and I am continually tossing until dawn.*

Thankfully God gave us the book of Job for sleepless nights and distressful times. Thankfully, God recorded Job's prayer of anguish, so we do not have to restrain our mouths; we can speak in the anguish of our spirit and complain in the bitterness of our soul (v. 11).

Pray Job's prayer from verses 12-21 as a faithful, prayerful watchman (Isaiah 62:6-7).

> *"LORD, am I the sea, or the sea monster, that You set a guard over me? If I say, 'My bed will comfort me, my couch will ease my complaint,' then You frighten me with dreams and terrify me by visions; so that my soul would choose suffocation, death rather than my pains. I waste away; I will not live forever. Leave me alone, for my days are but a breath. What is man that You magnify him, and that You are concerned about him, that You examine him every morning and try him every moment? Will You never turn Your gaze away from me, nor let me alone until I swallow my spittle? Have I sinned? What have I done to You, O Watcher of men? Why have You set me as Your target, so that I am a burden to myself? Why then do You not pardon my transgression and take away my iniquity? For now, I will lie down in the dust, and You will seek me, but I will not be. I need help, in Your name, Jesus~"*

AUGUST 19

Please read Job 8. Bildad is speaking.

Meditate on verses 1-2.

> *Then Bildad the Shuhite answered, "How long will you say these things, and the words of your mouth be a mighty wind?"*

Bildad the Shuhite could be nicknamed Bildad the Blunt. He speaks with no tact, calling Job a windbag and his children sinners who got what they deserved (vs. 2, 4). He shows no sympathy for Job, making no acknowledgment of his immense pain and suffering. Bildad simply states his assumption that if Job was righteous, God would bless him, and since he isn't being blessed, he is obviously being punished by God because of sin. He also counsels Job to manipulate God:

> *If you would seek God and implore the compassion of the Almighty, if you are pure and upright, surely now He would rouse Himself for you and restore your righteous estate.*
> —JOB 8:5-6

Again, God's Word is so convicting. How easy it is to be a blunt Bildad, assuming we understand God's ways and being quick to advise others to pray more, read their Bible more, go to church more, and sin less if they want to be blessed. Ask God to teach you what not to say and help you not be a spiritual bully like Bildad, using the words from Job 8:3, as a faithful, prayerful watchman (Isaiah 62:6-7).

> *"LORD God Almighty, You do not pervert justice,*
> *and You do not pervert what is right.*
> *Do not let me pervert who You are and what You say.*
> *In Your name, Jesus~"*

AUGUST 20

Please read Job 9. Job is speaking.

Meditate on verses 1-3.

> *Then Job answered, "In truth I know that this is so, but how can a man be in the right before God? If one wished to dispute with Him, He could not answer Him once in a thousand times."*

Unlike Job's pompous friends, Job figured out he does not have God figured out. He praises God's power and wisdom, humbly acknowledging his inability to understand the LORD and His ways. Job's friends counsel him to do things to be right with God and garner His favor. Job asks, "How can I be right with God? Even if I wash with snow and scrub myself with lye, God will send me to the pit" (vs. 2, 30-31). Job knows being right with God cannot come from one's self. His words sound similar to King David's:

> *Be gracious to me, O God, according to Your lovingkindness; according to the greatness of Your compassion blot out my transgressions. Wash me thoroughly from my iniquity and cleanse me from my sin. Purify me with hyssop, and I shall be clean; wash me, and I shall be whiter than snow.*
> —PSALM 51:1-2, 7

Humbly acknowledge God and your need for Him by praying Job 9:5-8, 10, and 30 as a faithful, prayerful watchman (Isaiah 62:6-7).

> *"God, You remove the mountains when You overturn them in Your anger. You shake the earth out of its place, and its pillars tremble. You command the sun not to shine and set a seal upon the stars. You alone stretch out the heavens and trample down the waves of the sea. You do great things, unfathomable, and wondrous works without number. You did the wondrous work of washing and cleansing me to be whiter than snow. Please do the same for _____.*
> *In Your name, Jesus~"*

AUGUST 21

Please read Job 10. Job is speaking.

Meditate on verses 1-2a.

> *I loathe my own life; I will give full vent to my complaint;*
> *I will speak in the bitterness of my soul. I will say to God...*

I love that Job's complaining prayer is recorded for eternity. You can complain it, I mean, pray it now, as a faithful, prayerful watchman (Isaiah 62:6-7). Because, even faithful watchmen have tough seasons in this life. Pray Job 10:2b-17.

> "LORD, do not condemn me; let me know why You contend with me. Is it right for You indeed to oppress, to reject the labor of Your hands, and to look favorably on the schemes of the wicked? Have You eyes of flesh? Or do You see as a man sees? Are Your days as the days of a mortal, or Your years as man's years, that You should seek for my guilt and search after my sin? According to Your knowledge, I am indeed not guilty, yet there is no deliverance from Your hand. Your hands fashioned and made me altogether, and would You destroy me? Remember now, that You have made me as clay; would You turn me into dust again? Did You not pour me out like milk and curdle me like cheese; clothe me with skin and flesh, and knit me together with bones and sinews? You have granted me life and lovingkindness, and Your care has preserved my spirit. Yet these things You have concealed in Your heart; I know that this is within You: If I sin, then You would take note of me, and would not acquit me of my guilt. If I am wicked, woe to me! And if I am righteous, I dare not lift up my head. I am sated with disgrace and conscious of my misery. Should my head be lifted up, You would hunt me like a lion, and again You would show Your power against me. You renew Your witnesses against me and increase Your anger toward me; hardship after hardship is with me.
> Help me, Jesus! For the sake of Your name~"

AUGUST 22

Please read Job 11. Zophar is speaking.

Meditate on verse 12.

> *An idiot will become intelligent when the foal*
> *of a wild donkey is born a man.*

Thankfully, Zophar only speaks twice in this book (Job 11; 20) because his arrogant severity is painful. His assessment of Job's situation is simple: God is sovereign and just; Job is sinful and getting less than he deserves (v. 6). He calls Job an idiot who will be intelligent the day a wild donkey gives birth to a human; in other words, never (v. 12). Wow, can you imagine having a friend like Zophar; can you imagine being a friend like he is? "Oh, LORD, make me aware when I am prideful and harsh and shut me up!"

Zophar ends his discourse with these promises of prosperity if Job will just straighten up:

- You will forget your troubles (v. 16).
- Your life will be brighter than noonday (v. 17).
- You will rest securely (v. 18).
- No one will disturb you (v. 19).
- Many will seek your favor (v. 19).

But, Zophar asserts if Job stays wicked, his eyes will fail, there will be no escape for him, and his only hope is to breathe his last (v. 20). Unbelievable!

Learn well from Zophar; there are some things we should NEVER say to others in the midst of their suffering. Thankfully God recorded his words, so we can know what they are. Pray Job 11:2-3 as a faithful, prayerful watchman (Isaiah 62:6-7).

> *"LORD, do not let _____ and me*
> *be talkative people with a multitude of words.*
> *Rebuke and silence us when we boast and scoff.*
> *Teach us what to say in Your name, Jesus~"*

AUGUST 23

Please read Job 12. Job is speaking.

Meditate on verses 1-2.

> *Then Job responded, "Truly then you are the*
> *people, and with you, wisdom will die!"*

Job responds to being called an idiot with quick wit and cutting sarcasm, referring to his friends being the ones miraculously birthed by a donkey (Job 11:12; 12:2). It is encouraging to see Job's smart comeback despite how horrible he feels.

After rebuking his friends, Job describes the amazing power of God. Pray these truths from Job 12:13-25 and 4 in declaration of who God is as a faithful, prayerful watchman (Isaiah 62:6-7).

> "LORD, with You are wisdom and might; to You belong counsel and understanding. Behold, You tear down, and it cannot be rebuilt; You imprison a man, and there can be no release. Behold, You restrain the waters, and they dry up, and You send them out, and they inundate the earth. With You are strength and sound wisdom, the misled and the misleader belong to You. You make counselors walk barefoot and make fools of judges. You loosen the bond of kings and bind their loins with a girdle. You make priests walk barefoot and overthrow the secure ones. You deprive the trusted ones of speech and take away the discernment of the elders. You pour contempt on nobles and loosen the belt of the strong. You reveal mysteries from the darkness and bring the deep darkness into light. You make the nations great, then destroy them; You enlarge the nations, then lead them away. You deprive of intelligence the chiefs of the earth's people and make them wander in a pathless waste. They grope in darkness with no light, and You make them stagger like a drunken man. LORD, I call on You. Please answer me in Your name, Jesus~"

AUGUST 24

Please read Job 13. Job is speaking.

Meditate on verse 3.

> *But I would speak to the Almighty,*
> *and I desire to argue with God.*

Job not only talks to his three friends; he talks to God. His friends are eager to give advice, but the book does not indicate they seek God's wisdom for how to give it, and they are rebuked by God for speaking incorrectly about Him (Job 42:7). To whom do you turn for advice and guidance? Are they Christians who spend time talking to God, reading His Word, and counseling Biblically?

This chapter gives other good counseling advice:

- Sometimes it is wise to be completely silent (v. 5).
- If one speaks a word from the LORD, it must be God's Word (v. 7).
- Be quiet and let others talk (v. 13).

Speak to the Almighty, arguing with Him if necessary (v. 3). Start with Job 13:20-28 as a faithful, prayerful watchman (Isaiah 62:6-7).

> *"LORD, only two things do not do to me,*
> *then I will not hide from Your face: Remove Your hand from*
> *me and let not the dread of You terrify me. Then call, and I will*
> *answer; or let me speak, then reply to me. How many are my*
> *iniquities and sins? Make known to me my rebellion and my sin.*
> *Why do You hide Your face and consider me Your enemy?*
> *Will You cause a driven leaf to tremble? Or will You pursue*
> *the dry chaff? For You write bitter things against me and*
> *make me to inherit the iniquities of my youth. You put my*
> *feet in the stocks and watch all my paths; You set a limit for*
> *the soles of my feet, while I am decaying like a rotten thing,*
> *like a garment that is moth-eaten. LORD, help me!*
> *In Your name, Jesus~"*

AUGUST 25

Please read Job 14. Job is speaking.

Meditate on verse 4.

Who can make the clean out of the unclean? No one!

Job's question is a good one, but his answer is wrong. Thankfully we know the correct answer.

If we walk in the Light as He Himself is in the Light, we have fellowship with one another, and the blood of Jesus His Son cleanses us from all sin. If we confess our sins, He is faithful and righteous to forgive us our sins and to cleanse us from all unrighteousness.
—1 JOHN 1:7, 9

We have been sanctified (made clean and holy) through the offering of the body of Jesus Christ once for all.
—HEBREWS 10:10

There are times when we feel like Job, overpowered and hopeless (vs. 19-20). But, unlike the Old Testament saints, who had the promise of Messiah, we have the fulfillment of that promise—Jesus. Hope in Him and use the words from Job 14:13-17 to pray as a faithful, prayerful watchman (Isaiah 62:6-7).

"Oh LORD God, thank You that I am hidden with Christ in You (Colossians 3:3). Conceal me until Your wrath returns to You, that You would set a limit for me and remember me! When I die, I will live again. All the days of my struggle I will wait until my change comes. You will call, and I will answer You; You will long for the work of Your hands. For now, You number my steps; You do not observe my sin. My transgression is sealed up in a bag, and You wrap up my iniquity. Thank You, in Your name, Jesus~"

AUGUST 26

Please read Job 15. Eliphaz is speaking.

Meditate on verses 24-25.

> *Distress and anguish terrify him; they overpower him like a king ready for the attack because he has stretched out his hand against God and conducts himself arrogantly against the Almighty.*

For a second time, Eliphaz criticizes Job, accusing him of not reverencing or meditating on the LORD. What an interesting accusation since we have yet to see Job's friends talking to God, yet every time Job speaks, it is not only to the friends but also to God.

Eliphaz describes his exhortations as "consolations from God" and "words spoken gently" (v. 11). All the while, calling Job "detestable and corrupt" and accusing him of drinking "iniquity like water" (v. 16). Gentle consolations indeed! And just in case he doesn't get another opportunity to speak, sadly he will, Eliphaz declares the reason God stretched out His hand against Job is because Job first arrogantly stretched out his hand against God (vs. 24-25). And, this time Eliphaz makes no prosperity prophecies (Job 5:17-27), only doom and gloom for poor Job (vs. 29-35). He should have taken his own advice, not answering Job with windy knowledge and useless talk (vs. 2-3).

It is easy to draw self-righteous conclusions when one is an observer of suffering rather than the receiver of it. Purpose not to be a disheartening Eliphaz. Ask God to make you a comforting friend, praying Job 15:2-3 and 11 as a faithful, prayerful watchman (Isaiah 62:6-7).

> *"LORD, make me a wise friend who does not answer with windy knowledge. Do not let me fill myself with the east wind; fill me with Your wisdom. Do not let me argue with useless talk or words that are not profitable. LORD, let me truly offer Your consolations to others. Let my words be spoken gently. In Your name, Jesus~"*

AUGUST 27

Please read Job 16. Job is speaking.

Meditate on verses 1-2 and 19.

> *Then Job answered, "I have heard many such things; sorry comforters are you all. Even now, behold, my witness is in heaven, and my advocate is on high."*

Job is fed up with his friends; they have done nothing to comfort him, but he has an advocate and a comforter who truly cares, and so do you.

> *My little children, I am writing these things to you so that you may not sin. And if anyone sins, we have an Advocate with the Father, Jesus Christ the righteous.*
> —1 JOHN 2:1

> *Blessed be the God and Father of our LORD Jesus Christ, the Father of mercies and God of all comfort, who comforts us in all our affliction so that we will be able to comfort those who are in any affliction with the comfort with which we ourselves are comforted by God. For just as the sufferings of Christ are ours in abundance, so also our comfort is abundant through Christ.*
> —2 CORINTHIANS 1:3-5

Perhaps you are in a difficult situation, and friends have let you down. Pour out your heart to God and let Him comfort you. As you experience His comfort, extend it to others.

Use Job's words from verses 7, 11, and 19 to tell the LORD how you really feel as His faithful, prayerful watchman (Isaiah 62:6-7).

> *"LORD, I'm exhausted, and I feel like You have handed me over to ruffians and tossed me into the hands of the wicked. LORD, I need Your help! You are my Witness and my Advocate. You are Jesus, the Righteous, in whose name I pray-"*

AUGUST 28

Please read Job 17. Job is speaking.

Meditate on verse 1a.

My spirit is broken.

The trial is not abating for Job. A broken man with dashed hopes, shattered dreams, and messed-up plans, he asks God for a pledge (vs. 3, 11, 15). Job needs a guarantee in this really difficult life (v. 3).

Sometimes life gets hard, even reaching Job-like proportions. For Christians, God gives us a pledge, a Guarantor, to whom we cling:

> *For indeed while we are in this tent, we groan, being burdened, because we do not want to be unclothed but to be clothed, so that what is mortal will be swallowed up by life. Now He who prepared us for this very purpose is God, who gave to us the* **Spirit** *as a* **pledge***. Therefore, being always of good courage, and knowing that while we are at home in the body, we are absent from the LORD, for we walk by faith, not by sight.*
> —2 CORINTHIANS 5:4-7

No matter what happens in this life, God wants you to "abound in hope by the power of the Holy Spirit" (Romans 15:13).

As a faithful, prayerful watchman (Isaiah 62:6-7), tell God how you feel, using the words from Job 17:1, 11, and 15, thanking Him for His pledge and Guarantor (v. 3).

> *"LORD, my spirit is broken; my days are extinguished, and it appears the grave is ready for me. My days are past; my plans and the wishes of my heart are torn apart. Where is my hope and who regards my hope? My hope is in You and Your Spirit, Jesus, my Pledge and Guarantor in this life and the life to come-"*

AUGUST 29

Please read Job 18. Bildad is speaking.

Meditate on verse 3.

> *Why are we regarded as beasts, as stupid in your eyes?*

Job regards Bildad as a beast because he behaves like one, savagely accusing Job of being wicked and not knowing God (vs. 5, 21). Be mindful of beastly Bildads who preach that it is not God's will to suffer. This is what God says about suffering:

> *Therefore, since Christ has suffered in the flesh, arm yourselves also with the same purpose, because he who has suffered in the flesh has ceased from sin, so as to live the rest of the time in the flesh no longer for the lusts of men, but for the will of God. Beloved, do not be surprised at the fiery ordeal among you, which comes upon you for your testing, as though some strange thing were happening to you, but to the degree that you share the sufferings of Christ, keep on rejoicing, so that also at the revelation of His glory, you may rejoice with exultation. If anyone suffers as a Christian, he is not to be ashamed but is to glorify God in this name. Therefore, those also who suffer according to the will of God shall entrust their souls to a faithful Creator in doing what is right.*
> —1 PETER 4:1-2, 12-13, 16, 19

Do not be wooed by false teachers and make false assumptions about those who are suffering. Be on your guard and purpose not to be a Bildad. Pray Job 18:3 over yourself and those for whom you stand guard as a faithful, prayerful watchman (Isaiah 62:6-7).

> *"LORD, do not let _____ and me be regarded as beasts and stupid in the eyes of others. Help us know and speak Your Words. In Your name, Jesus~"*

AUGUST 30

Please read Job 19. Job is speaking.

Meditate on verses 25-27.

> *As for me, I know that my Redeemer lives, and at the last He will take His stand on the earth. Even after my skin is destroyed, yet from my flesh I shall see God; whom I myself shall behold, and whom my eyes will see and not another. My heart faints within me!*

What an amazing statement of faith! Job is in the midst of:

- Darkness (v. 8)
- Stripped honor (v. 9)
- Brokenness (v. 10)
- Uprooted hope (v. 10)
- Estrangement from brothers and acquaintances (v. 13)
- Forgotten by intimate friends (v. 14)
- A stranger in his own house (v. 15)
- Offensive to his wife (v. 17)
- Despised by young children (v. 18)
- Bones cling to his skin (v. 20)
- Feels persecuted by God (v. 22)

Yet, despite everything, Job has confidence in his living Redeemer. He knows the day will come when the difficulties of this life will end, and he will see God.

Do you have that same assurance? Job's statement of faith can be yours, too. Pray Job 19:25-27 as a faithful, prayerful watchman (Isaiah 62:6-7).

> *"LORD, You are my Redeemer. I know You live, and at the last, You will take Your stand on the earth. Even after my skin is destroyed from my flesh, I shall see You, God. I shall behold You with my own eyes. LORD, _____ heart faints within them. Let them know You are their Redeemer, so they can see You, too. In Your name, my Redeemer, Jesus~"*

AUGUST 31

Please read Job 20. Zophar is speaking.

Meditate on verses 14 and 16.

> *His food in his stomach is changed to the venom of cobras within him.*
> *He sucks the poison of cobras; the viper's tongue slays him.*

It is unbelievable the way Zophar speaks to Job. This is the same friend who made the memorable quote: "An idiot will become intelligent when the foal of a wild donkey is born a man" (Job 11:12).

Now, he is obsessed with cobras. Let's nickname him Zophar the Zoologist. So far, we have Bildad the Blunt and Zophar the Zoologist. It will be fun to nickname Eliphaz in the next few days to help us remember these "friends" and how not to behave and what not to say in the presence of those who are suffering. As Christians, the goal would be not to even think such things about others. "Oh, LORD, forgive me and help this blunt zoologist think, speak, and act like You!"

Use the words from Job 20:2-3, praying to be a more Godly, faithful, and prayerful watchman (Isaiah 62:6-7).

> *"LORD, Your Word disquiets my thoughts, and I respond*
> *because of inward agitation with: 'LORD, forgive me!'*
> *Help me listen to reproof even when it insults me.*
> *Help me answer with Your Spirit of understanding.*
> *For the sake of Your name, Jesus~"*

SEPTEMBER

*On your walls, O Jerusalem,
I have appointed watchmen;
All day and all night they
will never keep silent.
You who remind the LORD,
take no rest for yourselves;
And give Him no rest until He establishes
And makes Jerusalem a
praise in the earth.*
ISAIAH 62:6-7, NASB

SEPTEMBER 1

Please read Job 21. Job is speaking.

Meditate on verse 4.

> *"As for me, is my complaint to man?*
> *And why should I not be impatient?"*

"No, Job, your complaint is to God, so why are you talking to your friends instead of the LORD?"

The story of Job started with most of his words spoken to God, but now he is talking more and more to his friends and less and less to God, and the conversation is crazy. Job is caught-up in a foolish argument. "Hush, Job! Talk to God!"

Have you ever been in a Job situation? Life is crazy and hard, and there are people with lots of advice for how to make it simple and easy. But the more you talk to humans the crazier the conversation and life becomes. Stop! The LORD says, "Hush, be still, cease striving, and know that I am God" (Psalm 46:10). Turn your conversations back to Him. He has the answers you need.

Use the words from Job 21:27 and 34 to talk to the LORD as a faithful, prayerful watchman (Isaiah 62:6-7).

> *"Behold, LORD, You know my thoughts and the plans I*
> *have, which are wrong for me. LORD, I need Your help!*
> *I want Your thoughts and plans! Others vainly comfort me, and their*
> *answers remain full of falsehood. I turn to You, LORD, only You can*
> *truly comfort me; Your answers remain full of faithfulness and truth.*
> *Let _____ turn to You,*
> *too, for the answers they need.*
> *In Your name, Jesus~"*

SEPTEMBER 2

Please read Job 22. Eliphaz is speaking.

Meditate on verses 1 and 4.

> Then Eliphaz the Temanite responded, "Is it because of your reverence that He reproves you, that He enters into judgment against you?"

Presuming Job was punished by God, No-Evidence-Eliphaz made up groundless accusations against his friend. In his mind, the punishment must fit the crime, and by all outward appearances, Job's judgment was great; therefore, his behavior was obviously wicked (v. 5). So, Eliphaz falsely accused Job of:

- Taking pledges from his brothers without cause, stripping them naked (v. 6)
- Withholding food and water from the weary and hungry (v. 7)
- Ignoring widows and orphans (v. 9)

Eliphaz wanted to justify in his mind why God did horrible things to Job. Convincing himself and others that Job did horrible things helped Eliphaz make sense of Job's situation. Eliphaz and his friends also wanted assurance they wouldn't experience such judgment from God, so they painted Job as being much more sinful than they.

No-Evidence-Eliphaz, Bildad the Blunt, and Zophar the Zoologist, three men rebuked by God for their slanderous behavior (Job 42:7-8). Learn well from what God recorded about them in His Word, so you can be a faithful friend to others in their time of need.

Pray Job 22:22 over yourself and those for whom you stand guard as a faithful, prayerful watchman (Isaiah 62:6-7).

> "LORD, let _____ and me receive instruction from Your mouth and establish Your Words in our heart. Not for the purpose of being blessed, but to know You. In Your name, Jesus~"

SEPTEMBER 3

Please read Job 23. Job is speaking.

Meditate on verse 5.

> *I would learn the words which He would answer*
> *and perceive what He would say to me.*

Perhaps you are like Job, in a difficult place, desperately desiring God's favor, but feeling like nothing pleases Him. Job spoke about God in this chapter. You can speak to God with Job 23 as His faithful, prayerful watchman (Isaiah 62:6-7).

> "LORD, please forgive me if my complaint is rebellion. I need to talk to You. Your hand is heavy despite my groaning. Oh, let me find You and come to Your seat! I present my case before You and fill my mouth with arguments. I learn the words You would answer and perceive what You say to me. Would You contend with me by the greatness of Your power? No, surely You pay attention to me. The upright reason with You, and I am delivered forever from You, my Judge. Behold, I go forward, but You are not there, and backward, but I cannot perceive You. When You act on the left, I cannot behold You. You turn on the right; I cannot see You. But You know the way I take. When You have tried me, I shall come forth as gold. My foot holds fast to Your path. I keep Your way and do not turn aside. I have not departed from the command of Your lips. I treasure the Words of Your mouth more than my necessary food. But You are unique, and who can turn You? What Your soul desires, You do. For You perform what is appointed for me, and many such decrees are with You. Therefore, I am dismayed at Your presence. When I consider, I am terrified of You. God, You make my heart faint, and Almighty, You dismay me. But I am not silenced by the darkness, nor the deep gloom which covers me. Because of You, Jesus~"

SEPTEMBER 4

Please read Job 24. Job is speaking.

Meditate on verse 1.

> *Why are times not stored up by the Almighty, and why do those who know Him not see His days?*

"Why, LORD? Why do You not judge those who seize what does not belong to them? Why does it seem You pay no attention to those who suffer? Why are murderers allowed to kill? Why do adulterers get away with infidelity? Why is a woman who wants a baby not able to conceive? Why do widows suffer? Why is a valiant man brought low by Your power? Why, LORD? Why do You allow suffering? Why is my family suffering? Why am I suffering? Why have You removed Your hand from us? Why, LORD, why?"

Perhaps you have questions to ask God. Do not hesitate to ask Him why He allows you to go through tough times. Ask Him how He is going to get you through those times. Ask Him when He will let the suffering cease. Ask Him what He wants you to do while you wait. Ask Him who else is going through difficulties that you can encourage. Ask Him where this trial will take you in your relationship with Him. Talk to the LORD, a lot. I wish Job had continued talking to God in the midst of his suffering instead of talking more and more to his friends, therefore, sounding more and more like them.

Ask the LORD your questions starting with Job 24:1, keeping in mind, as His faithful, prayerful watchman, your times are in His hand (Psalm 31:15; Isaiah 62:6-7).

> *"LORD Almighty, why are times not stored up by You, and why do those who know You not see Your days? LORD, why is this so difficult? Please answer for the sake of Your name, Jesus~"*

SEPTEMBER 5

Please read Job 25. Bildad is speaking.

Meditate on verse 1.

> *Then Bildad the Shuhite answered...*

Bildad answered with four sarcastic, rhetorical questions (vs. 3-4). How does God answer those questions?

- LORD, is there any number to Your troops?

    I have commanded My consecrated ones; I have even called My mighty warriors. The LORD of hosts is mustering the army for battle.
    —ISAIAH 13:3A, 4B

- Upon whom does Your light not rise?

    The people who walk in darkness will see a great light.
    —ISAIAH 9:2A

- How can I be just with You?

    Having been justified by faith, we have peace with God through our LORD Jesus Christ.
    —ROMANS 5:1

- How can I be clean?

    The blood of Jesus His Son cleanses us from all sin.
    —1 JOHN 1:7B

Bildad viewed humans as worms and maggots (v. 6); God sees us as worth saving. Use the words from Job 25:2 and 6 to pray over yourself and those for whom you stand guard as a faithful, prayerful watchman (Isaiah 62:6-7).

> "LORD, thank You that dominion and awe belong to You and so do I. Establish Your peace with _____ . Thank You that we are not maggots and worms in Your sight. Because of Your name, Jesus~"

SEPTEMBER 6

Please read Job 26. Job is speaking.

Meditate on verses 1-4.

> *Then Job responded, "What a help you are to the weak! How you have saved the arm without strength! What counsel you have given to one without wisdom! What helpful insight you have abundantly provided! To whom have you uttered words? And whose spirit was expressed through you?"*

Job answered Bildad with his own sarcasm: "A lot of help you are!" And, he expressed concern that Bildad spoke from a demonic spirit because his words did not reflect God's Spirit (v. 4). Thankfully, we don't have to listen to any more of Bildad, Zophar, and Eliphaz's words; their discourses ended with Bildad's maggot and worm spiel (Job 25:6).

Most of Job's words in this chapter are about God (vs. 6-14). Pray Job 26:7-14 to God as His faithful, prayerful watchman (Isaiah 62:6-7).

> *"LORD, You stretch out the north over empty space and hang the earth on nothing. You wrap up the waters in Your clouds, and the cloud does not burst under them. You obscure the face of the full moon and spread Your cloud over it. You have inscribed a circle on the surface of the waters at the boundary of light and darkness. The pillars of heaven tremble and are amazed at Your rebuke. You quiet the sea with Your power, and by Your understanding, You shattered Rahab (pride and arrogance[1]). By Your breath the heavens are cleared; Your hand has pierced the fleeing serpent. Behold, these are the fringes of Your ways, and how faint a word we hear of You! But Your mighty thunder, who can understand? I am in awe of You, Jesus~"*

---

1. Retrieved from www.blueletterbible.org/lang/lexicon/lexicon.cfm?Strongs=H7293&t=NASB

SEPTEMBER 7

Please read Job 27. Job is speaking.

Meditate on verses 3-5.

> *For as long as life is in me and the breath of God is in my nostrils, my lips certainly will not speak unjustly, nor will my tongue mutter deceit. Far be it from me that I should declare you right; till I die I will not put away my integrity from me.*

Despite being physically wasted, financially ruined, grieved beyond belief, and incessantly badgered by friends, Job refused to sin with his tongue by agreeing with the words of Eliphaz, Zophar, and Bildad. Recall Satan's goal in persecuting Job was to get him to lose his integrity (Job 2:3, 9). Job stood firm in the midst of his fiery ordeal.

The enemy wants to put you in a tight place, so you will do anything to get out, even compromising the truth of God's Word. Satan tempts you to espouse false teaching for a quick fix and promises of prosperity. Do not fall for his tricks. God's goal is not to give us an easy life; His goal is for us to become more Christlike through life's trials.

As you go through the trials, fix your eyes on Jesus and pray Job 27:2-6 as His faithful, prayerful watchman (Isaiah 62:6-7).

> "God Almighty, as You live, even if You take away my rights and embitter my soul, as long as life is in me and Your breath is in my nostrils, do not let my lips speak unjustly nor my tongue mutter deceit. Far be it from me to declare false teaching as right. Till I die, do not let me put away my integrity from me.
> Help me hold fast my righteousness and not let it go.
> Let not my heart reproach any of my days.
> Because of Your righteousness, Jesus~"

SEPTEMBER 8

Please read Job 28. Job is speaking.

Meditate on verse 12.

> *But where can wisdom be found? And where is the place of understanding?*

When Job lost everything, it put him in the position to see what really matters. More important than obtaining precious jewels and metals is obtaining wisdom. People can mine silver and gold (v. 1). They can extract iron, copper, and sapphires from rocks (vs. 2, 6). But, where can a person obtain wisdom? Acquiring wisdom is more desirable than owning topaz and pearls, and all the gold in the world cannot buy it (v. 15, 18-19). By the end of the chapter, Job had the answer to his questions:

- Where can wisdom be found?
    "*The fear of God is wisdom*" (v. 28).
- Where is the place of understanding?
    "*To depart from evil is understanding*" (v. 28).

The LORD used Job's suffering to give him something more precious than gold: God's wisdom and understanding. That is God's purpose for us in the midst of the trials—to give us the opportunity to obtain His wisdom and understanding.

Thank the LORD for the trials and pray Job 28:23-28 as a faithful, prayerful watchman (Isaiah 62:6-7).

> "*LORD God, You understand the way of wisdom, and You know its place. You look to the ends of the earth and see everything under the heavens. You imparted weight to the wind and meted out the waters by measure. You set a limit to the rain and a course for the thunderbolt. You saw wisdom and declared it. You established wisdom and searched it out. LORD, let _____ and me fear You, for that is wisdom. Let us depart from evil, for that is understanding. In Your name, Jesus~*"

SEPTEMBER 9

Please read Job 29. Job is speaking.

Meditate on verse 2.

> *Oh, that I were as in months gone by, as in*
> *the days when God watched over me.*

Have you ever been in the midst of suffering, feeling like God has removed His hand of blessing and protection from you? Job was in that place, and he speaks longingly about the bygone days when he had good health and the respect of others. But he has been dealt quite a blow, and all that was good in his life has been stripped from him. At least he still has the LORD, but Job even feels like He is far away.

Thankfully we have Job's words for our difficult seasons in this life. Use his words to express things that are on your heart. Pray Job 29:2-6 and 14 over yourself and those for whom you stand guard as a faithful, prayerful watchman (Isaiah 62:6-7).

> *"LORD, oh that _____ and I were as in months gone by, as in the days when You watched over us, when Your lamp shone over our heads, and by Your light, we walked through darkness, as we were in the prime of our days, when Your friendship, God, was over our house. Even though it doesn't feel like it, LORD Almighty, You are yet with us. Please continue to bathe our steps in butter, and let the rock pour out for us streams of oil! LORD Jesus, we have put on Your righteousness, and it clothes us. Your justice is our robe and turban.*
> *Thank You, in Your name, Jesus~"*

SEPTEMBER 10

Please read Job 30. Job is speaking.

Meditate on verse 20.

> *I cry out to You for help, but You do not answer me;*
> *I stand up, and You turn Your attention against me.*

Even though his words are difficult to hear, it is good to see Job speaking to God again. It has been 13 chapters since we heard him pray (Job 17). Now, in gnawing pain, he accuses God of cruelly persecuting him (vs. 17, 21). He feels like God is shooting at him with a bow and arrow as people abhorrently spit on him (vs. 10-11). With his diseased flesh dying on his feverish bones, Job is certainly not experiencing prosperity as promised by Eliphaz, Bildad, and Zophar (vs. 15, 30; Job 5:17-27; 8:20-22; 11:15-19). And so, he cries to God in his pain and confusion. Hang in there with Job; chapter 38 is coming when God helps us make sense of this entire mess.

In the meantime, use Job's prayer to cry out to the LORD because there are times when it feels like God is using us for target practice. Thankfully, we can tell Him how we feel. Pray Job 30:20-23 as a faithful, prayerful watchman (Isaiah 62:6-7).

> *"LORD, I cry out to You for help, but You do not answer me; I stand up, and You turn Your attention against me. You have become cruel to me. With the might of Your hand, You persecute me. You lift me up to the wind and cause me to ride, and You dissolve me in a storm. For I know that You will bring me to death and to the house of meeting for all living. Even so, I trust You, Jesus~"*

SEPTEMBER 11

Please read Job 31. Job is speaking.

Meditate on verses 2 and 4.

> *And what is the portion of God from above or the heritage of the Almighty from on high? Does He not see my ways and number all my steps?*

Job sincerely tried to please God, and he was truly puzzled by the accusations of his friends and his treatment by God and man. His final defense was a list of "Ifs." "If I had done this, then I deserve this miserable life, but I haven't!" Thankfully, we have the book of Job because sometimes things happen that make us say, "What did I do to deserve that!?"

Use Job's words to present your case to the LORD by praying Job 31:2, 4-7, 14, 23-24, 28, and 35 as His faithful, prayerful watchman (Isaiah 62:6-7).

> *"LORD God Almighty, what is Your portion for me? What is Your heritage from on high? Do You not see my ways and number all my steps? If I have walked with falsehood and my foot has hastened after deceit, weigh me with accurate scales and know my integrity. If my step has turned from the way, or my heart followed my eyes, or if any spot has stuck to my hands, then judge me, LORD. What can I do when You arise, God? And when You call me to account, what will I answer You? Calamity from You is a terror to me, God, and because of Your majesty I can do nothing. I have not put my confidence in gold and called fine gold my trust. I have not denied You, God. Oh, that I had one to hear me! Behold, here is my signature; Almighty God, please answer me! Answer the indictment which my adversary has written! In Your name, Jesus~"*

SEPTEMBER 12

Please read Job 32. Elihu is speaking.

Meditate on verse 17.

> *I too will answer my share; I also will tell my opinion.*

So, we are not the only ones listening to this conversation between Job and his three friends. A young man named Elihu has been there all the time, silently listening to every word. Afraid to interject his opinion earlier, he is about to burst because of the crazy conversation he has heard. Interestingly, God does not reprove Elihu, like He did Eliphaz, Zophar, and Bildad for the things he says (Job 42:7). His words are recorded for eternity, so it will be a great treasure hunt for the next five days to see what God wants us to learn from him.

In the meantime, use the words from Job 32:8, 10, and 17-20 to pray over yourself and those for whom you stand guard as a faithful, prayerful watchman (Isaiah 62:6-7), asking God to make you wise in what you say.

> *"LORD Almighty, by Your Spirit and breath,*
> *give _____ and me understanding.*
> *When others listen to us, let us tell them what You think. Let us*
> *answer with Your Word rather than our opinions. We are full of*
> *words; Holy Spirit, constrain us! Behold, our bellies are like unvented*
> *wine; like new wineskins, we are about to burst. Let us speak, not*
> *to get relief, but let us open our lips and answer as You lead.*
> *In Your name, Jesus~"*

SEPTEMBER 13

Please read Job 33. Elihu is speaking.

Meditate on verses 16-17.

> *Then He (God) opens the ears of men and seals*
> *their instruction, that He may turn man aside*
> *from his conduct and keep man from pride.*

Trials not only give us wisdom and understanding (Job 28:20, 28); they make us aware of pride in our lives (v. 17). God hates pride, so a wise person recognizes it, uproots it, and stops its growth.

> *The fear of the LORD is to hate evil; pride and arrogance*
> *and the evil way and the perverted mouth, I hate.*
> —PROVERBS 8:13

> *For all that is in the world, the lust of the flesh and*
> *the lust of the eyes and the boastful pride of life, is*
> *not from the Father but is from the world.*
> —1 JOHN 2:16

So, when the Father loves you enough to let you go through a trial, use it to obtain His wisdom and remove the pride lurking within you.

Pray Job 33:14-18, 26, and 28 over yourself and those for whom you stand guard as a faithful, prayerful watchman (Isaiah 62:6-7).

> *"LORD God, indeed, You speak once or twice;*
> *let _____ and me notice it. When You speak in a*
> *dream, in a vision of the night, when sound sleep falls on us and we*
> *slumber in our beds, open our ears and seal our instruction that You*
> *may turn us aside from our conduct and keep us from pride. Keep*
> *back our souls from the pit and our life from passing over into Sheol*
> *(the place of the dead). I pray, God, please accept us that we may*
> *see Your face with joy. Restore our righteousness. Thank You for*
> *redeeming our souls from going to the pit. Our lives shall see the light.*
> *Because You are the Light, Jesus~"*

SEPTEMBER 14

Please read Job 34. Elihu is speaking.

Meditate on verses 14-15.

> *If He (God) should determine to do so, if He should gather to Himself His spirit and His breath, all flesh would perish together, and man would return to dust.*

The greatest temptation in the midst of suffering is to fix your eyes on yourself and your situation instead of fixing your eyes on the LORD. God used Elihu to turn Job's attention back to Him. Picture what is described in the meditation verses. If God were to suck in His breath and His spirit, we would all physically die. That is sobering.

> *Then the LORD God formed man of dust from the ground and breathed into his nostrils the breath of life, and man became a living being.*
> —GENESIS 2:7

> *Thus says God the LORD, Who created the heavens and stretched them out, Who spread out the earth and its offspring, Who gives breath to the people on it and spirit to those who walk in it, "I am the LORD."*
> —ISAIAH 42:5-6A

God is the LORD. He is LORD of all the living, and He is LORD of you and your situation. Trust Him and pray Job 34:31-32 over yourself and those for whom you stand guard as a faithful, prayerful watchman (Isaiah 62:6-7).

> *"LORD, _____ and I have borne chastisement. Do not let us offend anymore. Teach us what we do not see. If we have done iniquity, help us not do it again. For the sake of Your name, Jesus~"*

SEPTEMBER 15

Please read Job 35. Elihu is speaking.

Meditate on verses 9-10a.

> *Because of the multitude of oppressions, they cry out;*
> *they cry for help because of the arm of the mighty.*
> *But no one says, "Where is God my Maker?"*

Prayers offered in the midst of suffering are often begging God to fix the situation and to fix it fast. Do you ever pray to know God better in the midst of the suffering? What would happen if your prayers changed from "LORD, please fix this mess" to "LORD, keep me in this difficult time until I know You"?

God's wants us to know He is LORD.

> *"Therefore behold, I am going to make them know—This*
> *time I will make them know My power and My might,*
> *and they shall know that My name is the LORD."*
> —JEREMIAH 16:21

The purpose of suffering is for obtaining wisdom, removing pride, and knowing God (Job 28:28; 33:17; 35:9-10). Thank God for the trials of life, purposing to know Him more and more.

Pray Job 35:9-12 over yourself and those for whom you stand guard as a faithful, prayerful watchman (Isaiah 62:6-7).

> *"LORD, _____ and I cry out because*
> *of the multitude of oppressions, and we cry for help because*
> *of the arm of the mighty. In the midst of this difficulty, we*
> *cry out to know You, God our Maker, Who gives songs in*
> *the night and Who teaches us more than the beasts of the*
> *earth and makes us wiser than the birds of the heavens.*
> *As we cry out, please answer us! Please remove our evil pride!*
> *For the sake of Your name, Jesus~"*

SEPTEMBER 16

Please read Job 36. Elihu is speaking.

Meditate on verse 13.

> *But the godless in heart lay up anger; they do not cry for help when He binds them.*

Beware of the anger that often comes in the midst of a trial. Search your heart for stored up anger, crying out to God for help in releasing it.

> *Rest in the LORD and wait patiently for Him; do not fret because of him who prospers in his way, because of the man who carries out wicked schemes. Cease from anger and forsake wrath; do not fret; it leads only to evildoing.*
> —PSALM 37:7-8

Turning from anger is easier said than done. Give your trials and anger to the LORD and pray Job 36:13, 15-19 and 21-22 over yourself and those for whom you stand guard as a faithful, prayerful watchman (Isaiah 62:6-7).

> *"LORD, do not let _____ and me be godless in heart and lay up anger. LORD, we cry to You for help for You have bound us. Please deliver us in our affliction and open our ears to hear You in our oppression. You entice us from the mouth of distress and offer us a broad place with no constraint and set before us a table full of fatness. Do not let us be full of judgment on the wicked that we are blind to what You are doing. Do not let judgment and justice take hold of us. Do not let wrath entice us to scoffing, and do not let the greatness of the ransom turn us aside from You. Riches and all the forces of our strength will not keep us from distress. Do not let us turn to evil, preferring it to our affliction. God, You are exalted in Your power. There is no Teacher like You. Teach us in Your name, Jesus~"*

SEPTEMBER 17

Please Please read Job 37. Elihu is speaking.

Meditate on verse 14b.

Stand and consider the wonders of God.

This chapter concludes 37 days of tragedy, finger-pointing, questioning, defending, and trying to make sense of trials and suffering. Thankfully, Job 37 points us to God, giving us a perfect segue into the final chapters of Job where we hear God speak. Elihu tells Job to stand up and think about the wonderful works of God (v. 14). It is a good command for us as well. Life can be hard, and we can be tempted to crawl under the covers when faced with difficulties, adding depression to our struggles. Heed this command from Job 37:14. If you are physically able, get up; go outside; look at the clouds; look at the stars; look at the birds, the trees, the rocks, the flowers; and think about how amazingly wonderful God is. Think about God and pray Job 37:5, 11-14, 16, and 22-24 over yourself and those for whom you stand guard as a faithful, prayerful watchman (Isaiah 62:6-7).

> *"LORD God, You thunder with Your voice wondrously, doing great things which _____ and I cannot comprehend. You load the thick clouds with moisture, and You disperse the cloud with Your lightning. It changes direction, turning around by Your guidance, that it may do whatever You command it on the face of the inhabited earth. Whether for correction, or for Your world, or for lovingkindness, You cause it to happen. We will stand and consider Your wonders, God. You are perfect in knowledge. Around You is awesome majesty. You are the Almighty; LORD, let us find You! You are exalted in power. You will not do violence to justice and abundant righteousness. We fear You. Give us Your wise heart.*
> *In Your name, Jesus~"*

SEPTEMBER 18

Please read Job 38. The LORD is speaking.

Meditate on verses 4 and 21.

> *Where were you when I laid the foundation of the earth? Tell Me, if you have understanding. You know, for you were born then, and the number of your days is great!*

With reproving sarcasm, the LORD asks Job 29 questions, jolting him back to reality. Let God's Words give you the jolt you need to remember who you are and Who God is. Pray Job 38:2-12, 21, 25-27, 36, and 41 as a faithful, prayerful watchman (Isaiah 62:6-7).

> *"LORD, forgive me for darkening counsel by words without knowledge. Forgive me for attempting to instruct You. LORD, I need You to instruct me! Only You were there when You laid the foundation of the earth. You set its measurements and laid its cornerstone. I will sing with the morning stars and shout for joy because of You. You enclosed the sea with doors and made a cloud its garment and thick darkness its swaddling band. You place boundaries on it and set a bolt and doors, saying, 'Thus far you shall come, but no farther, and here shall your proud waves stop.' You command the morning and cause the dawn to know its place. The number of my days is so finite; help me, LORD! You have cleft a channel for the flood and a way for the thunderbolt, to bring rain on a land without people, on a desert without a man in it, to satisfy the waste and desolate land and make the seeds of grass to sprout. LORD, please rain on my wasted and desolate soul. Let Your life sprout in me! Put wisdom in my innermost being and give understanding to my mind. God, I need Your nourishment! I'm crying out to You!*
> *In Your name, Jesus~"*

SEPTEMBER 19

Please read Job 39. The LORD is speaking.

Meditate on verses 9a, 11a, and 12.

> *Will the wild ox consent to serve you? Will you trust him because his strength is great? Will you have faith in him that he will return your grain and gather it from your threshing floor?*

The LORD asks Job fourteen questions about eight different animals: mountain goats, deer, donkeys, oxen, ostriches, horses, hawks, and eagles. "What do you really know about any of these animals, Job, and would you put your faith and trust in them? Who knows everything about these animals, Job, and will you put your faith and trust in Me?"

In the midst of Job's misery, God uses creation to teach Job Who He is and to counter the counsel of Job's friends who encouraged Job to earn God's favor by doing righteous deeds like feeding the hungry and caring for orphans and widows (Job 8:5-6; 11:13-19; 22:7-9). God wants Job to recognize works-based, self-reliant religion is as effective as putting his faith in a wild ox.

In the midst of suffering, continue to put your faith in God, trusting His strength to carry you through the trial. Putting your faith in wild donkeys and wild oxen will only get you kicked.

Use the words from Job 39:11-12 and 17 to pray over yourself and those for whom you stand guard as a faithful, prayerful watchman (Isaiah 62:6-7).

> "LORD, _____ and I trust You because Your strength is great. We leave our labor to You. LORD, we have been threshed, but we have faith in You to gather and return what is on the threshing floor of our lives. Do not let us forget wisdom; please give us a share of understanding.
> In Your name, Jesus~"

SEPTEMBER 20

Please read Job 40. The LORD and Job are talking.

Meditate on verses 1-5.

> Then the LORD said to Job, "Will the faultfinder contend with the Almighty? Let him who reproves God answer it." Then Job answered the LORD and said, "Behold, I am insignificant; what can I reply to You? I lay my hand on my mouth. Once I have spoken, and I will not answer; even twice, and I will add nothing more."

Accused by God of being a reproving faultfinder, Job realizes he has said enough, and it is time to stop talking. God's few, well-placed words brought immediate humility to this man; whereas, his friends' multiple attempts to heap conviction on him were ineffective. Be mindful when you should let the Holy Spirit convict others instead of your own words.

Let God's well-placed Words work in your life and use Job 40:6-14 to ask for forgiveness as a faithful, prayerful watchman (Isaiah 62:6-7).

> "LORD, I hear You answering me out of the storm. I no longer presume to instruct You; forgive my past attempts to do so. Forgive me for trying to annul Your judgment. I'm sorry for condemning You, so I might be justified. I do not have an arm like You, God, and I cannot thunder with a voice like Yours. Forgive me for adorning myself with eminence and dignity and clothing myself with honor and majesty. Forgive me for pouring out my overflowing anger and looking on everyone who is proud, wanting to make them low. Forgive me for looking on everyone who is proud, wanting to humble them, treading down the wicked where they stand, to hide them in the dust and bind them in the hidden place. LORD, I confess that only Your right hand can save me. Please save me in Your name, Jesus~"

SEPTEMBER 21

Please read Job 41. The LORD is speaking.

Meditate on verse 1.

> *Can you draw out Leviathan with a fishhook?*
> *Or press down his tongue with a cord?*

What is your Leviathan? What is the trial, the persecution, the burden you battle? The LORD asks Job 16 questions about his Leviathan, this monster causing him so much pain and trouble. God asks Job what he can do about Leviathan. And the answer is, nothing; Job is not capable of fighting Leviathan; only God can fight him. And so, we get to the heart of *Job*; the purpose of the trials is to bring us to the place of acknowledging we are not God, and we are powerless to fight Leviathan waging war against us. Only God can deal with the terror, pride, and fear consuming us (vs. 14, 15, 25). Allow what God has allowed in your life to work its purpose, giving up your pride and the control to Him. Relief comes with surrender to the Almighty.

Pray Job 41:8-10 and 34 over yourself and those for whom you stand guard as a faithful, prayerful watchman (Isaiah 62:6-7).

> *"LORD, I lay my hand one more time on this Leviathan in order to hand him to You. I will remember the battle because I do not want to do it again. Behold, my expectation has been false, and I was laid low at the sight of Leviathan. There is no one fierce enough who dares to arouse him, so I give him to You because no one can stand before You, God. Remove Leviathan from _____ and me, for he is king over all the sons of pride. Do not let him be king any longer over us. In Your name, King Jesus~"*

SEPTEMBER 22

Please read Job 42. Job is speaking.

Meditate on verses 3-4.

> *"'Who is this that hides counsel without knowledge?'*
> *Therefore, I have declared that which I did not understand,*
> *things too wonderful for me, which I did not know.*
> *'Hear, now, and I will speak; I will ask You, and You instruct me.'"*

God asked Job 64 questions in chapters 38-41; Job was able to answer one of them: "Who is this that hides counsel without knowledge?" (Job 38:2; 42:3).

"It is I, LORD, I have declared things that I really don't understand; I have talked of things about which I really know nothing" (v. 3).

Job then uses God's words to humbly ask Him to teach him (Job 38:3; 42:4).

The purpose behind Job's suffering is complete when he not only hears God but sees Him and is able to pray for his friends instead of bitterly arguing with them (vs. 5, 10).

Job learned so much about himself, others, and God because of suffering. What a blessing!

> *Consider it all joy, my brethren, when you encounter various trials, knowing that the testing of your faith produces endurance. And let endurance have its perfect result, so that you may be perfect and complete, lacking in nothing.*
> —JAMES 1:2-4

Pray Job 42:2-6 as a faithful, prayerful watchman (Isaiah 62:6-7).

> *"LORD, I know You can do all things, and no purpose of Yours can be thwarted. I have declared that which I did not understand, things too wonderful for me, which I did not know. I'm sorry, LORD. Now, I will ask You. Please instruct me, LORD. I have heard You by the hearing of the ear, but now, my eye sees You; therefore, I retract, and I repent in dust and ashes. Please forgive me.*
> *In Your name, Jesus~"*

This fourth volume of *The Watchman on the Wall* began with Psalm 118:24:

> *This is the day which the LORD has made;
> let us rejoice and be glad in it.*

Then continued with *1 & 2 Thessalonians*, encouraging you to be on the lookout for references to the Day of the LORD and Christ's return. Perhaps you gained insight into the LORD's return as you read and prayed *Matthew, Thessalonians*, and *Acts*. From now until December 31, the remainder of the devotionals will come from books of the Bible that specifically refer to the return of Christ and the Day of the LORD. The LORD has much to show us, so lift your head and fix your eyes on Jesus, for your redemption is drawing near (Hebrews 12:2; Luke 21:28). This will be an amazing 100-day journey!

SEPTEMBER 23

Please read Psalm 2.

Meditate on verses 11-12.

> *Worship the LORD with reverence and rejoice with trembling. Do homage to the Son, that He not become angry, and you perish in the way, for His wrath may soon be kindled. How blessed are all who take refuge in Him!*

Psalm 2 is a Messianic psalm. In fact, Jesus is speaking in verse 7:

> *"I will surely tell of the decree of the LORD: He said to Me, 'You are My Son; today I have begotten You.'"*

Notice the references to Christ: Anointed (v. 2), King (v. 6), and Son (vs. 7, 12). Observe the contrasts between the kings of the earth and the LORD's King. The LORD laughs and scoffs at earthly kings plotting against Him (vs. 1-4).

Take comfort from this psalm. The world around you may be in an uproar, and the earthly kings and rulers may think they are in charge, but God has already enthroned King Jesus on His holy mountain (v. 6).

Use Psalm 2:10-12 to pray and worship the LORD as a faithful, prayerful watchman (Isaiah 62:6-7).

> *"LORD, let _____ and me show discernment and pay attention to Your warning. We worship You with reverence and rejoice with trembling. We give homage to You, Jesus. We do not want You to become angry with us. Do not let us perish in the way of Your wrath that will soon be kindled. Bless us as we take refuge in You. In Your name, Jesus~"*

SEPTEMBER 24

Please read Psalm 23.

Meditate on what the LORD does for you for the sake of His name (vs. 2-3):

> *He makes me lie down in green pastures.*
> *He leads me beside quiet waters.*
> *He restores my soul.*
> *He guides me in the paths of righteousness.*

Despite the evil all around him, David knew God would take care of him for His name's sake. If you are in relationship with Jesus Christ, you, too, do not need to be afraid because God is true to His name, which is now part of your name: Christian. Be confident in Christ that His goodness and lovingkindness will follow you all the days of your life.

Pray Psalm 23 over yourself and those for whom you stand guard as a faithful, prayerful watchman (Isaiah 62:6-7).

> *"LORD, You are _____ and my shepherd; we shall not want. Make us lie down in green pastures. Lead us beside quiet waters. Restore our souls. Guide us in the path of righteousness for Your name's sake. Even though we walk through the valley of the shadow of death, let us not fear evil, for You are with us. Your rod and staff comfort us. Please prepare a table before us in the presence of our enemies. Anoint our heads with oil; let our cups overflow. Surely Your goodness and lovingkindness will follow us all the days of our lives! Let us dwell in Your house, LORD, forever. Because we belong to You, Jesus~"*

SEPTEMBER 25

Please read Psalm 27.

Meditate on verse 4.

> *One thing I have asked from the LORD, that I shall seek: that I may dwell in the house of the LORD all the days of my life, to behold the beauty of the LORD and to meditate in His temple.*

David's greatest desire was to be in the presence of the LORD forever. Is that your heart's desire, to be with Jesus all the time for eternity? If you are a Christian, God has granted you that request. Hear what Jesus says to you:

> *"I will ask the Father, and He will give you another Helper, that He may be with you forever; that is the Spirit of truth, whom the world cannot receive, because it does not see Him or know Him, but you know Him because He abides with you and will be in you. I will not leave you as orphans; I will come to you. After a little while the world will no longer see Me, but you will see Me; because I live, you will live also. In that day you will know that I am in My Father, and you in Me, and I in you."*
> —JOHN 14:16-20

What a magnificent promise—God with you forever! With the Holy Spirit inside you, praise the LORD with Psalm 27:1-3 as a faithful, prayerful watchman (Isaiah 62:6-7).

> *"LORD, You are my light and my salvation; whom shall I fear? LORD, You are the defense of my life; whom shall I dread? When evildoers come upon me to devour my flesh, make my adversaries and my enemies stumble and fall. Though a host encamp against me, my heart will not fear; though war arise against me, in spite of this, I shall be confident. Because You are my confidence, Jesus~"*

SEPTEMBER 26

Please read Psalm 37.

Meditate on verses 12-13 and 18-20a.

> *The wicked plots against the righteous and gnashes at him with his teeth. The LORD laughs at him, for He sees his day is coming. The LORD knows the days of the blameless, and their inheritance will be forever. They will not be ashamed in the time of evil, and in the days of famine they will have abundance. But the wicked will perish.*

What a contrast between the righteous and the wicked! Both have a day coming, that day when the righteous receive their eternal inheritance in the LORD and the wicked eternally perish.

There is no need to fret because of the wicked; instead, pray for them to become righteous through the blood of Jesus, for without Christ, we are all wicked. As you pray for others to know Jesus, think about these contrasts in Psalm 37:

1. Evildoers will be cut off, but those who wait for the LORD will inherit the land (v. 9).
2. The man of peace will have posterity, but transgressors will be altogether destroyed (vs. 37-38).
3. The posterity of the wicked will be cut off, but the salvation of the righteous is from the LORD (vs. 38-39).

Pray Psalm 37:27 and 39 over those for whom you stand guard as a faithful, prayerful watchman who need to be made righteous in Jesus (Isaiah 62:6-7).

> "LORD, let _____ depart from evil and do good, so they will abide forever. Salvation of the righteous is from You, LORD. Please save and make _____ righteous, so You will be their strength in time of trouble.
> In Your name, Jesus~"

SEPTEMBER 27

Please read Psalm 39.

Meditate on verse 10a.

> *Remove Your plague from me.*

As I write this devotional, we are in the midst of a world-wide plague. By the time you read this devotional, hopefully, the plague will be a distant memory, but if not, this is a psalm to pray in the midst of the plague. And even if you are reading it after the plague is over, there is probably something plaguing you, for that is the nature of our human existence. Thankfully, we serve a Living God who has been sovereign over lots of plagues in the past and is sovereign over the one you experience today.

Pray His Words from Psalm 39:4-8 and 10-12 over your plague as a faithful, prayerful watchman (Isaiah 62:6-7).

> *"LORD, make me to know my end and what is the extent of my days. Let me know how transient I am. Behold You have made my days as handbreadths and my lifetime as nothing in Your sight; surely every human at their best is a mere breath. Surely every human walks about as a phantom; surely we make an uproar for nothing; we amass riches and do not know who will gather them. And now, LORD, for what do I wait? My hope is in You. Deliver me from all my transgressions; make me not the reproach of the foolish. Remove Your plague from me; because of the opposition of Your hand I am perishing. With reproofs You chasten a man for iniquity; You consume as a moth what is precious to him; surely everyone is a mere breath. Hear my prayer, O LORD, and give ear to my cry; do not be silent at my tears, for I am a stranger with You, a sojourner like my fathers. Let me sojourn with You, Jesus~"*

SEPTEMBER 28

Please read Psalm 41.

Meditate on verse 1.

> *How blessed is he who considers the helpless; the*
> *LORD will deliver him in a day of trouble.*

David had problems with enemies; they poured out wickedness upon him, speaking evil against him, lying to him, and wanting him dead (vs. 5-8). Despite such horrific opposition, David helped others less fortunate than himself (v. 1). Observe the benefits of caring for the helpless:

1. The LORD delivers you in a day of trouble (v. 1).
2. The LORD protects you and keeps you alive (v. 2).
3. God calls you blessed and does not give you over to the desire of your enemies (v. 2).
4. The LORD sustains you on your sickbed, restoring you to health (v.3).

What an amazing protection plan David had with God! Instead of feeling sorry for himself and being the helpless one, he helped others, trusting God to deliver him from his enemies.

Are you in the midst of a difficult situation? Care for the needs of others. As you do, God will miraculously take care of you.

Pray Psalm 41:1 and 11-13 over yourself and those for whom you stand guard as a faithful, prayerful watchman (Isaiah 62:6-7).

> *"LORD, bless _____ and me as we consider*
> *the helpless. Deliver us in a day of trouble. Make us pleasing*
> *to You; do not let our enemy shout in triumph over us. Uphold*
> *us in our integrity and set us in Your presence forever.*
> *We will bless You, LORD, from everlasting to everlasting.*
> *Amen and Amen."*

SEPTEMBER 29

Please read Psalm 42.

Meditate on verses 6a and 8.

> *O my God, my soul is in despair within me. The LORD will command His lovingkindness in the daytime, and His song will be with me in the night, a prayer to the God of my life.*

The psalmist was desperate. God brought him to a seemingly hopeless place, so he could only be brought out of his despair by the LORD. Just as the refreshing stream satisfies a parched and panting deer, only God could quench his desperate thirst (vs. 1-2).

What situation threatens to roll over you and those you love? Has the LORD allowed it, so your only hope is to hope in Him? Pray to the God of your life, using the words from Psalm 42:1-2, 5-6, 8, and 11 as a faithful, prayerful watchman (Isaiah 62:6-7).

> *"As the deer pants for the water brooks, so my soul pants for You, O God. My soul thirsts for You, the living God; I come and appear before You. My soul is in despair; it is disturbed within me. I hope in You, God, for I shall again praise You for the help of Your presence. O my God, my soul is in despair within me; therefore, I remember You! LORD, command Your lovingkindness in the daytime! Let Your song be with me in the night. This is my prayer to You, the God of my life! My soul is in despair and disturbed within me! I hope in You, God, for I shall yet praise You, the help of my countenance and my God. In Your name, Jesus~"*

SEPTEMBER 30

Please read Psalm 77.

Meditate on verses 1-2.

> *My voice rises to God, and I will cry aloud; my voice rises to God, and He will hear me. In the day of my trouble, I sought the LORD; in the night, my hand was stretched out without weariness; my soul refused to be comforted.*

Asaph was distressed when he wrote this psalm, so distressed, he could not sleep, and so troubled, his soul refused to be comforted (vs. 2, 4). Perhaps the LORD's lovingkindness had ceased; maybe His promises had come to an end (v. 8).

As Asaph's grieving eyelids refused to close, he remembered God's deeds:

1. Your way, O God, is holy (v. 13).
2. You are God who works wonders (v. 14).
3. You make known Your strength among the peoples (v. 14).
4. You redeem Your people by Your power (v. 15).

Sometimes it seems like God has withdrawn His compassion. If you are experiencing one of those times, recall God's faithfulness toward you and those you love. Remember His paths are in the mighty waters; you may not be able to see His footprints but know that they are there (v. 19).

Pray Psalm 77:1 and 19-20 over yourself and those for whom you stand guard as a faithful, prayerful watchman (Isaiah 62:6-7).

> *"My voice rises to You, God, and I will cry aloud! My voice rises to You, God; please hear me! Keep _____ and me on Your path in these mighty waters; let us see and know Your footprints. Lead us like Your flock.*
> *By Your hand, Jesus~"*

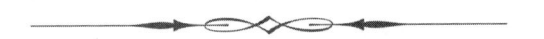

OCTOBER

*On your walls, O Jerusalem,
I have appointed watchmen;
All day and all night they
will never keep silent.
You who remind the LORD,
take no rest for yourselves;
And give Him no rest until He establishes
And makes Jerusalem a
praise in the earth.*
ISAIAH 62:6-7, NASB

OCTOBER 1

Please read Psalm 86.

Meditate on verse 3.

> *Be gracious to me, O LORD, for to You I cry all day long.*

Psalm 86 is a prayer of David. Perhaps you want to write your name next to David's in your Bible, making it your prayer, too.

David was afflicted, in need of God's help. Here are some of his prayer requests. Are they the same as yours?

- Preserve my soul and make it glad (vs. 2, 4).
- Give ear to my prayer and heed my supplications (v. 6).
- Teach me Your way, so I can walk in Your truth (v. 11).
- Unite my heart to fear Your name (v. 11).
- Turn to me and be gracious to me (vs. 3, 16).
- Grant me Your strength and save me (v. 16).
- Show me a sign for good (v. 17).
- Help me and comfort me (v. 17).

As a faithful, prayerful watchman (Isaiah 62:6-7), pray Psalm 86 as your personal prayer. Here are the first six verses to get you started:

> *"Incline Your ear, O LORD, and answer me, for I am afflicted and needy. Preserve my soul, for I am a Godly person. O my God, save me, Your servant, who trusts in You. Be gracious to me, O LORD, for to You I cry all day long. Make glad the soul of Your servant, for to You, O LORD, I lift up my soul. For You, LORD, are good, and ready to forgive, and abundant in lovingkindness to all who call upon You. Give ear, O LORD, to my prayer and give heed to the voice of my supplications! For the sake of Your name, Jesus~"*

OCTOBER 2

Please read Psalm 88.

Meditate on verse 10a.

Will You perform wonders for the dead?

The psalmist was in a low and depressed state. From the pit, he asked God six questions (vs. 10-12):

- Will You perform wonders for the dead?
- Will the departed spirits rise and praise You?
- Will Your lovingkindness be declared in the grave?
- Will Your faithfulness be declared in Abaddon (place of destruction)?
- Will Your wonders be made known in the darkness?
- Will Your righteousness be made known in the land of forgetfulness?

The answer to all of these questions is: "In Jesus Christ, YES!"

> *For the LORD Himself will descend from heaven with a shout, with the voice of the archangel and with the trumpet of God, and the dead in Christ will rise first. Then we who are alive and remain will be caught up together with them in the clouds to meet the LORD in the air, and so we shall always be with the LORD.*
> —1 THESSALONIANS 4:16-17

Perhaps you or those you love are in a dark place. Use the words from Psalm 88 to cry out to God then look up "because your redemption is drawing near" (Luke 21:28). Pray Psalm 88:1-2 and 13-14 over yourself and those for whom you stand guard as a faithful, prayerful watchman (Isaiah 62:6-7).

> *"O LORD, the God of my salvation, I have cried out by day and in the night before You. Let my prayer come before You; incline Your ear to my cry! O LORD, I cry to You for help, and in the morning, my prayer comes before You. O LORD, do not reject my soul and do not hide Your face from me. (Pour out your heart to God.) In Your name, Jesus~"*

OCTOBER 3

Please read Isaiah 2.

Meditate on verses 11-12.

> *The proud look of man will be abased, and the loftiness of man will be humbled, and the LORD alone will be exalted in that day. For the LORD of hosts will have a day of reckoning against everyone who is proud and lofty and against everyone who is lifted up, that he may be abased.*

The day of the LORD, the day of reckoning, the day when those who did not choose to apply the sacrifice of Christ as payment for their sins, will pay the consequences with eternal separation from God. Isaiah sets the stage in this chapter for why we need a Savior in order to escape God's day of reckoning.

The people in Isaiah's day were consumed with themselves, being influenced by the world instead of God. They had lots of stuff, and they worshiped their accomplishments instead of worshiping God. It is amazing how things have not changed in 2,700 years!

Verses 19-20 say men will go into caves and holes in the ground. They would rather hang out with moles and bats than humble themselves before God. Pride drives people to pathetic places.

God promises a day of reckoning against the proud, lofty, and lifted up (v. 12). Only those who are saved through faith in Jesus Christ will be reckoned as righteous on that day.

Pray Isaiah 2:5, 11, and 22 over yourself and those for whom you stand guard as a faithful, prayerful watchman (Isaiah 62:6-7).

> *"LORD, let _____ and me walk in Your light. Abase our proud look and humble our loftiness. LORD, You alone be exalted in our lives. Let us stop regarding and esteeming man, whose breath is in his nostrils. LORD, we regard and esteem You. In Your name, Jesus~"*

OCTOBER 4

Please read Isaiah 11.

Meditate on verses 10-11.

> *Then in that day, the nations will resort to the root of Jesse, who will stand as a signal for the peoples, and His resting place will be glorious. Then it will happen on that day, that the LORD will again recover the second time with His hand the remnant of His people who will remain from Assyria, Egypt, Pathros, Cush, Elam, Shinar, Hamath, and from the islands of the sea.*

Isaiah 11 describes Jesus (vs. 1-5) and what the world will be like under His rule (vs. 6-16). Christ will reign in righteousness, His unshakeable Kingdom characterized by peace. Israel will be recovered by the LORD's hand, and the earth will be full of the knowledge of the LORD. What a glorious day that will be!

As you wait for that day, the day of Christ's return, you are to become more like Him. Think about His characteristics from verse 2. Ask the LORD to increase in you: wisdom, understanding, counsel, strength, knowledge, and the fear of Him, praying Isaiah 11:2 and 9 over yourself and those for whom you stand guard as a faithful, prayerful watchman (Isaiah 62:6-7).

> *"LORD, let Your Spirit rest on _____ and me, the spirit of wisdom and understanding, the spirit of counsel and strength, the spirit of knowledge and the fear of the LORD. The earth will be full of the knowledge of You. Please fill us with that knowledge. In Your name, Jesus~"*

OCTOBER 5

Please read Isaiah 13.

Meditate on verses 6, 9, and 13.

> *Wail, for the day of the LORD is near! It will come as destruction from the Almighty. Behold, the day of the LORD is coming, cruel, with fury and burning anger, to make the land a desolation, and He will exterminate its sinners from it. Therefore, I will make the heavens tremble, and the earth will be shaken from its place at the fury of the LORD of hosts in the day of His burning anger.*

Let there be no doubt the day of the LORD is coming. Let there be no doubt the day of the LORD will be horrific for those who do not know Jesus as Savior, for God promises to exterminate the sinners from the land (v. 9). God describes His day of judgment as cruel, full of His fury and burning anger (vs. 9, 13).

Oh, how we need a Savior! Thanks be to God we have a Savior through Jesus Christ our LORD! Are you willing to share that Good News before Isaiah 13 is fulfilled?

Pray Isaiah 13:2-3 over yourself and those for whom you stand guard as a faithful, prayerful watchman (Isaiah 62:6-7).

> *"LORD, let _____ and me lift up Your standard on the bare hill and raise our voice to tell others about You. Let us wave our hand that others may see to enter the door of Your Kingdom. LORD, command us as Your consecrated ones. Call us as Your mighty warriors. We exult in Your name, Jesus~"*

OCTOBER 6

Please read Isaiah 19.

Meditate on verses 16 and 19.

> *In that day the Egyptians will become like women, and they will tremble and be in dread because of the waving of the hand of the LORD of hosts, which He is going to wave over them. In that day there will be an altar to the LORD in the midst of the land of Egypt, and a pillar to the LORD near its border.*

The LORD is burdened for Egypt, so burdened He dries up their water, removes their crops, fish, and manufacturing, and makes their leaders and wisest men stupid fools (vs. 5-11). God removes everything and everyone the Egyptians depend on, so they will depend on Him.

God has ways of getting our attention, doesn't He? What is He doing in our world right now to get our attention?

2,700 years ago, God spoke about a day when Egypt would need a Savior and a Champion to deliver them (v. 20). That day has come for Egypt and the rest of the world. Does the LORD have your attention?

Pray Isaiah 19:20-22 and 24 over yourself and those for whom you stand guard as a faithful, prayerful watchman (Isaiah 62:6-7).

> *"LORD, I cry to You because of our oppressors!*
> *_____ and I need a Savior and a Champion.*
> *We need You to deliver us. LORD, make Yourself known to us, so we will know You in that day. We worship You with sacrifice and offering; we make a vow to You and perform it. LORD, You are striking but healing us, so we will return to You. LORD, please respond to us and heal us! LORD, make us a blessing in the midst of the earth. In Your name, Jesus~"*

OCTOBER 7

Please read Isaiah 24.

Meditate on verses 21-23.

> *So, it will happen in that day, that the LORD will punish the host of heaven on high and the kings of the earth on earth. They will be gathered together, like prisoners in the dungeon, and will be confined in prison, and after many days, they will be punished. Then the moon will be abashed and the sun ashamed, for the LORD of hosts will reign on Mount Zion and in Jerusalem, and His glory will be before His elders.*

Isaiah 24 gives a vivid description of God's coming judgment on those who do not know Him as LORD and Savior. Prior to Christ's return, the earth is polluted and devoured by a curse because of its inhabitants (vs. 5-6). The LORD promises to completely despoil the earth, scatter its inhabitants, and not give preferential treatment to anyone because of their former rank or status (vs. 1-4). God will put an end to the world's party and fill the earth with songs glorifying the Righteous One (vs. 7-16).

Do you see any of Isaiah 24 starting to take place? What a great chapter to share with people about the coming day of the LORD! The only way to escape His wrath is through a relationship with Jesus Christ.

Pray Isaiah 24:16a over yourself and those for whom you stand guard as a faithful, prayerful watchman (Isaiah 62:6-7).

> *"LORD, on that day, let _____ and me be singing this song: 'Glory to the Righteous One.' In Your name, Jesus~"*

OCTOBER 8

Please read Isaiah 27.

Meditate on verse 1.

> *In that day the LORD will punish Leviathan the fleeing serpent, with His fierce and great and mighty sword, even Leviathan the twisted serpent, and He will kill the dragon who lives in the sea.*

"In that day," that day of the LORD, God will destroy the serpent—the dragon which is Satan (Revelation 12:9; 20:2, 10). In that day, God will forgive and restore Israel and gather people from the nations to worship Him (vs. 12-13).

It is exciting to read and think about end time prophecies. It is also sobering because like the dragon, the end of time will be a day of destruction for those who do not know the LORD.

Who do you know who needs to know Jesus, so they can be in the gathering of those who will worship Him? Do not hesitate to tell them the Good News of Jesus, for they must hear and believe before it is too late.

> *So faith comes from hearing, and hearing by the Word of Christ.*
> —ROMANS 10:17

As a faithful, prayerful watchman (Isaiah 62:6-7), pray Isaiah 27:5 and 9 over those who need Jesus, asking God to give you the opportunity to tell them how to have peace with Him.

> *"LORD, let _____ rely on You for protection. Let them make peace with You. Let them make peace with You. Let them come to You to have their iniquity forgiven because You paid the full price for pardoning their sin. By Your blood, Jesus~"*

OCTOBER 9

Please read Isaiah 34.

Meditate on verses 1a, 2, 5, and 8a.

> *Draw near, O nations, to hear; and listen, O peoples!*
> *For the LORD'S indignation is against all the nations, and His wrath against all their armies; He has utterly destroyed them; He has given them over to slaughter. For My sword is satiated in heaven; behold it shall descend for judgment upon Edom and upon the people whom I have devoted to destruction. For the LORD has a day of vengeance...*

Isaiah 34 describes God's day of vengeance, a time when His indignation and wrath are poured out on all of mankind who do not know Him as Savior. God hates it when people, like Edom (Esau), despise the birthright He gives them, their birthright to become a child of His, selling it for a bowl of the world's "red stuff" (Genesis 25:30-34; Malachi 1:3). People who choose the way of the world rather than the way of Jesus Christ are forewarned they will be utterly destroyed and given over to slaughter (v. 2).

Yet, God desires for all men to be saved and come to knowledge of the truth (1 Timothy 2:3-4). Salvation is why the LORD invites all people to hear and listen (v. 1).

As a faithful, prayerful watchman (Isaiah 62:6-7), pray Isaiah 34:1 and 16 over the "Edoms" in your life who need salvation from the coming wrath of God.

> *"LORD, please let _____ draw near to hear and listen. May they seek and read from Your Book, LORD. Holy Spirit, gather them to You!*
> *In Your name, Jesus~"*

OCTOBER 10

Please read Isaiah 35.

Meditate on verse 4.

> *Say to those with anxious heart, "Take courage, fear not. Behold, your God will come with vengeance; the recompense of God will come, but He will save you."*

A day is coming when the wilderness and desert will have pools and springs of water and blossom profusely (vs. 1-2). A road, the Highway of Holiness, will be there (v. 8). There the redeemed will walk with everlasting joy radiating from their faces (vs. 9-10).

What a breath of fresh air in the midst of God's day of vengeance! The day of the LORD is a day of rejoicing for those who know Him. If that day were today, whom do you know that would not be walking the Highway of Holiness? Pray for them to ask Christ, the Living Water, to come and forever change their desert of a life (v. 1, 5; John 7:38).

Pray Isaiah 35:5-6 and 10 over those for whom you stand guard as a faithful, prayerful watchman (Isaiah 62:6-7).

> *"LORD, _____ is spiritually blind, deaf, lame, and mute. Let Your waters break forth in the wilderness of their life. Open their eyes and unstop their ears. Let them leap like a deer and shout for joy. LORD, ransom them, so they will return to You with joyful shouting. May everlasting joy be upon their heads. Let them find gladness and joy. Let sorrow and sighing flee away from them. In Your name, Jesus~"*

OCTOBER 11

Please read Isaiah 61.

Meditate on verses 1-2a.

> *The Spirit of the LORD GOD is upon me because the LORD has anointed me to bring good news to the afflicted; He has sent me to bind up the brokenhearted, to proclaim liberty to captives and freedom to prisoners, to proclaim the favorable year of the LORD and the day of vengeance of our God.*

This chapter is filled with good news. The day of the LORD, the day of God's vengeance, is a great day for those who belong to Him. It is a day when God turns hopeless situations into victories: freedom for prisoners, comfort for those who mourn, rising up from former devastations, a double portion replacing shame and humiliation, everlasting joy... (vs. 1-7).

What does the day of the LORD hold for you and those you love? Will it be a day of mourning or a day of rejoicing?

As a faithful, prayerful watchman (Isaiah 62:6-7), pray Isaiah 61:3 and 10 over those who need Jesus as their LORD and Savior.

> *"LORD, grant comfort to _____ who is mourning. Give them a garland instead of ashes, the oil of gladness instead of mourning, the mantle of praise instead of a spirit of fainting. Let them be called 'oaks of righteousness,' the planting of the LORD, that You may be glorified. Let them rejoice greatly in You, LORD. Let their soul exult in You, my God. Clothe them with garments of salvation. Wrap them with Your robe of righteousness, as a bridegroom decks himself with a garland, and as a bride adorns herself with her jewels.*
> *In Your name, Jesus~"*

OCTOBER 12

Please read Ezekiel 13.

Meditate on verses 3 and 5.

> *Thus says the LORD GOD, "Woe to the foolish prophets who are following their own spirit and have seen nothing. You have not gone up into the breaches, nor did you build the wall around the house of Israel to stand in the battle on the day of the LORD."*

Ezekiel prophesied 600 years before Peter wrote his letter to believers, but their words are interestingly similar and accurately describe false teachers today.

> *But false prophets also arose among the people, just as there will also be false teachers among you, who will secretly introduce destructive heresies, even denying the Master who bought them, bringing swift destruction upon themselves.*
> —2 PETER 2:1

Be mindful, there have always been false teachers, inspired by Satan, the father of lies, who whispers, "Did God really say...?"; he continues to plant the same seed of doubt he planted in Adam and Eve 6,000 years ago (Genesis 3:1). A teacher is false if they teach contrary to God's Word, filtering it through a sieve, choosing what they prefer not to apply to their lives and those of their followers. False teachers—their eternal judgment and destruction awaits them on the day of the LORD (2 Peter 2:3-9).

Let God's Word fill the breaches in your life and the lives of those you love; let it build strong walls around your life, so the lies of Satan cannot destroy you (v. 5).

As a faithful, prayerful watchman (Isaiah 62:6-7), pray Ezekiel 13:22 over yourself to speak God's Words accurately.

> *"LORD, do not let me dishearten the righteous with falsehood when You did not cause them grief. Help me encourage the wicked to turn from their wicked way and preserve their life. In Your name, Jesus~"*

OCTOBER 13

Please read Ezekiel 30.

Meditate on verses 1-3.

> *The Word of the LORD came again to me saying, "Son of man, prophesy and say, 'Thus says the LORD GOD, "Wail, 'Alas for the day!'" For the day is near; even the day of the LORD is near; it will be a day of clouds, a time of doom for the nations.'"*

Observe what God declares He will do, so people will know He is the LORD.

- "The pride of her power will come down. They will be desolate in the midst of the desolated lands. And they will know that I AM the LORD" (vs. 6-8).
- "I will destroy the idols. I will pour out my wrath on Sin, the stronghold of Egypt. And they will know that I AM the LORD" (vs. 13, 15, 19).
- "I will strengthen the arms of the king of Babylon and put My sword in his hand, and I will break the arms of Pharaoh; the arms of Pharaoh will fail. Then they will know that I AM the LORD" (vs. 24-25).
- "When I scatter the Egyptians among the nations and disperse them among the land, then they will know that I AM the LORD" (v. 26).

What is God doing in your day, so you know He is the LORD? He wants people to know He is LORD before the coming of that day of doom for those who do not know Him. As a faithful, prayerful watchman (Isaiah 62:6-7), pay attention to the LORD and pray Ezekiel 30:19 over those who need to know Him.

> *"LORD, You will execute judgment on Egypt and all who do not know You. Please let _____ know You are the LORD before it is too late. In Your name, Jesus~"*

OCTOBER 14

Please read Ezekiel 38.

Meditate on verse 18.

> *"It will come about on that day, when Gog comes against the land of Israel," declares the LORD GOD, "that My fury will mount up in My anger."*

In the last days, God uses Gog to bring an army from many nations against Israel, showing His majesty to the nations of the world (vs. 14-16). Picture the battle. Gog's army arrives, and the LORD's fury mounts up (v. 18). In His zeal and blazing wrath, there is a great earthquake in the land of Israel (v. 19). The fish, birds, beasts, all creeping things, and all humans on the face of the earth shake at God's presence (v. 20). Mountains are thrown down; pathways collapse, and every wall falls to the ground (v. 20). The LORD casts His sword against Gog and judges him with blood and pestilence, raining down hail, fire, and brimstone on Gog and his troops (vs. 21-22). In all of this God magnifies Himself, shows Himself holy, and makes Himself known to the nations, so they know without a doubt, He is the LORD (vs. 22-23).

A day is coming when everyone will know God is the LORD. Pray for God to magnify Himself in your life and the lives of those for whom you stand guard as a faithful, prayerful watchman (Isaiah 62:6-7), using the words from Ezekiel 38:23.

> *"LORD, You will magnify Yourself, sanctify Yourself, and make Yourself known in the sight of many nations, and they will know that You are the LORD. LORD, magnify Yourself, sanctify Yourself, and make Yourself known in _____ and me. Let us never forget that You are the LORD. In Your name, LORD Jesus~"*

OCTOBER 15

Please read Daniel 1.

Meditate on verse 8.

> *But Daniel made up his mind that he would not defile himself with the king's choice food or with the wine which he drank, so he sought permission from the commander of the officials that he might not defile himself.*

The year was 605 BC, and the first wave of exiles was forced-marched from Jerusalem to Babylon. These exiles were Jerusalem's best: smart, good-looking, strong, and capable of serving in King Nebuchadnezzar's court (v. 4). With royal blood flowing through their own veins (v. 3), these young men were made eunuchs by the Babylonians; their family tree ended with them (Isaiah 39:5-7 KJV).

Despite such a dismal future, Daniel, about 15-years-old, made the choice to stay true to his Godly values, rather than give-in to a Babylonian lifestyle. With his mind set like concrete, he refused to defile himself (v. 8). Daniel's bold obedience to God will bring a cascade of blessings for the rest of his life.

As you read this amazing book, write a list of Daniel characteristics. Ask God to make you and those you love like this Godly man.

Pray Daniel 1:8-9, 17, and 20-21 over yourself and those for whom you stand guard as a faithful, prayerful watchman (Isaiah 62:6-7).

> *"LORD, please help _____ and me make up our minds that we will not defile ourselves with the things of this world. As we do, grant us favor and compassion in the sight of our bosses. God give us knowledge and intelligence in every branch of literature and wisdom. Let us even understand all kinds of visions and dreams. In every matter of wisdom and understanding about which we are consulted, make us ten times better than all others. Let us faithfully continue in Your name, Jesus~"*

OCTOBER 16

Please read Daniel 2.

Meditate on verse 5.

> *The king replied to the Chaldeans, "The command from me is firm: if you do not make known to me the dream and its interpretation, you will be torn limb from limb and your houses will be made a rubbish heap."*

What a demanding boss! Have you ever worked for someone like this guy? King Nebuchadnezzar not only wanted his dream interpreted; he wanted his wise men to tell him what he dreamt. Unbelievable!

Notice Daniel's calm demeanor in this horrible situation. He responded with discretion and discernment (v. 14). He asked appropriate questions (v. 15). He bravely requested more time from the king (v. 16). He told his prayer partners, and they asked for "compassion from the God of heaven concerning this mystery" (vs. 17-18). God answered those prayers, revealing to Daniel the dream and its meaning—amazing!

When Daniel was ushered into the king's presence, he boldly declared: "No wise men, conjurers, magicians, nor diviners were able to declare the dream. However, there is a God in heaven who reveals mysteries" (vs. 27-28).

Daniel turned the attention of this pagan king to Almighty God, so that even Nebuchadnezzar acknowledged God is a "God of gods, Lord of kings, and revealer of mysteries" (v. 47).

Pray for God to make you and those you love a brave, discerning "Daniel" by praying Daniel 2:14, 18, and 47 as a faithful, prayerful watchman (Isaiah 62:6-7).

> *"LORD, help _____ and me reply to others with discretion and discernment. God of heaven, we need Your compassion concerning this mystery so that we will not be destroyed. You are God of gods and LORD of kings and revealer of mysteries. We trust in Your name, Jesus~"*

OCTOBER 17

Please read Daniel 3.

Meditate on these three words from verse 18.

But if not...

If you grew up learning Bible stories, Shadrach, Meshach, Abed-nego, and the fiery furnace was probably one of them. In 1940, the British knew this story and exactly what "But if not" meant. Those words were the rallying cry for the people of England to send every boat possible to rescue Allied troops surrounded by Hitler's forces at Dunkirk in May of that year. The troops were miraculously saved when more than 300,000 men refused to bow and surrender to the Nazis and their evil ideology. Just like the three brave Hebrew young men, they did not compromise their convictions.

Today's temptations to compromise Biblical truths are shockingly similar to the times of Daniel and his friends. "Would it hurt to change God's Word on this issue?" When you are threatened for taking a stand for Christ and His Word, finish the sentence, "But if not..." with an unwavering declaration to remain firm for God.

Pray Daniel 3:16-18 and 28 over yourself and those for whom you stand guard as a faithful, prayerful watchman (Isaiah 62:6-7).

"LORD, give _____ and me wisdom for when we do not need to give an answer concerning a matter. God, we serve You, and we know You are able to deliver us from this fiery situation and out of the hand of _____. But even if You do not, let it be known we are not going to serve the gods of this world or worship any golden image or opportunity. Blessed are You, our God! Deliver us! We put our trust in You! In Your name, Jesus~"

OCTOBER 18

Please read Daniel 4.

Meditate on verses 30-31.

> *The king reflected and said, "Is this not Babylon the great, which I myself have built as a royal residence by the might of my power and for the glory of my majesty?" While the word was in the king's mouth, a voice came from heaven, saying, "King Nebuchadnezzar, to you it is declared: sovereignty has been removed from you."*

Have you ever been full of yourself, content and prosperous, believing Satan's lies that you are an accomplished, self-made individual? King Nebuchadnezzar was in that disastrously deluded place, when God spoke into his pride, sentencing him to seven years as a wild, grass-grazing beast (vs. 32-33). Looking up to heaven and coming to his senses, Nebuchadnezzar finally honored the LORD Most High (v. 34). How might life have been different if he turned from his pride years earlier?

Learn from Nebuchadnezzar's arrogant mistakes, humbly asking God to reveal pride in your life.

Pray Daniel 4:34-37 over yourself and those for whom you stand guard as a faithful, prayerful watchman (Isaiah 62:6-7).

> *"LORD, raise _____ and my eyes to heaven and let reason return to us. I bless You, Most High, and praise and honor You who lives forever, for Your dominion is an everlasting dominion, and Your kingdom endures from generation to generation. All the inhabitants of the earth are accounted as nothing, but You do according to Your will in the host of heaven and among the inhabitants of earth. No one can ward off Your hand or say to You, 'What have You done?' I praise, exalt, and honor You, King of heaven, for all Your works are true and Your ways just, and You are able to humble those who walk in pride. I come humbly in Your name, Jesus~"*

OCTOBER 19

Please read Daniel 5.

Meditate on verses 22-23.

> *Yet you, his son, Belshazzar, have not humbled your heart, even though you knew all this, but you have exalted yourself against the LORD of heaven; and they have brought the vessels of His house before you, and you and your nobles, your wives and your concubines have been drinking wine from them; and you have praised the gods of silver and gold, of bronze, iron, wood and stone, which do not see, hear or understand. But the God in whose hand are your life-breath and all your ways, you have not glorified.*

Belshazzar irreverently praised false gods while consuming wine from goblets stolen from the temple in Jerusalem (vs. 1-4). Suddenly, fingers appeared, writing a message for this arrogant king (v. 5). Faithful Daniel is once again brought in to provide the interpretation, telling Belshazzar God had put an end to his kingdom because Belshazzar was found deficient (vs. 13, 25-28). That very night, Belshazzar was killed, and the kingdom of Babylon divided between the Medes and Persians and ruled by King Darius (vs. 28, 30-31).

Contrast the deficient, arrogant Belshazzar with Daniel. Daniel is described as having illumination, insight, knowledge, an extraordinary spirit, and extraordinary wisdom (vs. 11-12, 14). Before interpreting the handwriting on the wall, he unashamedly declares: "The Most High God is ruler over the realm of mankind, and He sets over it whomever He wishes" (v. 21).

Pray for God to make you and those you love like Daniel. Pray Daniel 5:11-12 as a faithful, prayerful watchman (Isaiah 62:6-7).

> *"Holy God, Your Spirit is in _____ and me. Let Your illumination, insight, and wisdom be in us. Because of Your extraordinary Spirit, let knowledge, insight, interpretation of dreams, explanation of enigmas, and solving of difficult problems be found in us. For the glory of Your name, Jesus~"*

OCTOBER 20

Please read Daniel 6.

Meditate on verse 16b.

> *Your God whom you constantly serve will Himself deliver you.*

Approximately 66 years passed between Daniel 1 and 6. This familiar story of Daniel and the lions' den happened when Daniel was in his 80's; he faithfully served in government jobs his entire adult life. Working for pagan bosses in a land that was not his home, Daniel did not compromise His Godly values. He was so faithful the only thing he could be found guilty of was being faithful (v. 5).

This chapter contains many of Daniel's Godly characteristics. Treasure hunt the chapter for qualities you want the LORD to make permanent in your life and the lives of those you love.

Pray Daniel 6:3-4, 10, 16, 23, and 26-28 over yourself and those for whom you stand guard as a faithful, prayerful watchman (Isaiah 62:6-7).

> *"LORD, help _____ and me distinguish ourselves because we possess Your extraordinary Spirit. Make us faithful; let no negligence or corruption be found in us. No matter what happens keep us kneeling, praying, and giving thanks before You, God. May we constantly serve You! God deliver us from evil.*
> *Let no injury be found on us because we trust in You, God.*
> *Let everyone fear and tremble before You, God, for You are the living God, enduring forever. Your kingdom is one which will not be destroyed, and Your dominion will be forever. You deliver and rescue and perform signs and wonders in heaven and on earth.*
> *You have also delivered _____ from the power of _____.*
> *Please let us enjoy success.*
> *In Your name, Jesus~"*

OCTOBER 21

Please read Daniel 7.

Meditate on verse 13.

> *I kept looking in the night visions, and behold, with the clouds of heaven One like a Son of Man was coming, and He came up to the Ancient of Days and was presented before Him.*

As you continue praying Daniel, followed by Revelation in a few weeks, you have the privilege of reading descriptions of end time visions God gave Daniel and John. Keep your focus on the main character in both books. Some of His names are: Ancient of Days, Highest One, King of Kings, and LORD of LORDS (vs. 13, 27; Revelation 19:16). He controls the events described in both books, so there is no need to fear the future.

Bible scholars differ on which kingdoms are represented by the four great beasts in the Daniel 7 vision. We believe the kingdoms parallel the four kingdoms represented in Nebuchadnezzar's statue vision: Babylon, Medo-Persia, Greece, and Rome (Daniel 2). The Precept upon Precept Bible studies of *Daniel* and *Revelation* are excellent for learning more.[1]

For now, fix your eyes on Jesus and pray Daniel 7:13-14 and 27 as a faithful, prayerful watchman (Isaiah 62:6-7).

> *"Jesus, Son of Man, dominion, glory, and a kingdom has been given to You by the Ancient of Days, that all the peoples, nations, and people of every language might serve You. Your dominion is an everlasting dominion which will not pass away, and Your kingdom is one which will not be destroyed. I look forward to the day when the sovereignty, the dominion, and the greatness of all the kingdoms under the whole heaven will be given to Your people, the saints of the Highest One. Your kingdom will be an everlasting kingdom, and all the dominions will serve and obey You.*
> *Let _____ become Your saint before it is too late.*
> *In Your name, Highest One, Jesus~"*

---

1. shop.precept.org/pages/precept-upon-precept

OCTOBER 22

Please read Daniel 8.

Meditate on verses 16 and 19.

> *And I heard the voice of a man between the banks of Ulai, and he called out and said, "Gabriel, give this man an understanding of the vision." He said, "Behold, I am going to let you know what will occur at the final period of the indignation, for it pertains to the appointed time of the end."*

Thankfully, God lets us glimpse into the future, for it gives us confidence as we see the world falling apart, that things are actually coming together for that glorious day when Christ the Cornerstone fulfills the statue vision in Daniel 2 (Acts 4:11).

> *Inasmuch as you saw that a stone was cut out of the mountain without hands and that it crushed the iron, the bronze, the clay, the silver and the gold, the great God has made known to the king what will take place in the future, so the dream is true, and its interpretation is trustworthy.*
> —DANIEL 2:45

Keep in mind these are appointed times ordained by the Commander of the host, the Commander of your life (vs. 11, 19). So, do not fear when you see the Prince of princes being opposed because He will break the opposer; you have God's Word on it (v. 25).

Pray Daniel 8:16 and 25 over yourself and those for whom you stand guard as a faithful, prayerful watchman (Isaiah 62:6-7).

> *"LORD, give _____ and me an understanding of the visions in Your Word. Do not let us be deceived by Satan's shrewdness. Do not let his influence cause deceit to succeed in our lives. Do not let us be like him, magnifying ourselves in our heart. Do not let us be at ease so he is able to destroy us. Prince of princes, we look forward to the day the opposer is broken. In Your name, Jesus~"*

OCTOBER 23

Please read Daniel 9.

Meditate on verses 2-3.

> *I, Daniel, observed in the books the number of the years which was revealed as the Word of the LORD to Jeremiah the prophet for the completion of the desolations of Jerusalem, namely, seventy years. So, I gave my attention to the LORD God to seek Him by prayer and supplications, with fasting, sackcloth, and ashes.*

Daniel read God's Word given to the prophet Jeremiah. You can read those same Words in Jeremiah 25:8-14. Observing God's Word caused Daniel to pay attention to God, which made Daniel aware of his own sinfulness, bringing him to a place of confession and prayer (vs. 3-19). During his intense prayer time, Gabriel appeared and gave Daniel a foundational prophecy for understanding end times (vs. 24-27) and revealed an incredible truth to Daniel:

> *He (Gabriel) gave me instruction and talked with me and said, "O Daniel, I have now come forth to give you insight with understanding. At the beginning of your supplications the command was issued, and I have come to tell you, for you are highly esteemed; so give heed to the message and gain understanding of the vision.*
> —DANIEL 9:22-23

When Daniel began praying, God told Gabriel to go and give Daniel insight with understanding into the message and vision. God does the same for you as you observe His Word, paying attention to and talking to Him.

Pray Daniel 9:19 over yourself and those for whom you stand guard as a faithful, prayerful watchman (Isaiah 62:6-7).

> *"O LORD, hear! O LORD, forgive! O LORD, listen and take action! For Your own sake, O my God, do not delay because _____ and I are called by Your name, Jesus-"*

OCTOBER 24

Please read Daniel 10.

Meditate on verse 12.

> *Then he said to me, "Do not be afraid, Daniel, for from the first day that you set your heart on understanding this and on humbling yourself before your God, your words were heard, and I have come in response to your words."*

Contrast Daniel's anguish and lack of strength with the man in linen's care for Daniel. Daniel was at the end of himself, yet despite being so weak and scared, Daniel set his mind to understand God's message. God sent the man in linen in response to Daniel's prayers, strengthening and giving him even more understanding of God's Word.

Do not grow weary and lose heart in prayer and reading the Bible. As you abide in Christ and His Word, God will touch you and strengthen you (v. 18). A miracle happens every time you feel like you cannot take another step, yet you open your Bible to receive God's peace, strength, and encouragement for another day.

Pray Daniel 10:12, 18-19, and 21 over yourself and those for whom you stand guard as a faithful, prayerful watchman (Isaiah 62:6-7).

> *"LORD, please make _____ and me like Daniel. Let us set our hearts on understanding Your Word and humbling ourselves before You, God. LORD, hear our prayers and come in response to our words. Please touch us again and strengthen us. Let us hear You say, 'O _____ of high esteem, do not be afraid. Peace be with you; take courage and be courageous!' As soon as You speak, we receive strength. LORD, continue to speak because You have strengthened us. Tell us what is in Your Writing of Truth. In Your name, Jesus~"*

OCTOBER 25

Please read Daniel 11.

Meditate on verses 32b-33a.

The people who know their God will display strength and take action. Those who have insight among the people will give understanding to the many.

When God gave Daniel the visions in Daniel 7-12, the world was ruled by Persia. Soon Greece would conquer the world followed by the Roman empire. The first part of this chapter prophesies the fall of the Persian empire followed by the rise of the Greek empire. Starting with verse 36, the focus shifts to end time events. The king who magnifies himself and speaks monstrous things against God is the Little Horn in Daniel 7:8, the insolent king in Daniel 8:23, the man of lawlessness and the son of destruction in 2 Thessalonians 2:3, the antichrist in 1 John 2:18, and the beast in Revelation 13. Be aware of his tactics so you are not deceived and turned to godlessness (v. 32).

Be encouraged as you see God's Word being fulfilled before your eyes. As you read and study the Bible, "give understanding to the many" (v. 33).

Pray Daniel 11:32-33 and 35 over yourself and those for whom you stand guard as a faithful, prayerful watchman (Isaiah 62:6-7).

> *"LORD, do not let _____ and me be deceived by smooth words and turned to godlessness. Let us never act wickedly toward Your covenant. Make us people who know You, God. Let us display strength and take action. Give us insight among the people so we can give understanding to the many. LORD, when we fall, use it to refine, purge, and make us pure until the end time because it is still to come at the appointed time. In Your name, Jesus~"*

OCTOBER 26

Please read Daniel 12.

Meditate on this command in verse 13.

But as for you, go to the end.

Ponder these truths about Daniel:

- God introduced Daniel when he was approximately 15 years old, a youth who made up his mind not to defile himself (Daniel 1:3-8).
- Daniel served under pagan, human kings - 8 kings and 2 world kingdoms for approximately 66 years (Daniel 1:21; 5:30-31).
- Daniel interpreted the dreams and visions of kings from the age of 16 until he was in his 80's (Daniel 2; 4; 5).
- Daniel was given visions of kings and kingdoms (at least 20 kings and 5 kingdoms) from the time he was approximately 67 years old until he was 85 years old (Daniel 7-12).
- Daniel's calling when he was in his 80's (v. 13): **"Go to the end!"**

God's calling on your life is the same - keep going! No matter how old or young you are God wants faithful people to make up their mind to faithfully serve Him, giving a lost world insight into who He is.

Pray Daniel 12:10 and 13 over yourself and those for whom you stand guard as a faithful, prayerful watchman (Isaiah 62:6-7).

"LORD, purge, purify, and refine _____ and me. Please give us insight to understand. Strengthen us to go to the end. Let us enter into rest and rise again for our allotted portion at the end of the age. Because we belong to You, Jesus~"

OCTOBER 27

Please read Joel 1.

Meditate on verses 2 and 15.

> *Hear this, O elders, and listen, all inhabitants of the land. Has anything like this happened in your days or in your fathers' days? Alas for the day! For the day of the LORD is near, and it will come as destruction from the Almighty.*

Judah was in the midst of famine and plague when God said, "Wake-up!" (v. 5). The gnawing, swarming, creeping, stripping locusts they experienced would be mild compared to the coming day of the LORD (vs. 4, 15).

> *But the day of the LORD will come like a thief, in which the heavens will pass away with a roar and the elements will be destroyed with intense heat, and the earth and its works will be burned up.*
> —2 PETER 3:10

What is going on in the world right now? As we write this devotional, a devastating virus is wreaking havoc around the world, causing much fear and concern. God wants us to use these events—plagues, famines, wildfires, disease—to tell our children and grandchildren about the LORD, so they will tell the next generation because the day of the LORD is coming when it will be too late to receive the LORD's salvation (2 Peter 3:14-15).

Pray Joel 1:2-3, 15, and 19 as a faithful, prayerful watchman (Isaiah 62:6-7).

> *"LORD, has anything like this happened in my days or in my father's days? Let me tell my children about it and let them tell their children and their children to the next generation. For the day of the LORD is near, and it will come as destruction from You, the Almighty. To You, O LORD, I cry! Please save _____ before it is too late.*
> *In Your name, Jesus~"*

OCTOBER 28

Please read Joel 2.

Meditate on verse 32a.

> *And it will come about that whoever calls on the name of the LORD will be delivered.*

"LORD" in the meditation verse is the Hebrew word *Yehovah*; it means "the self-Existent, Eternal One," and it is the proper name of the one true God.[1] This most holy name for God is first seen in Genesis 2:4:

> *This is the account of the heavens and the earth when they were created, in the day that the LORD God made earth and heaven.*

And, this is the name Paul ascribes to Jesus in Romans 10 where he quotes Joel 2:32:

> *If you confess with your mouth Jesus as LORD, and believe in your heart that God raised Him from the dead, you will be saved, for "WHOEVER WILL CALL ON THE NAME OF THE LORD WILL BE SAVED."*
> —ROMANS 10:9, 13

Jesus is God, the self-Existent, Eternal One, Creator and Savior of the world. Appeal to Him with Joel 2:11-14 and 32 as a faithful, prayerful watchman (Isaiah 62:6-7).

> *"LORD, You utter Your voice before Your army; surely Your camp is very great. Make _____ and me strong as we carry out Your Word. The day of the LORD is indeed great and very awesome, and who can endure it? Let _____ return to You with all their heart and with fasting, weeping, and mourning. Let us rend our hearts and not our garments and return to You, LORD our God, for You are gracious and compassionate, slow to anger, abounding in lovingkindness and relenting of evil. LORD, please turn and relent and leave a blessing behind You. Please let _____ call on Your name, LORD, so they will be delivered.*
> *In Your name, LORD Jesus-"*

1. Retrieved from www.blueletterbible.org/lang/lexicon/lexicon.cfm?Strongs=H3068&t=NASB

OCTOBER 29

Please read Joel 3.

Meditate on verse 13.

> *Put in the sickle, for the harvest is ripe. Come, tread, for the wine press is full; the vats overflow, for their wickedness is great.*

The meditation verse sounds similar to these verses in Isaiah and Revelation:

> *I (the LORD) have trodden the wine trough alone, and from the peoples there was no man with Me. I also trod them in My anger and trampled them in My wrath, and their lifeblood is sprinkled on My garments, and I stained all My raiment. I trod down the peoples in My anger and made them drunk in My wrath, and I poured out their lifeblood on the earth.*
> —ISAIAH 63:3, 6

> *So, the angel swung his sickle to the earth and gathered the clusters from the vine of the earth and threw them into the great wine press of the wrath of God. And the wine press was trodden outside the city, and blood came out from the wine press, up to the horses' bridles, for a distance of two hundred miles.*
> —REVELATION 14:19-20

Let there be no doubt a day is coming when all the wicked, those who are not made righteous through the blood of Jesus, will be trampled in His wrath. Pray for them, using Joel 3:14 as their faithful, prayerful watchman (Isaiah 62:6-7).

> *"LORD, there are multitudes, multitudes in the valley of decision! For the day of the LORD is near in the valley of decision. LORD, _____ is in the valley of decision! Let them choose You before it is too late. In Your name, Jesus~"*

OCTOBER 30

Please read Amos 1.

Meditate on verses 1a, 2a, and 3a.

> *The words of Amos, who was among the sheepherders from Tekoa. He said, "The LORD roars from Zion and from Jerusalem He utters His voice." Thus says the LORD, "For three transgressions of Damascus and for four I will not revoke its punishment."*

Amos raised sheep, and by his own admission, was not groomed to be a prophet (Amos 7:14), but God used this humble sheepherder to speak to His people 2,800 years ago, and his words still speak to us today. Ask the LORD to use His Words to shepherd you to be the Godly person He wants you to be.

The LORD addressed five people groups in this chapter, some you can find in today's news: Damascus, Gaza, Tyre, Edom, and Ammon (vs. 3, 6, 9, 11, 13). Their sins were numerous and still plague us today: trampling on others, deportation of entire populations, breaking covenants, no compassion, uncontrolled anger, and killing babies in the womb (vs. 3, 6, 9, 11, 13).

God repeated Himself five times concerning these sins saying:

> *Thus says the LORD, "For three transgressions and for four, I will not revoke its punishment. So, I will..."*
> —AMOS 1:3-4, 6-7, 9-14

Let God's repeated phrases penetrate your mind and heart and appeal to Him with Amos 1:2 as a faithful, prayerful watchman (Isaiah 62:6-7).

> *"LORD, You roar from Zion, and from Jerusalem, You utter Your voice. Please roar and utter Your voice in _____ and my life. Let us heed Your Words so our pasture grounds can stop mourning and our summits no longer dry up. In Your name, Jesus~"*

OCTOBER 31

Please read Amos 2.

Meditate on verse 4.

> *Thus says the LORD, "For three transgressions of Judah and for four I will not revoke its punishment, because they rejected the law of the LORD and have not kept His statutes; their lies also have led them astray, those after which their fathers walked.*

The pattern continues in the second chapter of *Amos*: "Thus says the LORD, 'For three transgressions and for four I will not revoke its punishment, because…'" (vs. 1, 4, 6). Sadly, Judah and Israel are now included with the six Gentile nations in God's judgement (Amos 1:3, 6, 9, 11, 13; 2:1, 4, 6). Sadder still is the fact that Judah and Israel have God's Law; they are God's chosen people; they know better, yet like the heathen nations surrounding them, they pile sin on top of sin, ignoring God's Word and incurring His wrath.

Just like Amos 1, the sins listed in this chapter are still committed today: desecration of human remains, rejecting God's Law and ignoring His statutes, following lies, human trafficking, extortion, immorality, idolatry, and oppression (vs. 1, 4, 6-8). This list of sins is overwhelming and so tragic, and most of God's indictments are against His people who know better. "O LORD, remove the blinders from our eyes, so we can examine our lives and repent of our sins against You."

Use the words from Amos 2:4 and 13, asking God for forgiveness and restoration as a faithful, prayerful watchman (Isaiah 62:6-7).

> *"LORD, please forgive me for rejecting Your Law and not keeping Your statutes. Do not let lies lead me astray. Do not let me walk in the lies of this world. LORD, I want to bring You joy and not weigh You down as a wagon is weighed down when filled with sheaves. In Your name, Jesus~"*

November

*On your walls, O Jerusalem,
I have appointed watchmen;
All day and all night they
will never keep silent.
You who remind the LORD,
take no rest for yourselves;
And give Him no rest until He establishes
And makes Jerusalem a
praise in the earth.*
Isaiah 62:6-7, NASB

NOVEMBER 1

Please read Amos 3.

Meditate on verse 2. The LORD is speaking.

> *"You only have I chosen among all the families of the earth;*
> *therefore, I will punish you for all your iniquities."*

As a child did you ever say to your parents when being disciplined, "But, my friend did the same thing, and they didn't get punished." To which your parent replied, "Your friend is not my child; it isn't my responsibility to discipline them. You are my child, and it is my responsibility to discipline you."

God took the same firm and loving care of Israel. He rescued them from Egypt; He gave them His Law. As His chosen people, He was their Father, and He expected them to obey.

God not only chose Israel; He has chosen you. And with the privilege of being chosen, comes the expectation of obedience and the loving discipline of the Father when we disobey.

> *God deals with you as with sons; for what son is there*
> *whom his father does not discipline? He disciplines us*
> *for our good, so that we may share His holiness.*
> —HEBREWS 12:7B, 10B

Thank the LORD for taking a personal interest in you and pray Amos 3:2, 8, and 10 over yourself and those for whom you stand guard as a faithful, prayerful watchman (Isaiah 62:6-7).

> *"LORD, thank You for choosing _____ and me*
> *among all the families of the earth. Thank You for taking the*
> *punishment for all our iniquities, Jesus. Now, a lion has roared!*
> *Who will not fear? LORD God, You have spoken! Let us prophesy*
> *Your Words, so others can know how to do what is right and*
> *no longer hoard up violence and devastation in their lives.*
> *For the sake of Your name, Jesus~"*

NOVEMBER 2

Please read Amos 4.

Meditate on verse 9.

> *"I smote you with scorching wind and mildew, and the caterpillar was devouring Your many gardens and vineyards, fig trees, and olive trees; yet you have not returned to Me," declares the LORD.*

In the midst of grievous sin and idolatry, the LORD wanted to get Israel's attention, so they would return to Him. But the people were so blinded by their ungodly behavior that even plague, drought, famine, and war did not wake them up to their iniquities and bring them to repentance. You can hear God's frustration as He declares, "I overthrew you, yet you have not returned to Me" (v. 11).

People have not changed; most do not fall to their knees in repentance when there is an earthquake, plague, or wildfire. In fact, one is often met with indignation by Christians and non-Christians alike when God's judgment is attributed to tragedies. The event is usually referred to as a natural disaster or blamed on global warming rather than the consequences of sin and God's wake-up call to our relationship with Him.

As you continue to read the Bible, notice what God does and His purpose behind His actions. Notice the things going on in your world. What is God doing? How will you respond?

Pray Amos 4:12-13 over yourself and those for whom you stand guard as a faithful, prayerful watchman (Isaiah 62:6-7).

> *"LORD, You declare, 'Prepare to meet your God!' Let _____ and me be well-prepared. For behold, You form mountains and create the wind and declare Your thoughts to man. You make dawn into darkness and tread on the high places of the earth. LORD God of hosts is Your name, Jesus~"*

NOVEMBER 3

Please read Amos 5.

Meditate on verses 4, 6a, and 14.

> *For thus says the LORD to the house of Israel, "Seek Me that you may live Seek the LORD that you may live. Seek good and not evil, that you may live, and thus may the LORD God of hosts be with you, just as you have said!"*

Restoration and reconciliation are always on the heart and mind of God. No matter how grievous the sin and complicated the situation, the cry of God is: "Seek Me! I will be with you and let you live!"

The lie of Satan is: "You messed up so badly, God will never forgive you. Your life is ruined. There is no hope for you."

Do not believe the lie of the one who comes to kill, steal, and destroy (John 10:10). Believe Jesus, who came to give life, so you can have it abundantly (John 10:10).

> *Seek the LORD while He may be found; call upon Him while He is near. Let the wicked forsake his way and the unrighteous man his thoughts; and let him return to the LORD, and He will have compassion on him, and to our God, for He will abundantly pardon.*
> —ISAIAH 55:6-7

Pray Amos 5:8, 12, and 14 over yourself and those for whom you stand guard as a faithful, prayerful watchman (Isaiah 62:6-7).

> *"LORD, You made the Pleiades and Orion, and You change deep darkness into morning. You darken day into night, and You call for the waters of the sea and pour them out on the surface of the earth. LORD, You know _____ and my transgressions are many and our sins are great. Forgive us, LORD. We seek good and not evil that we may live. LORD God of hosts be with us, just as You have said! In Your name, Jesus~"*

NOVEMBER 4

Please read Amos 6.

Meditate on verses 1 and 8.

> *Woe to those who are at ease in Zion and to those who feel secure in the mountain of Samaria, the distinguished men of the foremost of nations, to whom the house of Israel comes. The LORD GOD has sworn by Himself, the LORD God of hosts has declared: "I loathe the arrogance of Jacob and detest his citadels; therefore, I will deliver up the city and all it contains."*

God pronounces judgment on His people for being at ease and feeling secure. Take His Words to heart, for the very thing that makes God furious would be described as success by many people today.

God says "Woe" to those who are indifferent and self-indulgent (vs. 1, 3, 6). God says "Woe" to those who are lazy and gluttonous (v. 4). God says "Woe" to those who are prideful and arrogant (v. 8). God says "Woe" to those who do not mention the name of God, convincing themselves He doesn't notice their behavior (v. 10).

Examine your life in the Light of God's Word. Have you fallen into sinful ease, embracing the world's comforts and pleasures, self-indulging instead of meeting the needs of those around you?

Use the words from Amos 6:1, 4, 6, and 8 to confess and repent as a faithful, prayerful watchman (Isaiah 62:6-7).

> *"LORD, please forgive me for being at ease and self-secure. Forgive me for reclining and sprawling in luxury and eating gluttonously. Forgive me for anointing myself with the finest of oils but not grieving over the ruin of others. Forgive me for my arrogance. I do not want You to loathe my behaviors, LORD. Help me change to gain Your perspective, see with Your eyes, and walk in Your ways. In Your name, Jesus~"*

NOVEMBER 5

Please read Amos 7.

Meditate on verses 4-6.

> *Thus the LORD GOD showed me, and behold, the LORD GOD was calling to contend with them by fire, and it consumed the great deep and began to consume the farmland. Then I said, "LORD GOD, please stop! How can Jacob stand, for he is small?" The LORD changed His mind about this. "This too shall not be," said the LORD GOD.*

When you pray, do you ever think, "What difference does my prayer make? God is going to do what He wants to do anyway."

The LORD God Almighty, considers our prayers as He controls the universe—mindboggling! How wonderful to know as you walk and talk with Jesus, He really hears your prayers, and what you pray really makes a difference. Amos 7 is an amazing affirmation of that fact. So, heed God's commands to pray:

> *Devote yourselves to prayer, keeping alert in it with an attitude of thanksgiving.*
> —COLOSSIANS 4:2

> *With all prayer and petition, pray at all times in the Spirit, and with this in view, be on the alert with all perseverance and petition for all the saints.*
> —EPHESIANS 6:18

> *The effective prayer of a righteous man can accomplish much.*
> —JAMES 5:16B

Pray Amos 7:2 and 5-6 as you intercede on behalf of those for whom you stand guard as a faithful, prayerful watchman (Isaiah 62:6-7).

> *"LORD God, please pardon! How can _____ stand for they are small? LORD God, please stop! How can _____ stand for they are small? LORD, please change Your mind about this and let it not be. Because of Your mercy, Jesus~"*

NOVEMBER 6

Please read Amos 8.

Meditate on verse 11.

> *"Behold, days are coming," declares the LORD GOD, "when I will send a famine on the land, not a famine for bread or a thirst for water, but rather for hearing the Words of the LORD."*

The Israelites experienced this famine of God's Word when some of them were scattered and destroyed by the Assyrians in 722 BC and more of them exiled by the Babylonians beginning in 605 BC. God's last recorded words in the Old Testament came through the prophet Malachi around 433 BC. It would be 400 years before the LORD spoke again through John the Baptist: "Behold, the Lamb of God who takes away the sin of the world!" (John 1:29). "And the Word became flesh and dwelt among us, and we saw His glory, glory as the only begotten from the Father, full of grace and truth" (John 1:14).

Miraculously we have Jesus, the Word of God in the flesh. And, at the time of writing this devotional, we have God's written Word translated in its entirety into nearly 700 languages; almost 3,400 of the world's 7,353 languages have some portion of the Bible in their language.[1] We have the privilege of living in a time when access to God's Word is easier than it has ever been. Take advantage of this gift God has graciously afforded us, being careful not to create a famine of the Word in your own life.

Use the words from Amos 8:11-12 to pray for those who need God's Word, as their faithful, prayerful watchman (Isaiah 62:6-7).

> *"LORD, please stop the famine in _____ life for hearing Your Words. They are staggering. Please let them seek You and Your Word   Please let them find You in Your Word before it is too late. In Your name, Jesus~"*

---

1. Retrieved from Wycliffe Global Alliance: www.wycliffe.net/resources/scripture-access-statistics/

NOVEMBER 7

Please read Amos 9.

Meditate on verse 10.

> *All the sinners of My people will die by the sword, those who say, "The calamity will not overtake or confront us."*

It is easy to become distracted by the world's calamities; thankfully this chapter refocuses our attention on the LORD. Fix your eyes on Him by praying Amos 9:1-6, 8, and 10 as a faithful, prayerful watchman (Isaiah 62:6-7).

> *"LORD, I see You standing beside the altar, saying, 'Smite the capitals so that the thresholds will shake and break them on the heads of them all!' LORD, You slay with the sword; the fugitive will not flee, and the refugee will not escape. Though they dig into Sheol, from there Your hand takes them, and though they ascend to heaven, from there You bring them down. Though they hide on the summit of Carmel, You search them out and take them, and though they conceal themselves from Your sight on the floor of the sea, from there You command the serpent and it bites them. Though they go into captivity before their enemies, from there You command the sword to slay them, and You set Your eyes against them for evil and not for good. LORD GOD of hosts, You touch the land so it melts, and all those who dwell in it mourn, and all of it rises up like the Nile and subsides like the Nile of Egypt. LORD, You build Your upper chambers in the heavens and have founded Your vaulted dome over the earth. You call for the waters of the sea and pour them out on the face of the earth. The LORD is Your name. Your eyes are on the sinful kingdom, and You will destroy it from the face of the earth; nevertheless, You will not totally destroy the house of Jacob. All the sinners of Your people will die by the sword, those who say, 'The calamity will not overtake or confront us.' LORD, please let _____ stop saying those words and come to You. In Your name, Jesus~"*

NOVEMBER 8

Please read Obadiah 1.

Meditate on verses 1a and 3a.

> *The vision of Obadiah. Thus says the LORD GOD concerning Edom—*
> *"The arrogance of your heart has deceived you."*

Edom is another name for Esau, the twin brother of Jacob, who is also called Israel (Genesis 25:21-30; 32:28). The brothers' relationship was contentious, even in the womb, and Esau's attitude toward his brother trickled down to his descendants, so much so, God pronounces judgement on the Edomites approximately 1,200 years after Jacob and Esau were alive.

The heart of Edom's issues is their pride (v. 3). Pride made the Edomites violent toward Israel (v. 10). They gloat and rejoice when bad things happen to Israel (vs. 12-13).

Their haughty attitude infuriates God, and He pronounces judgment on their head for what they have done (v. 15).

Arrogance, violence, gloating, snubbing, boasting—does the Holy Spirit convict your heart of any of those charges like He does mine? "Oh, LORD, let me see with Your eyes and hear with Your ears the things I say and do. Please forgive me and make me more and more like You."

Use the words from Obadiah 1:3, 10-13, 15, and 18 to pray over yourself and those for whom you stand guard as a faithful, prayerful watchman (Isaiah 62:6-7).

> *"LORD, the arrogance of _____ and my heart has deceived us. In the loftiness of our dwelling place, You will bring us down to earth. LORD, forgive our arrogance, violence, haughtiness, gloating, and boasting. Remove them from our lives, so You do not have to return them on our heads. Be the fire and the flame that burns sin from our lives.*
> *In Your name, Jesus~"*

NOVEMBER 9

Please read Nahum 1.

Meditate on verse 2.

> *A jealous and avenging God is the LORD; the LORD is avenging and wrathful. The LORD takes vengeance on His adversaries, and He reserves wrath for His enemies.*

Were there things in this chapter that surprised you about God? These truths are important to remember. People enjoy talking about the love and mercy of God, but His jealousy and wrath are often shunned with words like, "Well, the god I worship isn't vengeful." Know with Biblical certainty the one who says those words does not know God.

You have God's Word, so you are privileged to know the LORD. Tell Him that you know Him by praying Nahum 1:2-7 and 14b as a faithful, prayerful watchman (Isaiah 62:6-7).

> *"LORD, You are a jealous and avenging God. You are avenging and wrathful. You take vengeance on Your adversaries, and You reserve wrath for Your enemies. LORD, You are slow to anger and great in power, and You will by no means leave the guilty unpunished. In whirlwind and storm is Your way, and clouds are the dust beneath Your feet. You rebuke the sea and make it dry. You dry up all the rivers. Mountains quake because of You, and the hills dissolve; indeed, the earth is upheaved by Your presence, the world and all the inhabitants in it. Who can stand before Your indignation? Who can endure the burning of Your anger? Your wrath is poured out like fire, and the rocks are broken up by You. LORD, You are good, a stronghold in the day of trouble, and You know those who take refuge in You. LORD, You are my stronghold; I take refuge in You. Please let _____ stop being contemptible and turn to You. In Your name, Jesus~"*

NOVEMBER 10

Please read Nahum 2.

Meditate on verse 13.

> *"Behold, I am against you," declares the LORD of hosts.*
> *"I will burn up her chariots in smoke, a sword will devour*
> *your young lions; I will cut off your prey from the land, and*
> *no longer will the voice of your messengers be heard."*

God prophesied through Nahum concerning Nineveh, the capital of Assyria (Nahum 1:1). Jonah spoke God's Word to the people of Nineveh 100 years earlier (Jonah 1:1-2). That generation of Ninevites heeded God's Word and turned from their wicked way (Jonah 3). Now, a new generation spurned God's Word and arrogantly believed they were impregnable and undefeatable. God had other plans.

"In 612 BC, the city of Nineveh was sacked and burned by the allied forces of the Persians, Medes, Babylonians, and others who then divided the region between them. The area was sparsely populated thereafter, and slowly, the ancient ruins became buried in earth" (Nineveh—Ancient History Encyclopedia).[1] History backs up what God says in the Bible.

"Behold, I am against you," declares the LORD of hosts (v. 13a). What scary words to hear from the Commander in Chief over all the armies in heaven![2] Thankfully, the opposite is true for Christians:

> *If God is for us, who is against us?*
> —ROMANS 8:31B

As a faithful prayerful watchman (Isaiah 62:6-7), use the words from Nahum 2:13 to pray for those who need to stop fighting against God, so God will not be against them.

> *"LORD, please let _____ turn to You, so*
> *You will no longer be against them. Please let them hear*
> *the voice of Your messengers before it is too late.*
> *For the sake of Your name, Jesus~"*

---

[1]. Retrieved from www.ancient.eu/nineveh/
[2]. Retrieved from www.blueletterbible.org/Comm/guzik_david/StudyGuide2017-Nah/Nah-2.cfm?a=902003

NOVEMBER 11

Please read Nahum 3.

Meditate on verses 1 and 4.

> *Woe to the bloody city, completely full of lies and pillage; her prey never departs. All because of the many harlotries of the harlot, the charming one, the mistress of sorceries, who sells nations by her harlotries and families by her sorceries.*

Nineveh was a violent, evil mess. How quickly the people forgot God's Word preached by Jonah:

> *Then the people of Nineveh believed in God. When the word reached the king of Nineveh, he issued a proclamation and it said, "Let men call on God earnestly that each may turn from his wicked way and from the violence which is in his hands." When God saw their deeds, that they turned from their wicked way, then God relented concerning the calamity which He had declared He would bring upon them. And He did not do it.*
> —JONAH 3:5A, 6A, 7A, 8B, 10

Sadly, 100 years later, the Ninevites laid God's Word aside, exchanging conviction of sin for the charms of sensual unfaithfulness (v. 4). God was furious and promised to expose their disgrace and throw their filthiness back in their face, making them a disgusting spectacle (vs. 5-6).

Think about your life and the life of your nation. Was there a time when God's Word impacted you more than it does today, or does it convict you more now than ever? Learn from Nineveh. Do not be deceived by the world's delights.

Use the words from Nahum 3:18-19 to pray for yourself and those for whom you stand guard as a faithful, prayerful watchman (Isaiah 62:6-7).

> *"LORD, wake-up our shepherds, raise up our nobles, and gather our people. Only You can bring relief for our breakdown and cure our wound. LORD, make us stop continually passing on our evil. Save us before it is too late. In Your name, Jesus~"*

NOVEMBER 12

Please read Zephaniah 1.

Meditate on verses 14-15.

> *Near is the great day of the LORD, near and coming very quickly; listen, the day of the LORD! In it the warrior cries out bitterly. A day of wrath is that day, a day of trouble and distress, a day of destruction and desolation, a day of darkness and gloom, a day of clouds and thick darkness.*

Let there be no doubt in your mind about the coming of the day of the LORD. The prophets Isaiah, Ezekiel, Joel, Amos, Obadiah, Zephaniah, and Malachi all wrote specifically about it (Isaiah 13:6, 9; Ezekiel 13:5; 30:3; Joel 1:15; 2:1, 11; 3:14; Amos 5:18, 20; Obadiah 1:15; Zephaniah 1:7, 14; 2:2-3; Malachi 3:2). Peter preached about the day of the LORD (Acts 2:20) and exhorts us with these words:

> *But the day of the LORD will come like a thief, in which the heavens will pass away with a roar and the elements will be destroyed with intense heat, and the earth and its works will be burned up. Since all these things are to be destroyed in this way, what sort of people ought you to be in holy conduct and Godliness.*
> —2 PETER 3:10-11

Take God's Words to heart, telling others about the day of the LORD before it is too late.

Pray Zephaniah 1:12 and 17 over yourself and those for whom you stand guard as a faithful, prayerful watchman (Isaiah 62:6-7).

> *"LORD, do not let _____ and me become stagnant in spirit. Do not let us say in our hearts, 'The LORD will not do good or evil!' Let us tell people You will bring distress on men. Let _____ stop walking like the blind because they sin against You. Let them turn to You, so their blood will not be poured out like dust and their flesh like dung. In Your name, Jesus~"*

NOVEMBER 13

Please read Zephaniah 2.

Meditate on verses 1-3.

> *Gather yourselves together, yes, gather, O nation without shame, before the decree takes effect—the day passes like the chaff—before the burning anger of the LORD comes upon you, before the day of the LORD's anger comes upon you. Seek the LORD, all you humble of the earth who have carried out His ordinances; seek righteousness, seek humility. Perhaps you will be hidden in the day of the LORD's anger.*

The LORD issues an invitation: The day of God's anger is coming. Repent and seek Him before it is too late.

> *You yourselves know full well that the day of the LORD will come just like a thief in the night. While they are saying, "Peace and safety!" then destruction will come upon them suddenly like labor pains upon a woman with child, and they will not escape.*
> —1 THESSALONIANS 5:2-3

Let God's Word give you urgency to tell others about the day of the LORD, for "behold, now is the acceptable time; behold, now is the day of salvation" (2 Corinthians 6:2b). Let your days not pass like chaff, the worthless part of the wheat that blows away in the wind. Let your days be fruitful because you walk with Jesus and tell others about Him, so they do not have to experience the day of the LORD's anger (v. 2).

Pray Zephaniah 2:2-3 over yourself and those for whom you stand guard as a faithful, prayerful watchman (Isaiah 62:6-7).

> *"LORD, do not let _____ and my days pass like chaff. Before the day of Your anger comes, let us seek You. Make us the humble of the earth who carry out Your ordinances. Let us seek righteousness and humility. Please hide us in the day of Your anger. In Your name, Jesus~"*

NOVEMBER 14

Please read Zephaniah 3.

Meditate on verses 8-9.

> *"Therefore, wait for Me," declares the LORD, "For the day when I rise up as a witness. Indeed, My decision is to gather nations, to assemble kingdoms, to pour out on them My indignation, all My burning anger; for all the earth will be devoured by the fire of My zeal. For then I will give to the peoples purified lips, that all of them may call on the name of the LORD, to serve Him shoulder to shoulder."*

For those who do not know Jesus, the day of the LORD will be horrific, for God will pour out His wrath on a Christ-rejecting world. But, for those who know Him as LORD and Savior, it will be a glorious day, a day of joy when God will:

- take away His judgments against you
- clear away your enemies
- be in your midst as LORD and King
- remove your fear of disaster (v. 15).

What does the day of the LORD hold for you and those you love? Pray for those who do not know Jesus to believe in Him before it is too late. Teach them what you have learned about the day of the LORD.

Pray Zephaniah 3:16-17 as a faithful, prayerful watchman (Isaiah 62:6-7).

> *"LORD, in that day, let it be said to _____ and me, 'Do not be afraid; do not let your hands fall limp. The LORD your God is in your midst, a victorious warrior. He will exult over you with joy. He will quiet you in His love. He will rejoice over you with shouts of joy.' Thank You, in Your name, Jesus~"*

NOVEMBER 15

Please read Zechariah 14.

Meditate on verse 9.

> *And the LORD will be king over all the earth; in that day the LORD will be the only one, and His name the only one.*

Zechariah 14 describes the time when Christ returns with His holy ones, Christians, to rule the earth. It gives added details to the events recorded in Revelation 19:1-21 and 20:1-6. It is exciting to know a day is coming when "Jerusalem will dwell in security" (v. 11). It is also sobering to know a day is coming when the enemies of God will experience a plague where "their flesh will rot while they stand on their feet, and their eyes will rot in their sockets, and their tongue will rot in their mouth" (v. 12). As this panic from the LORD befalls them, their livestock will also experience this same flesh rotting plague (vs. 13, 15).

In the past, we may have been tempted to think such a thing would never happen in our lifetime; however, our own recent worldwide plague makes this chapter in Zechariah not so farfetched. What God declares will happen. This is not a fictional scene from a movie; this is not man's imagination. This is the Word of God, and this is the Truth (Psalm 119:160). Whom will you tell before it is too late?

Today, pray Zechariah 14:9 and 11 as a faithful, prayerful watchman (Isaiah 62:6-7).

> *"LORD, _____ and I look forward to the day You are king over all the earth, the day when You, LORD, are the only one and Your name the only one. We look forward to the day when people will live in Jerusalem, and there will no longer be a curse, for Jerusalem will dwell in security. Because of Your name, Jesus~"*

NOVEMBER 16

Please read Malachi 1.

Meditate on verse 6.

> *"A son honors his father, and a servant his master. Then if I am a father, where is My honor? And if I am a master, where is My respect?" says the LORD of hosts to you, O priests who despise My name. But you say, "How have we despised Your name?"*

Four hundred years before coming to earth in human flesh, God spoke one more time to His people through the prophet Malachi. His message begins with, "I have loved you" (v. 2). The people responded like spoiled, disrespectful children: "How have You loved us?" (v. 2). As the book continues, God the Father patiently answers the children's questions.

As you read *Malachi*, think about how you talk to God. Do you ever sound like an insolent child, questioning God's motives and actions? Amazingly, God lets us ask Him anything. Consider asking Him what He notices about your heart and attitude when you talk to Him. Ask Him to shape your attitudes toward Him and what He is doing in your life.

Use the words from Malachi 1:5-6 and 11a to give respectful honor to the LORD, as His faithful, prayerful watchman (Isaiah 62:6-7).

> *"LORD, be magnified beyond the border of Israel! Father, I honor You. Master, I respect You. LORD of hosts, may I never despise Your name. From the rising of the sun even to its setting, Your name will be great among the nations. Because Your name is Jesus~"*

NOVEMBER 17

Please read Malachi 2.

Meditate on verses 7-8.

> *"For the lips of a priest should preserve knowledge, and men should seek instruction from his mouth; for he is the messenger of the LORD of hosts. But as for you, you have turned aside from the way; you have caused many to stumble by the instruction; you have corrupted the covenant of Levi," says the LORD of hosts.*

God was not pleased 2,400 years ago. The priests caused many to stumble because they refused to truthfully teach God's Word (vs. 6-8). People wanted God's favor without seeking His forgiveness (v. 13). Divorce was rampant (vs. 14-16). People called evil "good," and they questioned, "Where is God?" as their lives crumbled under unchecked sin (v. 17). Wow! This chapter sounds like it was written today.

God and His Word do not change with the times. Times change when impacted by God and His Word.

As a faithful, prayerful watchman (Isaiah 62:6-7), pray to uphold God's Word, using the words from Malachi 2:5-7.

> *"LORD, thank You for Your covenant of life and peace with _____ and me. Your Words are an object of reverence to us, so we revere You and stand in awe of Your name. May true instruction be in our mouths, and unrighteousness not be found on our lips. May we walk with You in peace and uprightness and turn many back from iniquity. May our lips preserve knowledge; let people seek instruction from our mouths. Let us be Your messengers, LORD of hosts. For the sake of Your name, LORD Jesus~"*

NOVEMBER 18

Please read Malachi 3.

Meditate on verses 13 and 16.

> *"Your words have been arrogant against Me," says the LORD.*
> *"Yet you say, 'What have we spoken against You?'"*
>
> *Then those who feared the LORD spoke to one another,*
> *and the LORD gave attention and heard it, and a*
> *book of remembrance was written before Him for those*
> *who fear the LORD and who esteem His name.*

The questions continue in Malachi 3. "How shall we return?" and "What have we spoken against You?" spill from the mouths of those unwilling to take responsibility for their actions (vs. 7, 13).

Then suddenly the questions cease, and the LORD turns His attention from the arrogant God-questioners to the humble God-fearers (vs. 16-18). As God listens to this quite different conversation, He is so touched He has a book of remembrance written about them, making those who esteem His name His own precious possession, promising to spare them from His judgment (vs. 16-17).

With whom do you most identify from Malachi: God-questioner or God-fearer? Pray Malachi 3:16-18 over yourself and those for whom you stand guard as a faithful, prayerful watchman (Isaiah 62:6-7).

> *"LORD, may _____ and I fear You! As we speak*
> *to one another, please give attention and hear our words. Write*
> *about us in Your book of remembrance, as those who fear You and*
> *esteem Your name. LORD, make us Yours, preparing us as Your*
> *own possession and sparing us as a man spares his own son who*
> *serves him. LORD, You distinguish between the righteous and*
> *the wicked, between one who serves God and one who does not*
> *serve You. Make us Your righteous ones who serve You always.*
> *For the sake of Your name, Jesus~"*

NOVEMBER 19

Please read Malachi 4.

Meditate on verse 2.

> *But for you who fear My name, the sun of righteousness will rise with healing in its wings, and you will go forth and skip about like calves from the stall.*

God's final recorded words in the Old Testament are the closing verses of Malachi, describing the coming day of the LORD (vs. 1, 5). It is a day of health, youthful vitality, and restoration for those who fear God's name (vs. 2, 6). But for the arrogant and wicked, it is a day of consuming fire (v. 1).

What does the day hold for you and those you love?

Pray God's final Old Testament message from Malachi 4:1-6 over yourself and those for whom you stand guard as a faithful, prayerful watchman (Isaiah 62:6-7).

> *"LORD, do not let _____ and me be arrogant evildoers for whom the day is coming burning like a furnace. Please save us from the chaff; do not set us ablaze! Do not leave us without root or branch! Let us fear Your name, so the sun of righteousness will rise on us with healing in its wings. Let us go forth and skip about like calves from the stall. Save _____ from being the wicked who will be ashes under the soles of our feet on the day which You are preparing, LORD of hosts. Let us remember Your law of Moses, Your servant, even the statutes and ordinances which You commanded. Thank You for sending Elijah the prophet before the coming of Your great and terrible day, LORD. Restore the hearts of the fathers to their children and the hearts of the children to their fathers, so that You will not come and smite the land with a curse. In Your name, Jesus~"*

NOVEMBER 20

Please read Mark 13.

Meditate on verses 4-5.

> *Tell us, when will these things be, and what will be the sign when all these things are going to be fulfilled? And Jesus began to say to them, "See to it that no one misleads you."*

Mark 13 is a treasure chest of end-time prophecies as revealed by Jesus. Observe His Words carefully, so no one misleads you.

- Many will come claiming to be Jesus (v. 6).
- Wars and rumors of wars must first take place (v. 7).
- There will be earthquakes and famines in various places—these are the beginning of the birth pangs (v. 8).
- You will be delivered to the courts and stand before authorities to testify for Christ's sake (v. 9).
- The Gospel must first be preached to all the nations (v. 10).
- Family members will betray each other to death, and children will rise up against parents and put them to death (v. 12).
- You will be hated because of the name of Jesus (v. 13).

Do you think we are in the labor pains of Christ's return?

> *Even so, you too, when you see these things happening, recognize that He is near, right at the door.*
> —MARK 13:29

Jesus is coming soon. As a faithful, prayerful watchman (Isaiah 62:6-7), pray to be on the alert, using the words from Mark 13:33-37.

> *"LORD, let _____ and me take heed and keep on the alert, for we do not know when the appointed time will come. Help us stay on the alert as Your doorkeepers, doing Your assigned tasks. Let us be on the alert, for we do not know when You will return, Master. If You come suddenly, do not find us asleep. May we all be on the alert! For the sake of Your name, Jesus~"*

NOVEMBER 21

Please read Luke 21.

Meditate on verses 25-26.

> *There will be signs in sun and moon and stars, and on the earth dismay among nations, in perplexity at the roaring of the sea and the waves, men fainting from fear and the expectation of the things which are coming upon the world; for the powers of the heavens will be shaken.*

This chapter is full of end time prophecies declared by Jesus. Some of them have been fulfilled, like verse 6 when the temple was destroyed in 70 AD. Others are happening even as you read this, like the meditation verses describe (vs. 25-26).

This chapter is also filled with commands from Jesus, like verse 28: "Straighten up and lift up your heads because your redemption is drawing near."

Ask God to show you areas in your life where you need to straighten up. Time on earth is short. It is time to lift our heads and fix our eyes on Jesus.

Pray Luke 21:8a, 28, 34, and 36 over yourself and those for whom you stand guard as a faithful, prayerful watchman (Isaiah 62:6-7).

> *"LORD, do not let _____ and me be misled. Help us to straighten up, lift up our heads, and recognize our redemption is drawing near. Let us be on guard, so our hearts will not be weighed down with dissipation, drunkenness, and the worries of life. Do not let the day come upon us suddenly like a trap. Let us keep on the alert at all times, praying that we may have strength to escape all these things that are about to take place. In order to stand before You, Jesus~"*

NOVEMBER 22

Please read 1 Timothy 1.

Meditate on verse 12.

> *I thank Christ Jesus our LORD, who has strengthened me because He considered me faithful, putting me into service.*

Paul left Timothy in Ephesus to teach the believers how to function as a church (vs. 3-4). Before giving guidelines for church administration, Paul thanked Jesus for strengthening him and putting him into service despite his past life as a blasphemer, persecutor, and violent aggressor—the foremost of sinners (vs. 12-15). If Jesus Christ saved Paul and let him serve the church, then no one in Ephesus was hopeless for eternal life and serving the LORD.

This letter is for you and those you love. Are you praying for someone who appears will never follow Christ? Be encouraged by blasphemous, violently aggressive Paul, who because of the LORD, became a faithful servant to eternal, immortal King Jesus. If God can save Paul, He can save anyone!

Pray 1 Timothy 1:12-17 over yourself and those for whom you stand guard as a faithful, prayerful watchman (Isaiah 62:6-7).

> *"LORD Jesus Christ, strengthen _____ and me. Please consider us faithful and put us into service. Show us Your mercy, grace, faith, and love, which are only found in You. Thank You for coming into the world to save sinners. Please demonstrate Your perfect patience and let _____ believe in You for eternal life. Now to You, Jesus, the King eternal, immortal, invisible, the only God, be honor and glory forever and ever. Amen~"*

NOVEMBER 23

Please read 1 Timothy 2.

Meditate on verses 1-4.

> *First of all, then, I urge that entreaties and prayers, petitions and thanksgivings, be made on behalf of all men, for kings and all who are in authority, so that we may lead a tranquil and quiet life in all Godliness and dignity. This is good and acceptable in the sight of God our Savior, who desires all men to be saved and to come to the knowledge of the truth.*

Paul commanded Timothy to fight the good fight, keep the faith, and keep a good conscience (1 Timothy 1:18-19). Some people in the church rejected doing those things, and their faith suffered shipwreck (1 Timothy 1:19-20). How could the shipwreck of one's faith be averted? Pray! Pray for yourself and pray for everyone else. The way to fight the good fight is with prayer. It was the first thing God told the Ephesian Christians to do, and He wants you to do the same. Your faith and the faith of others is at stake. God wants all people to be saved, and He wants you to pray for their salvation.

Pray 1 Timothy 2:4 over those for whom you stand guard as a faithful, prayerful watchman (Isaiah 62:6-7).

> *"LORD, You say in Your Word You desire for all people to be saved and come to the knowledge of the truth. Please save _____ . For the sake of Your name, Jesus~"*

NOVEMBER 24

Please read 1 Timothy 3.

Meditate on verse 15.

> *But in case I am delayed, I write so that you will know how one ought to conduct himself in the household of God, which is the church of the living God, the pillar and support of the truth.*

The meditation verse contains the definition of church. The church belongs to the living God and is His household, the pillar and support of the truth (v. 15). Does your church fit that description? Do the people take a stand for the truth of God's Word, or does they capitulate to worldly ideology? Pray for your church to be a pillar of truth and for every individual to possess the 25 Godly characteristics listed in this chapter.

Pray 1 Timothy 3:2-11 and 15 over yourself and your church as a faithful, prayerful watchman (Isaiah 62:6-7).

> *"LORD, let every member of Your church be: above reproach, faithful to one spouse, temperate, prudent, respectable, hospitable, able to teach, not addicted to wine, not pugnacious, gentle, peaceable, free from the love of money, able to manage their own household well, able to keep their children under control with dignity, able to take care of the church of God, not conceited, not falling into the condemnation of the devil, good reputation outside of church, not falling into reproach and the snare of the devil, dignified, not double-tongued, not fond of sordid gain, holding to the mystery of the faith with a clear conscience, not malicious gossips, faithful in all things. God, let us know how to conduct ourselves in Your household, which is the church of the living God. Let us be the pillar and support of the truth. For the sake of Your name, Jesus~"*

NOVEMBER 25

Please read 1 Timothy 4.

Meditate on verse 1.

> *But the Spirit explicitly says that in later times some will fall away from the faith, paying attention to deceitful spirits and doctrines of demons.*

Here is a warning from God. In the last days, people will remove themselves from the truth of God because they pay attention to and are deceived by the demonic. Today, witches, zombies, vampires, and walking dead things fascinate many. These topics are not merely adult entertainment, but are in children's books, movies, and television shows. These ideas are propagated by liars, searing one's conscience like a branding iron (v. 2). Ouch!

As Christians, we are called to be pillars and supporters of the truth (1 Timothy 3:15). It is vital to discipline ourselves for the purpose of Godliness rather than be disciplined by the demonic (v. 7). Be careful not to let books, shows, and games creep into your home which are the deceit of Satan.

Pray 1 Timothy 4:7 and 12-16 over yourself and those for whom you stand guard as a faithful, prayerful watchman (Isaiah 62:6-7).

> *"LORD, let _____ and me have nothing to do with worldly fables. Instead, help us discipline ourselves for the purpose of Godliness. In our speech, conduct, love, faith, and purity, let us show ourselves an example of those who believe. Help us give attention to the reading of Scripture, to exhortation, and to teaching the Word. Do not let us neglect the spiritual gift within us. Help us be absorbed in the things of You, God, so our progress will be evident to all. Help us pay close attention to ourselves and what we teach, persevering in Your things, God, ensuring salvation for ourselves and those who hear. In Your name, Jesus~"*

NOVEMBER 26

Please read 1 Timothy 5.

Meditate on verse 22b.

Keep yourself free from sin.

God's Word is so practical. In this part of Paul's letter to Timothy, specific principles were given for men and women of all ages and in various life situations: married, widowed, leading a church, dealing with sin, and working with others. Paul even addressed stomach ailments. God cares about every detail of your life, and He wants you to live the plans and purposes He has for you.

Most of God's will for your life is contained in the Bible. Remain faithful to study and live His Word.

Pray 1 Timothy 5:21-22 over yourself and those for whom you stand guard as a faithful, prayerful watchman (Isaiah 62:6-7).

"LORD, may _____ and I maintain Your principles. Let us do nothing in a spirit of partiality. Do not let us share in the sins of others. Keep us free from sin. In Your name, Jesus~"

NOVEMBER 27

Please read 1 Timothy 6.

Meditate on verse 20.

> *O Timothy, guard what has been entrusted to you, avoiding worldly and empty chatter and the opposing arguments of what is falsely called "knowledge."*

Paul closed his letter to Timothy with a plea to guard the truth entrusted to him. Paul knew when people believed ideas opposite of God's Word, they would stray from true faith in God (v. 21).

Insert your name in place of "Timothy" in the meditation verse.

> *O _____, guard what has been entrusted to you, avoiding worldly and empty chatter and the opposing arguments of what is falsely called "knowledge."*

God begs you to avoid what the world calls "knowledge." If what you read and learn is in opposition to the Bible, it is a lie. God's Word is timeless truth; hold fast the Word of Life, so you will not be deceived by Satan, the father of lies (Philippians 2:16; John 8:44).

Pray 1 Timothy 6:4-6 and 11-12 over yourself and those for whom you stand guard as a faithful, prayerful watchman (Isaiah 62:6-7).

> *"LORD, do not let _____ and me be conceited, understanding nothing. Let us flee from controversial questions, disputes about words, envy, strife, abusive language, evil suspicions, and constant friction between men of depraved mind deprived of the truth. Make us Godly and content. Let us pursue righteousness, Godliness, faith, love, perseverance, and gentleness. Let us fight the good fight of faith and take hold of the eternal life to which we were called. Let _____ make the good confession of faith in the presence of many witnesses. In Your name, Jesus~"*

NOVEMBER 28

Please read 2 Timothy 1.

Meditate on verse 7.

> *God has not given us a spirit of timidity, but of power and love and discipline.*

Paul's first letter to Timothy was filled with instructions for leading the church in Ephesus. A few years passed; now Paul's beloved son in the faith needed a letter of personal encouragement.

Even a faithful bond-servant of Christ gets discouraged at times, so although Paul was close to death, imprisoned in Rome, and rejected by many of his friends, he wrote this letter to exhort and encourage Timothy.

There are at least 30 exhortations from Paul to Timothy in this letter, commands to be strong and diligent, to remember Jesus, to do certain things and to avoid doing other things. They are wise words from a concerned spiritual father, and they are words from a loving Heavenly Father to you.

No matter what is happening in your life, remember God saved you and gave you a holy calling (v. 9). Let God's Words encourage you today.

Pray 2 Timothy 1:7-9 and 14 over yourself and those for whom you stand guard as a faithful, prayerful watchman (Isaiah 62:6-7).

> *"LORD, You have not given _____ and me a spirit of timidity, but of power and love and discipline. Let us not be ashamed of Your testimony, LORD. Let us not forget You saved us and called us with a holy calling, not according to our works, but according to Your own purpose and grace granted to us in You, Christ Jesus, from all eternity. Holy Spirit, You dwell in us. Please guard the treasure entrusted to us. In Your name, Jesus~"*

NOVEMBER 29

Please read 2 Timothy 2.

Meditate on verses 8-9.

> *Remember Jesus Christ, risen from the dead, descendant of David, according to my Gospel, for which I suffer hardship even to imprisonment as a criminal, but the word of God is not imprisoned.*

In the midst of discouragement, it is important to remember.

- Remember Jesus Christ (v. 8).
- Remember He rose from the dead (v. 8).
- Remember God's Word is not imprisoned (v. 9).
- Remember salvation in Jesus Christ brings eternal glory (v. 10).
- Remember if we die with Christ, we will also live with Christ (v. 11).
- Remember if we endure with Christ, we will reign with Christ (v. 12).
- Remember Jesus remains faithful—He cannot deny Himself (v. 13).

Remember, remember, remember. No matter what is happening to you and those you love, remember who Christ is and who you are in Him. Be encouraged in Christ and His Word.

Pray 2 Timothy 2:1 over yourself and those for whom you stand guard as a faithful, prayerful watchman (Isaiah 62:6-7).

> *"LORD, make _____ and me strong in the grace that is in You, Christ Jesus~"*

NOVEMBER 30

Please read 2 Timothy 3.

Meditate on verse 1.

> *But realize this, that in the last days difficult times will come.*

The last days started after Christ's ascension (Acts 1). Timothy and Paul were living in the last days, and so are you. In the last days, people will be:

- lovers of self and lovers of money instead of lovers of God
- boastful, arrogant, and conceited
- revilers and disobedient to parents
- ungrateful, unholy, and unloving
- irreconcilable and malicious gossips
- without self-control
- brutal, treacherous, and reckless
- haters of good and lovers of pleasure
- holding to a form of godliness, yet denying its power (vs. 2-5)

People have not changed in 2,000 years; we need Christ and His Word to change us for good.

Pray 2 Timothy 3:16-17 over yourself and those for whom you stand guard as a faithful, prayerful watchman (Isaiah 62:6-7).

> *"All Scripture is inspired by You, God. Let it teach, reprove, correct, and train _____ and me in righteousness. Make us Your people, adequate and equipped for every good work. In Your name, Jesus~"*

DECEMBER

*On your walls, O Jerusalem,
I have appointed watchmen;
All day and all night they
will never keep silent.
You who remind the LORD,
take no rest for yourselves;
And give Him no rest until He establishes
And makes Jerusalem a
praise in the earth.*
ISAIAH 62:6-7, NASB

DECEMBER 1

Please read 2 Timothy 4.

Meditate on verses 3-4.

> *For the time will come when they will not endure sound doctrine; but wanting to have their ears tickled, they will accumulate for themselves teachers in accordance to their own desires and will turn away their ears from the truth and will turn aside to myths.*

Today's meditation verses sound as if they were recently written, just like the list of the ungodly in 2 Timothy 3:2-5. God's Word is eternal and continues to be profitable for teaching, reproof, correction, and training in righteousness (2 Timothy 3:16).

Does 2 Timothy 4:3-4 reprove you? What teachers and teachings do you follow? Do you merely want your ears tickled, or do you really want to know Truth? Are you part of a church where the Bible is preached and taught as the inerrant Word of God, the supreme and final authority for life and faith? Or does your church capitulate to pop-culture and political correctness, and personal preference?

Pray 2 Timothy 4:2 and 5 over yourself and those for whom you stand guard as a faithful, prayerful watchman (Isaiah 62:6-7).

> *"LORD, in these last days, let _____ and me preach the Word; be ready in season and out of season; reprove, rebuke, and exhort with great patience and instruction. Let us be sober in all things, endure hardship, do the work of an evangelist, and fulfill our ministry.*
> *In Your name, Jesus~"*

DECEMBER 2

Please read 1 Peter 1.

Meditate on verse 25.

> *But the Word of the LORD endures forever, and*
> *this is the Word which was preached to you.*

Peter was the disciple who denied knowing Jesus three times the night before the crucifixion (Luke 22:54-62). Peter was part of Jesus' inner circle of friends, yet that night, more motivated by fear than love for his LORD, he did the regrettable. Thankfully, he did not kill himself, like Judas did (Matthew 27:3-5). Instead, Peter let Jesus forgive and restore him. After the resurrection, Jesus graciously came to Peter, asking if he loved Him and exhorting him three times to shepherd His sheep (John 21:15-17). Peter wrote two letters as part of obeying his LORD's command to tend the lambs. Thankfully, as a lamb of God, you have these enduring letters to tend your heart and the hearts of those God calls you to shepherd.

As a faithful, prayerful watchman (Isaiah 62:6-7), pray 1 Peter 1:3-5 over those who need to be born again, so they can become a lamb of God.

> *"Blessed are You, God and Father of our LORD Jesus Christ.*
> *According to Your great mercy, please cause _____ to*
> *be born again to a living hope through the resurrection of Jesus*
> *Christ from the dead. Let them obtain an inheritance which is*
> *imperishable and undefiled and will not fade away, reserved in*
> *heaven for them. Protect them by Your power, God, through*
> *faith for a salvation ready to be revealed in the last time.*
> *For the sake of Your name, Jesus~"*

DECEMBER 3

Please read 1 Peter 2.

Meditate on verse 25.

> *For you were continually straying like sheep, but now you have returned to the Shepherd and Guardian of your souls.*

A good shepherd makes sure the sheep are fed. Peter took the LORD's sheep to the Word of God for nourishment.

> *Like newborn babies, long for the pure milk of the Word, so that by it you may grow in respect to salvation.*
> —1 PETER 2:2

Peter exhorts his readers to long for God's Word, to crave and desire it like a newborn baby craves the mama's milk. As a child of God, your spiritual nourishment comes from the Bible. What happens to a newborn who is not given milk to drink? God uses this comparison to help you understand how vitally important it is to your Christian growth to spend time in God's Word every day, throughout the day.

Pray 1 Peter 2:2 and 25 over yourself and those for whom you stand guard as a faithful, prayerful watchman (Isaiah 62:6-7).

> *"LORD, like newborn babies, help _____ and me long for the pure milk of Your Word, so that by it we may grow in respect to salvation. LORD, _____ is continually straying like sheep; let them return to You the Shepherd and Guardian of their souls. In Your name, Jesus~"*

DECEMBER 4

Please read 1 Peter 3.

Meditate on verse 15.

> *Sanctify Christ as LORD in your hearts, always being ready to make a defense to everyone who asks you to give an account for the hope that is in you, yet with gentleness and reverence.*

"Sanctify Christ as LORD in your heart" (v. 15). What an interesting command! Sanctify—set apart Christ as LORD—Master—God—Sovereign in your heart. Have you made Jesus LORD of your life? Is He your Master, the One in charge of you? Is Jesus your God and Sovereign, your Supreme Ruler? It may be easy to say, "Jesus is LORD," but what does that look like applied to your life? These are important questions to answer because Jesus says:

> *"Many will say to Me on that day, 'Lord, Lord, did we not prophesy in Your name, and in Your name cast out demons, and in Your name perform many miracles?' And then I will declare to them, 'I never knew you; depart from me, you who practice lawlessness.'"*
> —MATTHEW 7:22-23

Jesus died for you, so you can be brought to God (v. 18). If you haven't already, make Him God of your life today.

As a faithful, prayerful watchman (Isaiah 62:6-7), pray 1 Peter 3:15 over those who need to make Jesus their LORD.

> *"LORD, let _____ sanctify You as LORD in their hearts. Help me always be ready to make a defense to everyone who asks me to give an account for the hope that is in me. Let me do it with gentleness and reverence. In Your name, Jesus~"*

DECEMBER 5

Please read 1 Peter 4.

Meditate on verse 7.

> *The end of all things is near; therefore, be of sound judgment and sober spirit for the purpose of prayer.*

Wow, what a sobering thought! The end of all things is near. Therefore, what are we to be doing and what kind of people should we be? The time is past for pursuing worldly things; the time is now for pursuing God's will (vs. 2-3). The time is past for carrying out fleshly desires; the time is now to carry out God's desires. May the remainder of our time on earth be consumed by the things of God.

Ask God to give you an eternal perspective. Time is short; focus on Christ and what positively impacts His Kingdom.

Pray 1 Peter 4:1-2 and 7-11 over yourself and those for whom you stand guard as a faithful, prayerful watchman (Isaiah 62:6-7).

> *"LORD Jesus Christ, arm _____ and me with Your purpose. As we suffer in the flesh, let us cease from sin, so as to live the rest of the time in the flesh no longer for the lusts of men, but for Your will, God. The end of all things is near; therefore, let us have sound judgment and a sober spirit for the purpose of prayer. Help us keep fervent in our love for one another because love covers a multitude of sins. Let us be hospitable to one another without complaint. With the gifts You give us, let us serve one another as good stewards of Your grace. Help us speak Your utterances, God. Help us serve by the strength You supply, so that in all things You will be glorified through Jesus Christ. To You, Jesus, belongs the glory and dominion forever and ever. Amen~"*

DECEMBER 6

Please read 1 Peter 5.

Meditate on verse 2a.

Shepherd the flock of God among you.

Peter took seriously Jesus' command to shepherd His sheep (John 21:15-17). His obedience is seen in this letter which still shepherds the flock of God today.

Who has the LORD placed in your realm of influence to shepherd? He trusts you to eagerly feed His flock, being an example for them to follow (vs. 2-3). Jesus, the Chief Shepherd promises you a reward for being a good shepherd, the unfading crown of glory (v. 4).

As you shepherd the flock God entrusts to you, pray 1 Peter 5:2-3 over yourself to be a faithful shepherd and verses 6-11 over yourself and your flock as their faithful, prayerful watchman (Isaiah 62:6- 7).

"LORD, help me shepherd the flock You place among me. Let me exercise oversight not under compulsion, but voluntarily, according to Your will, God, and not for sordid gain, but with eagerness. Do not let me lord over those allotted to my charge but help me prove to be an example to the flock. LORD, help _____ and me humble ourselves under Your mighty hand, that You may exalt us at the proper time. Help us cast all our anxiety upon You because You care for us. Give us sober spirits; keep us on the alert, so our adversary, the devil, will not devour us. Let us resist him, firm in our faith, knowing the same experiences of suffering are being accomplished by our brethren who are in the world. God of all grace, after we have suffered for a little while, You will call us to Your eternal glory in Christ. Perfect, confirm, strengthen, and establish us. To You, Jesus, be dominion forever and ever. Amen~"

DECEMBER 7

Please read 2 Peter 1.

Meditate on verses 12-13.

> *Therefore, I will always be ready to remind you of these things, even though you already know them, and have been established in the truth which is present with you. I consider it right, as long as I am in this earthly dwelling, to stir you up by way of reminder.*

Peter was about to die, and the sheep entrusted to him were on his mind. He wrote another letter reminding them of things they already knew. Once he departed this earthly dwelling, Peter did not want them to forget the truth.

As you shepherd the flock God has given you, remember His divine power gives you everything you need to tend them. Like Peter, remind them of God's truths, being diligent to ensure they can recall those truths at any time.

Pray 2 Peter 1:4-8 over yourself and those for whom you stand guard as a faithful, prayerful watchman (Isaiah 62:6-7).

> *"LORD, as partakers of Your divine nature and having escaped the corruption that is in the world by lust, let _____ and me apply all diligence in our faith. LORD, supply us with moral excellence, knowledge, self-control, perseverance, Godliness, brotherly kindness, and love. Let these qualities be increasingly ours, so we will be neither useless nor unfruitful in the true knowledge of You, our LORD Jesus Christ. In whose name I pray-"*

DECEMBER 8

Please read 2 Peter 2.

Meditate on verses 1-2.

> *But false prophets also arose among the people, just as there will also be false teachers among you, who will secretly introduce destructive heresies, even denying the Master who bought them, bringing swift destruction upon themselves. Many will follow their sensuality, and because of them the way of the truth will be maligned.*

Peter warned his readers of false teachers. They introduce destructive heresies, follow their sensuality, and malign the truth (vs. 1-2). With eyes full of adultery, they never cease from sin (v. 14).

More than 2,000 years have passed, but our world is eerily similar to Peter's. There are false teachers, even in churches, teaching heresy as if it was truth. God's Word does not change; He still hates sin. God hates sin because it destroys lives. The world's legalization and condoning of sin does not change what God says about it. Sin ruins lives even if legalized. What God called immoral and wrong in the Old Testament was immoral and wrong in the New Testament and is immoral and wrong today.

Do not be swayed from the truth of the Bible. Do not let a preacher, teacher, family member, or friend convince you that God or His Word has changed. Stand firm! Live to please God rather than men.

Pray 2 Peter 2:9 over yourself and those for whom you stand guard as a faithful, prayerful watchman (Isaiah 62:6-7).

> *"LORD, make _____ and me*
> *Godly and rescue us from temptation.*
> *Save _____ so they are no longer*
> *with the unrighteous, kept under punishment*
> *for the day of judgment.*
> *In Your name, Jesus~"*

DECEMBER 9

Please read 2 Peter 3.

Meditate on verses 3-4a and 10.

> *Know this first of all, that in the last days mockers will come with their mocking, following after their own lusts, and saying, "Where is the promise of His coming?" But the day of the LORD will come like a thief, in which the heavens will pass away with a roar and the elements will be destroyed with intense heat, and the earth and its works will be burned up.*

What a sobering chapter describing the Day of LORD—the day of judgment and destruction of the ungodly and the day of new heavens and a new earth for the righteous (vs. 7, 10, 12). God promises the day is coming; therefore, how should we live today? Live your life investing in the eternal—people and God's Word. Diligently share the Word of God with others, praying they will choose God's salvation and not be destroyed.

Pray 2 Peter 3:11-12a, 14, and 18 over yourself and those for whom you stand guard as a faithful, prayerful watchman (Isaiah 62:6-7).

> *"LORD, make _____ and me people of holy conduct and Godliness, looking for and hastening the coming of Your day, God. May we be diligent to be found by You in peace, spotless and blameless. Let us grow in the grace and knowledge of You, our LORD and Savior Jesus Christ. To You be the glory, both now and to the day of eternity. Amen."*

DECEMBER 10

Please read Revelation 1.

Meditate on this phrase from verse 1.

The Revelation of Jesus Christ...

What a blessing to hold in your hand a letter written to churches revealing our Savior, Jesus Christ! As you read the words of this prophecy, you get a sneak peek into the end of time and God's coming judgement, but do not be too focused on those things; fix your eyes on Jesus because He is the focus of this book.

When I (Marsha) studied *Revelation* using *Precept Upon Precept* Bible studies, I was taught to take it literally because John is describing what he saw in his vision (vs. 11, 19). Part of the Bible study was drawing what was depicted in chapters 4-22. It was an amazing way to handle *Revelation*. You may want to get 19 pieces of paper and do the same.

Ask the LORD to give insight with understanding into this revelation of Jesus, getting to know Him like you never have before.

As a faithful watchman (Isaiah 62:6-7), pray Revelation 1:8 and 14-18, acknowledging Jesus.

> *"LORD God, You are the Alpha and the Omega, who is and who was and who is to come, the Almighty. Your head and Your hair are white like white wool, like snow, and Your eyes are like a flame of fire. Your feet are like burnished bronze, when it has been made to glow in a furnace, and Your voice is like the sound of many waters. In Your right hand You hold seven stars and out of Your mouth comes a sharp two-edged sword, and Your face is like the sun shining in its strength. I will not be afraid because You are the first and the last, the living One; You were dead, and behold, You are alive forevermore, and You have the keys of death and Hades. You are the LORD God, Almighty Jesus~"*

DECEMBER 11

Please read Revelation 2.

Meditate on verse 29.

He who has an ear, let him hear what the Spirit says to the churches.

John recorded seven messages to seven churches, and we are commanded to hear what the Spirit said. Consider reading the messages three times: observing Jesus, repenting of sin, and noticing the reward for overcoming.

As you fix your eyes on Jesus, you see He is:

- The One holding the seven stars in His right hand and walking among the seven golden lampstands (v. 1).
- The first and the last, who was dead, and has come to life (v. 8).
- The One with the sharp two-edged sword (v. 12).
- The Son of God, with eyes like a flame of fire and feet like burnished bronze (v. 18).

Ask the LORD to convict you of sins listed in this chapter. Have you lost your first love for Jesus (v. 4)? Do you hold to the teaching of false teachers, denying God's truth (vs. 14-15, 20)?

Repent and pray to be an overcomer. Pray Revelation 2:7, 10, 17, and 26 over yourself and those for whom you stand guard as a faithful, prayerful watchman (Isaiah 62:6-7).

"LORD, let _____ and me hear what Your Spirit says to the churches. Let us overcome and eat of the tree of life in the Paradise of God. Make us faithful until death and give us the crown of life. Help us overcome and give us some of Your hidden manna and a white stone with a new name written on it. LORD, let us overcome and keep Your deeds until the end. Give us authority over the nations. For the sake of Your name, Jesus~"

DECEMBER 12

Please read Revelation 3.

Meditate on verse 2. Jesus is giving a command.

> *"Wake up, and strengthen the things that remain, which were about to die, for I have not found your deeds completed in the sight of My God."*

Here is a wake-up call. What needs strengthening in your walk with Christ: daily Bible reading, talking and listening to Jesus, walking in the Spirit's power, memorizing God's Word, fellowshipping with believers, and studying God's Word? Do not let these Christian disciplines die; ask God to complete them on your journey with Him.

Continue to observe Jesus in this chapter. He:

- is the One with the seven spirits of God and the seven stars (v. 1).
- is holy and true (v. 7).
- has the key of David; what He opens no one shuts and what He shuts no one opens (v. 7).
- is the Amen, the faithful and true Witness, the Beginning, the Origin and Source of creation (v. 14).

Pray Revelation 3:5, 10, 12, and 21-22 over yourself and those for whom you stand guard as a faithful, prayerful watchman (Isaiah 62:6-7).

> *"LORD, make _____ and me overcomers clothed in white garments, whose names will not be erased from the book of life. Jesus, confess our name before Your Father and His angels. Help us keep the Word of Your perseverance and keep us from the hour of testing. Make us pillars in Your temple who will not go out from it anymore. Write Your name on us, God, and the name of Your city, the new Jerusalem. Make us overcomers who sit down with You on Your throne just as You have overcome and sit down with Your Father on His throne. LORD, we have ears; let us hear what Your Spirit says to the churches. In Your name, Jesus~"*

DECEMBER 13

Please read Revelation 4.

Meditate on verses 9-10.

> *And when the living creatures give glory and honor and thanks to Him who sits on the throne, to Him who lives forever and ever, the twenty-four elders will fall down before Him who sits on the throne, and will worship Him who lives forever and ever, and will cast their crowns before the throne.*

As you continue reading *Revelation*, remember you are simply reading John's description of what he saw in his vision from Jesus about Jesus and things that must soon take place (Revelation 1:1). It would be like you describing a dream you had last night. So, try to picture in your mind what John saw in his mind 2,000 years ago.

John gives a glorious description of God on His throne and the response of those privileged to see Him. Notice what happens when the four living creatures praise the LORD (v. 9). The 24 elders worship Him, too, casting their gold crowns at His feet (v. 10).

Purpose to be a living creature with your eyes fixed on Jesus, constantly giving glory, honor, and thanks to Him. As you do, notice the impact on others who will worship Him, too.

Praise the LORD with Revelation 4:8b and 11 as a faithful, prayerful watchman (Isaiah 62:6-7).

> *"Holy, holy, holy are You LORD God, the Almighty, Who was and Who is and Who is to come. Worthy are You, my LORD and my God, to receive glory and honor and power; for You created all things, and because of Your will they existed and were created. LORD, let me say these Words day and night, forever and ever. To the glory of Your name, Jesus~"*

DECEMBER 14

Please read Revelation 5.

Meditate on verse 9.

> *And they sang a new song, saying, "Worthy are You to take the book and to break its seals; for You were slain and purchased for God with Your blood men from every tribe and tongue and people and nation."*

Picture in your mind the worship taking place around God's throne when Jesus, the Lion, stands at the throne, appearing as a slain Lamb, and takes the book from God's right hand. Jesus the Overcomer is on the scene, and every created thing exuberantly rejoices.

Will you join them? Do not be tempted to join the doom and gloom throng of the world, grumbling their way through life. If the blood of Jesus purchased you, you are one of those singing praises to the Lion of Judah, the Lamb of God. Let Revelation 5 become your reality today. Start by praising Jesus with verses 9-10 and 12-14 as a faithful, prayerful watchman (Isaiah 62:6-7).

> *"LORD Jesus, worthy are You to take the book and to break its seals; for You were slain and purchased for God with Your blood people from every tribe and tongue and people and nation. Lamb of God, thank You for purchasing me! Make _____ and me to be a kingdom and priests to our God and let us reign upon the earth. Worthy are You, Lamb that was slain to receive power and riches and wisdom and might and honor and glory and blessing. To You who sits on the throne and to the Lamb be blessing and honor and glory and dominion forever and ever. Amen and Amen and Amen and Amen~"*

DECEMBER 15

Please read Revelation 6.

Notice the repeated phrase "when the Lamb broke...."

Meditate on verse 1a.

> *Then I saw when the Lamb broke one of the seven seals...*

Keep in mind that while *Revelation* gives us a glimpse into end time events, it dramatically reveals who Jesus is. In this chapter, rather than focusing on the various colored horses focus on the One in charge of the horses. By simply breaking a seal, the Lamb sets into motion events impacting the entire world. Be amazed by Him and His power.

The last three verses of this chapter are tragic. After the Lamb breaks six seals, notice how those left on the earth are cowering in caves, begging rocks to fall on them, so they do not have to face the Lamb. Rather than run to "the Lamb of God who takes away the sin of the world" (John 1:29), they run from Him. Do not let sin drive you to the pathetic place of running from God. Run to Him before it is too late.

Pray for those, who need to be saved by the Lamb, not to be like those in Revelation 6:15-17 as their faithful, prayerful watchman (Isaiah 62:6-7).

> *"LORD, please make _____ stop hiding in caves and among the rocks of the mountains. May they stop hiding from Your presence. Lamb of God, let them fall before Your throne and receive Your salvation, so they do not experience Your wrath. For the great day of their wrath will come, and they will not be able to stand without You. For the sake of Your name, Jesus~"*

DECEMBER 16

Please read Revelation 7.

Meditate on verse 17a.

> *The Lamb in the center of the throne will be their shepherd.*

As you continue to move through *Revelation*, keep your eyes on the Lamb. Notice He is in the center of the throne, and because of His blood, people are removed from the great tribulation (vs. 14, 17). People, too numerous to count, from every nation, tribe, and tongue stand before the Lamb worshiping Him (vs. 9-10). Will you and those you love be in that great multitude?

Pray Revelation 7:9-12 and 14-17 over yourself and those for whom you stand guard as a faithful, prayerful watchman (Isaiah 62:6-7).

> *"O Lamb of God, I want to be with that great multitude from every nation, tribe, people, and tongue, standing before the throne and before You, clothed in a white robe with palm branches in my hand. LORD, let _____ be there, too! I fall on my face and worship You, God, saying, 'Amen, blessing and glory and wisdom and thanksgiving and honor and power and might be to You my God forever and ever. Amen.' Lamb of God, take us out of the great tribulation because we have washed our robes and made them white in Your blood. Because of You, we are before Your throne, God, and we will serve You day and night in Your temple. LORD, You sit on the throne; spread Your tabernacle over us. Thank You that we will no longer hunger nor thirst anymore, nor will the sun beat down on us, nor any heat because You are our Shepherd, Lamb of God, and You are in the center of the throne. Guide us to the springs of the water of life and wipe every tear from our eyes. For the sake of Your name, Jesus~"*

DECEMBER 17

Please read Revelation 8.

Meditate on verses 3-4.

> *Another angel came and stood at the altar, holding a golden censer; and much incense was given to him, so that he might add it to the prayers of all the saints on the golden altar which was before the throne. And the smoke of the incense, with the prayers of the saints, went up before God out of the angel's hand.*

> *May my prayer be counted as incense before You; the lifting up of my hands as the evening offering.*
> —PSALM 141:2

The Lamb has broken six seals; men slay each other; there are earthquakes, famine, and pestilence (Revelation 6). The earth is a mess when the Lamb breaks the seventh seal, ushering in seven angels with seven trumpets (vs. 1-2). These trumpets will be quickly blown, one after the other, and things will get much worse. Before the trumpets are blown, an angel holding a container filled with incense comes to the throne of God and mixes the incense with the prayers of the Christians. God breathes in these fragrant prayers.

Picture what is happening in this chapter. The LORD is about to act in such a powerful way that the entire universe will be rocked. But, before the first trumpet is blown, God pauses for 30 minutes to breathe in your prayers. Amazing!

Keeping these truths in mind, pray for the Lamb to break seals on the hearts of those you love, using the words from Revelation 8:1, as their faithful, prayerful watchman (Isaiah 62:6-7).

> *"LORD, please breathe in my prayers and break the seal that is on the heart of _____ before it is too late. In Your name, Jesus the Lamb~"*

DECEMBER 18

Please read Revelation 9.

Meditate on verses 13-15.

> *Then the sixth angel sounded, and I heard*
> *a voice from the four horns of the*
> *golden altar which is before God, one saying*
> *to the sixth angel who had the*
> *trumpet, "Release the four angels who are*
> *bound at the great river Euphrates."*
> *And the four angels, who had been prepared*
> *for the hour and day and month*
> *and year, were released, so that they would kill a third of mankind.*

Let there be no doubt in your mind Who is in charge of the events in *Revelation*. The One Who sits on the throne has prepared four angels for a precise moment in time to kill a third of mankind who do not have His seal on their foreheads (v. 4). As that truth soaks in, ask the LORD what exactly He has prepared for you today. For whom does He want you to pray? What does He want you to do? Whom does He want you to tell about Him and His precise plan for their life?

Your life is very important to God. Make every moment count as you walk and talk with Jesus, being all He has prepared you to be.

Use the words from Revelation 9:20-21 to pray for repentance in your life and the lives of those for whom you stand guard as a faithful, prayerful watchman (Isaiah 62:6-7).

> *"LORD, I repent of the works of my hands that*
> *are not Your works. LORD, forgive me!*
> *Please let _____ repent of the works*
> *of their hands, so they stop worshiping*
> *demons and idols of gold, silver, brass, stone,*
> *and wood, which can neither see, hear,*
> *nor walk. Let them repent of their murders,*
> *sorceries, immorality, and their thefts.*
> *Before it is too late, Jesus~"*

DECEMBER 19

Please read Revelation 10.

Meditate on verses 10-11.

> *I took the little book out of the angel's hand and ate it, and in my mouth, it was sweet as honey; and when I had eaten it, my stomach was made bitter. And they said to me, "You must prophesy again concerning many peoples and nations and tongues and kings."*

God's Word is so powerful, and when you start to devour it, discovering its mysteries, it will be sweet to the taste.

> *How sweet are Your words to my taste! Yes, sweeter than honey to my mouth! From Your precepts I get understanding; therefore, I hate every false way.*
> —PSALM 119:103-104

The more you eat God's Word, the more it also hits you in the gut that everything God says is the truth, and He is coming again to judge those who do not know Him as Savior and LORD; therefore, the time is now for revealing the mystery of Jesus to others (1 Timothy 3:16).

Pray to fearlessly proclaim the truth of Christ as a faithful, prayerful watchman (Isaiah 62:6-7). Start by declaring Revelation 10:6-7.

> *"LORD, You live forever and ever. You created heaven and the things in it, and the earth and the things in it, and the sea and the things in it. I know You will not delay much longer, and Your mystery, which You preached to Your servants the prophets will be finished. Help me live to tell others Your mystery before it is too late. In Your name, Jesus~"*

DECEMBER 20

Please read Revelation 11.

Meditate on verses 3-4.

> *And I will grant authority to my two witnesses, and they will prophesy for twelve hundred and sixty days, clothed in sackcloth. These are the two olive trees and the two lampstands that stand before the LORD of the earth.*

You may have learned the two witnesses in *Revelation* are perhaps Moses, Elijah, and/or Enoch. Ponder for a moment the possibility of the two witnesses being the church. Jesus said at the beginning of His revelation the lampstands are churches (Revelation 1:20). And, the psalmist declared that he was like an olive tree in God's house (Psalm 52:8).

Reread this chapter, picturing yourself as one of the witnesses because that is who Jesus declared you to be:

> *You will receive power when the Holy Spirit has come upon you, and you shall be My witnesses both in Jerusalem, and in all Judea and Samaria, and even to the remotest part of the earth.*
> —ACTS 1:8

Ask the LORD to make you His bold witness and pray Revelation 11:15-18 as His faithful, prayerful watchman (Isaiah 62:6-7).

> *"LORD, the kingdom of the world has become Your Kingdom, the Kingdom of Christ, and You will reign forever and ever. I fall on my face and worship You! I give You thanks, O LORD God, the Almighty, who are and who were because You have taken Your great power and have begun to reign. LORD, the time is coming for the dead to be judged and for Your bond-servants, the prophets and the saints and those who fear Your name, the small and the great, to be rewarded. Please let _____ become your saint and bond-servant before You destroy those who destroy the earth. In Your name, Jesus~"*

DECEMBER 21

Please read Revelation 12.

Meditate on verse 10.

> *Then I heard a loud voice in heaven, saying, "Now the salvation, and the power, and the kingdom of our God and the authority of His Christ have come, for the accuser of our brethren has been thrown down, he who accuses them before our God day and night."*

Throughout the book of *Revelation*, Jesus is revealed as the One to receive all glory, honor, and praise because He has all authority and power (Revelation 4:8, 11; 5:12-14; 7:10-12; 11:15-17; 12:10). Keep that fact in mind when you feel overwhelmed by Satan and the world. The truth is "the salvation, and the power, and the kingdom of God and the authority of Christ" came when Satan was kicked out of heaven (v. 10). Do not be deceived by Satan's accusations (v. 10). If you are a Christian, you have already overcome because of the blood of the Lamb (v. 11). Satan's time is short (v. 12). Press on in the strength of the LORD.

As a faithful, prayerful watchman (Isaiah 62:6-7), praise the LORD with Revelation 12:10-11 and pray for others to overcome Satan with the blood of the Lamb.

> *"The salvation and the power and the kingdom of our God and the authority of His Christ have come, for the accuser of our brethren has been thrown down. Jesus, defend me when Satan accuses me before God day and night. LORD, the only way to overcome is by the blood of the Lamb. Please let _____ overcome by Your blood. Let the word of our testimony be that we did not love our life even when faced with death. Because of Your blood, Jesus~"*

DECEMBER 22

Please read Revelation 13.

Meditate on verses 1 and 11.

> *And the dragon stood on the sand of the*
> *seashore. Then I saw a beast coming up*
> *out of the sea, having ten horns and seven heads,*
> *and on his horns were ten diadems,*
> *and on his heads were blasphemous names.*
> *Then I saw another beast coming*
> *up out of the earth; and he had two horns like*
> *a lamb, and he spoke as a dragon.*

Thankfully, we have God's Word, so we can be aware of Satan and his tactics. In this chapter, God shows us how the dragon and the two beasts attempt to mimic the Trinity. The dragon gives the first beast his power and throne; together, they work with a second beast who looks like a lamb but speaks like the dragon (vs. 2, 11). Do not be deceived by this evil trio; only God is Three in One.

A day is coming when the beast who speaks like the dragon will deceive those who dwell on the earth, and they will be marked as belonging to him (vs. 14-17). Have you been marked by the Holy Spirit, proving you belong to God through the blood of the Lamb? If you have an ear, hear what God reveals to you in this chapter, sharing it with everyone in your realm of influence (v. 9).

As a faithful, prayerful watchman (Isaiah 62:6-7), pray Revelation 13:8 over those who need Jesus.

> *"LORD, do not let _____ be one*
> *of those who dwells on the earth and*
> *worships the beast. LORD, please let their*
> *name have been written from*
> *the foundation of the world in the book of life*
> *of the Lamb who has been slain.*
> *In Your name, Jesus~"*

DECEMBER 23

Please read Revelation 14.

Meditate on verses 9-10.

> *Then another angel, a third one, followed them, saying with a loud voice, "If anyone worships the beast and his image, and receives a mark on his forehead or on his hand, he also will drink of the wine of the wrath of God, which is mixed in full strength in the cup of His anger; and he will be tormented with fire and brimstone in the presence of the holy angels and in the presence of the Lamb."*

As you read *Revelation*, you may be thinking, "Wow, this sounds like things happening today!" Recently, a high-ranking government official, who is a Christian, said, "Do not feed the beast." His wise advice was given for a situation where believers were persecuted by nonbelievers. Do not focus on Satanic beasts; God will take care of them. Focus on those who need Jesus because you know how the story ends; those who do not know Him will be put into the wine press of the wrath of God, and they will be tormented day and night (vs. 10, 19-20). You have the eternal Gospel (v. 6). Share it with others before it is too late.

Pray Revelation 14:6-7 and 12 over yourself and those for whom you stand guard as a faithful, prayerful watchman (Isaiah 62:6-7).

> *"LORD, You have given _____ and me the eternal Gospel to preach to those who live on the earth and to every nation and tribe and tongue and people. LORD, help us preach it!*
> *Let _____ fear You and give You glory because the hour of Your judgment is coming. We worship You who made the heaven and the earth and sea and springs of waters.*
> *Give us perseverance. Help us keep Your commandments and our faith in You, Jesus~"*

DECEMBER 24

Please read Revelation 15.

Meditate on verses 2-3.

> *And I saw something like a sea of glass mixed with fire, and those who had been victorious over the beast and his image and the number of his name, standing on the sea of glass, holding harps of God. And they sang the song of Moses, the bond-servant of God, and the song of the Lamb, saying, "Great and marvelous are Your works, O LORD God, the Almighty; righteous and true are Your ways, King of the nations!"*

Thankfully, Jesus included lots of worship throughout the vision He gave John because arrogant, blasphemous beasts can wear a person down (Revelation 13:5-6). Not surprisingly, even as we write these devotionals for *Revelation*, real-life "beasts" are speaking blasphemies about the Bible and a stand we took for God's Word. Persevering for the cause of Christ is exhausting; that is why it must be done in God's strength and not our own. Worshiping the One who gives the strength is vital for being victorious in Jesus.

Revelation 4, 5, 7, 11, 12, and 15 contain beautiful worship verses. Praise Jesus with them. Praise Him with Revelation 15:2-4 as His faithful, prayerful watchman (Isaiah 62:6-7).

> *"Great and marvelous are Your works, O LORD God, the Almighty! Righteous and true are Your ways, King of the nations! Who will not fear, O LORD, and glorify Your name? For You alone are holy; for all the nations will come and worship before You, for Your righteous acts have been revealed. Make us victorious over the beast and his image and the number of His name. By the power of Your name, Lamb of God, LORD Jesus~"*

DECEMBER 25

Please read Revelation 16.

Meditate on verses 5-7.

> *And I heard the angel of the waters saying, "Righteous are You, who are and who were, O Holy One, because You judged these things; for they poured out the blood of saints and prophets, and You have given them blood to drink. They deserve it." And I heard the altar saying, "Yes, O LORD God, the Almighty, true and righteous are Your judgments."*

Seven seals, seven trumpets, seven bowls—God's judgment poured out on mankind who refuse to be covered by the blood of the Lamb. Since the beginning of time, Satan's desire is to delude the minds of humans, so they question and deny the authority of God. "Did God really say…" (Genesis 3:1). And, now you see the end results of the devil's schemes: humans, the crown of God's creation, covered in His wrath, blaspheming Him instead of repenting so as to give the Almighty glory (v. 9).

Genesis 3 and Revelation 16, tragic bookends of God's Word for those who believe Satan's lies and follow the created rather than the Creator. Let these chapters motivate you to tell others the truth about Jesus. Pray for God to give them ears to hear.

Do you know people who already behave like those in Revelation 16, blaspheming God when things are bad? Pray for them to repent before it is too late, using Revelation 16:9, 11, and 21 as their faithful, prayerful watchman (Isaiah 62:6-7).

> *"LORD, please let _____ stop blaspheming Your name. Let them repent and give You glory. Let them stop blaspheming You, God of heaven, because of their pains and sores. May they repent of their deeds. Let them stop blaspheming You, God, before the plague becomes extremely severe. For the sake of Your name, Jesus~"*

DECEMBER 26

Please read Revelation 17.

Meditate on verses 15-17.

> *And he said to me, "The waters which you saw where the harlot sits, are peoples and multitudes and nations and tongues. And the ten horns which you saw, and the beast, these will hate the harlot and will make her desolate and naked and will eat her flesh and will burn her up with fire. For God has put it in their hearts to execute His purpose by having a common purpose, and by giving their kingdom to the beast, until the Words of God will be fulfilled."*

Much is revealed in this chapter, and a most important revelation is that God is in charge of the beast, kings, peoples, multitudes, nations, and tongues; they will execute His plans.

Hear what God told the prophet Isaiah:

> *"Remember the former things long past, for I am God, and there is no other; I am God, and there is no one like Me, declaring the end from the beginning, and from ancient times things which have not been done, saying, 'My purpose will be established, and I will accomplish all My good pleasure.'"*
> —ISAIAH 46:9-10

Take confidence in God that His purpose for you and those you love is established; live for Him to accomplish all His good pleasure in your life.

Pray Revelation 17:14 over yourself and those for whom you stand guard as a faithful, prayerful watchman (Isaiah 62:6-7).

> *"Lamb of God, Your Word says the beast and ten kings will wage war against You, but You will overcome them because You are LORD of lords and King of kings, and _____ and I will be with You because we are the called and chosen and faithful. Lamb of God, please let _____ be with us, too.*
> *In Your name, Jesus~"*

DECEMBER 27

Please read Revelation 18.

Meditate on verse 14.

> *The fruit you long for has gone from you,*
> *and all things that were luxurious*
> *and splendid have passed away from you and*
> *men will no longer find them.*

Can you imagine a day when there will no longer be stuff to buy? Jesus gave John a vision of all the merchants on earth mourning and crying because they are no longer making any money off of people buying their stuff (v. 11). Can you imagine a day when "cargoes of gold and silver and precious stones and pearls and fine linen and purple and silk and scarlet, and every kind of citron wood and every article of ivory and every article made from very costly wood and bronze and iron and marble, and cinnamon and spice and incense and perfume and frankincense and wine and olive oil and fine flour and wheat and cattle and sheep, and cargoes of horses and chariots and slaves and human lives" will no longer exist (vs. 12-13)? When that day comes will you rejoice, or will you cry because there will no longer be a reason to go shopping?

Examine your life. Are you investing in stuff that will be destroyed in the wrath of God, or are you investing in things with eternal value—people and God's Word?

Pray Revelation 18:4-5 over yourself and those for whom you stand guard as a faithful, prayerful watchman (Isaiah 62:6-7).

> *"LORD, let _____ and me heed the*
> *command to 'Come out of Babylon the great.'*
> *Do not let us participate in her sins. Keep us*
> *from sins that pile up as high as heaven.*
> *Thank You that You remember our sin no more (Jeremiah 31:34).*
> *Because of Your blood, Lamb of God, Jesus~"*

DECEMBER 28

Please read Revelation 19.

Meditate on verses 9a and 17.

> *Then he said to me, "Write, 'Blessed are those who are invited to the marriage supper of the Lamb.'"*
>
> *Then I saw an angel standing in the sun, and he cried out with a loud voice, saying to all the birds which fly in midheaven, "Come, assemble for the great supper of God."*

What a stark contrast of two suppers taking place at the end of time—the marriage supper of the Lamb and the great supper of God. Which one will you and those you love attend? It is really important to take God's Word to heart, knowing a day will come when every human ever created will either say, "Hallelujah! Salvation and glory and power belong to our God," or they will experience His wrath (vs. 1, 17-18).

Tell others what you are learning in *Revelation*, especially those who have not yet accepted God's invitation to the marriage supper of the Lamb, praying for them to accept before it is too late.

Praise the LORD with the words you will say at the Lamb's supper from Revelation 19:1-3, 6-7, 11, 13, and 16 as His faithful, prayerful watchman (Isaiah 62:6-7).

> *"Hallelujah! Salvation and glory and power belong to You, my God, because Your judgments are true and righteous, for You will judge the great harlot who is corrupting the earth with her immorality, and You will avenge the blood of Your bond-servants on her. Hallelujah! Her smoke will rise up forever and ever. Hallelujah! For LORD God Almighty, You reign, and the marriage of the Lamb will come. Let _____ and me make ourselves ready as Your bride. Because You are Faithful and True, the Word of God, King of kings, and LORD of lords, Jesus~"*

DECEMBER 29

Please read Revelation 20.

Meditate on verse 6.

> *Blessed and holy is the one who has a part in the first resurrection; over these the second death has no power, but they will be priests of God and of Christ and will reign with Him for a thousand years.*

What a foundational chapter for understanding death and resurrection! There are two deaths and two resurrections. Christians experience only one death—that physical death when you get to leave your earthly body to be with Jesus (2 Corinthians 5:6-8). For those who do not know Jesus, there are two deaths—the one when their physical body dies, and the one when their names are not found written in the book of life, and they are condemned to eternity separated from God in the lake of fire (vs. 14-15).

Christians will be in the first resurrection when Christ returns to earth with those who belong to Him (v. 6; 1 Thessalonians 4:14). Those who do not know Jesus will experience the second resurrection when they will be judged according to their deeds then thrown into the lake of fire (vs. 12-15).

It seems like an easy choice—follow Christ and die once, being in the glorious first resurrection, or deny Christ and die twice, being in the dreaded second resurrection. To be clear, you want no part in the second death and the second resurrection. Tell those you love what Revelation 20 says about death and resurrection. As their faithful, prayerful watchman (Isaiah 62:6-7), pray for them to be in the first resurrection, using the words from Revelation 20:6.

> *"LORD, please make _____ a blessed and holy one who has a part in the first resurrection. Let the second death have no power over them. Make them Your priests, God, and let them reign with You, Christ, for a thousand years. In Your name, Jesus~"*

DECEMBER 30

Please read Revelation 21.

Meditate on verse 4.

> *He (God) will wipe away every tear from their eyes; and there will no longer be any death; there will no longer be any mourning, or crying, or pain; the first things have passed away.*

Can you imagine the day when there will be no more death, pain, sickness, crying, depression, anxiety, weariness…in your life? God says when He creates the new heavens and earth, those painful things from your past will not be remembered or come to your mind (Isaiah 65:17). And Jesus says you won't even question Him about any of those things (John 16:23). How glorious it is through the blood of Jesus to overcome everything that wants to overcome you (v. 7)!

In the midst of this life on earth, which can be very difficult, keep your eyes fixed on the Lamb. Let Him shed His light on your situation, revealing His glory in the good times and the bad. Keep in mind a day is coming when you won't remember or wonder why bad things happened today.

Pray Revelations 21:7-8 and 27 over yourself and those for whom you stand guard as a faithful, prayerful watchman (Isaiah 62:6-7).

> *"LORD, let _____ and me overcome and inherit You! Be our God! We want to be Your children! Because of You, we are not cowardly, unbelieving, abominable, murderers, immoral, sorcerers, idolaters, and liars, whose part will be in the lake that burns with fire and brimstone, which is the second death. LORD, please let _____ choose You, so they will not experience the second death. Let their names be written in the Lamb's book of life. In Your name, Jesus~"*

DECEMBER 31

Please read Revelation 22.

Meditate on verse 6.

> *And he said to me, "These Words are faithful and true," and the LORD, the God of the spirits of the prophets, sent His angel to show to His bond-servants the things which must soon take place.*

As a bond-servant of Jesus Christ, you, like John, have had the privilege of seeing things that are already taking place and will continue to happen. It is encouraging to know God is in charge. You have also had the privilege of knowing Jesus better as you observed His *Revelation*. Notice His "I AM" statements in this final chapter:

- "I AM coming quickly" (v. 7).
- "I AM coming quickly, and My reward is with Me to render to every man according to what he has done" (v. 12).
- "I AM the Alpha and the Omega, the first and the last, the beginning and the end" (v. 13).
- "I AM the root and the descendant of David, the bright morning star" (v. 16).
- "I AM coming quickly" (v. 20).

Jesus says three times in this chapter, "I AM coming quickly" (vs. 7, 12, 20). As His faithful bond-servant (vs. 3, 6, 9), tell others He is coming soon. As a faithful, prayerful watchman (Isaiah 62:6-7), pray for them using the words from Revelation 22:3-4, 14, 17, and 20.

> *"LORD, make _____ Your bond-servant who will serve You and see Your face. Put Your name on their forehead. Let them wash their robes so they have the right to the tree of life and enter by the gates into the city. LORD, let them come. Let me invite them to come. They are thirsty. May they wish to take the water of life without cost. LORD, You are coming quickly. Amen. Come, LORD Jesus~"*

Scripture Index

NUMBERS	January 10 - February 14
DEUTERONOMY	February 15 - March 10
JOSHUA	April 17 - May 10
1 CHRONICLES	May 11 - June 8
2 CHRONICLES	June 9 - July 14
JOB	August 12 - September 22
PSALM 2	September 23
PSALM 23	September 24
PSALM 27	September 25
PSALM 37	September 26
PSALM 39	September 27
PSALM 41	September 28
PSALM 42	September 29
PSALM 77	September 30
PSALM 86	October 1
PSALM 88	October 2
PSALM 118	January 1
ISAIAH 2	October 3
ISAIAH 11	October 4

ISAIAH 13	October 5
ISAIAH 19	October 6
ISAIAH 24	October 7
ISAIAH 27	October 8
ISAIAH 34	October 9
ISAIAH 35	October 10
ISAIAH 61	October 11
EZEKIEL 13	October 12
EZEKIEL 30	October 13
EZEKIEL 38	October 14
DANIEL	October 15 - 26
JOEL	October 27 - 29
AMOS	October 30 - November 7
OBADIAH	November 8
NAHUM	November 9 - 11
ZEPHANIAH	November 12 - 14
ZECHARIAH 14	November 15
MALACHI	November 16 - 19
MATTHEW	March 20 - April 16
MARK 13	November 20
LUKE 21	November 21
ACTS	July 15 - August 11
1 THESSALONIANS	January 2 - January 6
2 THESSALONIANS	January 7 - January 9
1 TIMOTHY	November 22 - 27
2 TIMOTHY	November 28 - December 1
1 PETER	December 2 - 6
2 PETER	December 7 - 9
REVELATION	December 10 - 31

Topical Index

BANNED THINGS
April 22, 23; May 12

BLESSINGS
February 15, 21; March 18, 24; May 1, 5, 13, 14, 21

CHRIST'S RETURN AND THE DAY OF THE LORD
January 5, 6, 7, 8, 9; April 12, 13; September 23;
October 3, 4, 5, 6, 7, 8, 9, 10, 11, 12, 13, 14, 22, 25, 27, 28, 29;
November 12, 13, 14, 15, 19, 20, 21, 25, 30;
December 1, 5, 9, 15, 28, 29, 30

CHURCH
February 5; April 11; July 5, 7, 23; August 3; November 24

COMMITMENT
January 16, 17; May 10; June 14, 24; July 27; August 4, 5

Confession and Repentence
January 14, 21, 30; March 6, 23; May 31; June 29;
July 17, 19; November 4, 11; December 18

Courage
May 18, 29; June 1, 23; July 10; August 6, 10

Discernment and Wisdom
May 23; June 9, 10, 17, 27; September 8; October 16, 19

Established and Faithful
January 2, 4, 11; February 8, 9, 19, 26; March 1; April 28, 30;
May 9, 11, 24, 27; June 15, 16, 25; July 2, 6, 9, 20, 25;
August 13; October 15, 17, 20, 26;
November 22, 28, 29; December 4, 7, 11, 12, 26

Fear
February 17; March 29; April 5; June 28; November 18

God's Word
January 3; February 22, 25; March 2, 14; April 24; May 25;
July 18; October 23, 30; November 1, 6, 7, 17, 27; December 3, 8

God's Wrath and Judgment
February 23; November 2, 9; December 23, 25

The Heart and Humility
January 24; February 7, 29; April 6; June 19, 20;
July 3, 4, 8, 11, 14; September 13; November 8

Help!
January 25; April 14, 26, 27, 29; May 3, 15, 28;
September 28, 29, 30; October 2

Holiness
January 15; February 27, 28; March 8, 10

Holy Spirit
July 15, 16, 21, 28, 29, 30

Jesus
January 28, 29; February 13, 18; December 10, 31

The Journey
January 19; February 10, 16; March 16, 27;
April 2, 17, 19; September 24, 27; December 6

Listen
March 30; April 1, 3

Marriage and Family
March 9; April 7; June 7

Men
May 17; June 6

Obedience
January 18, 22, 23, 26, 31; February 2, 14, 20; March 11, 12, 13, 15, 20, 21, 22, 25, 28, 31; April 4, 9, 15, 16, 25; May 4; June 18; July 22

Pain and Suffering
August 14, 15, 18, 21, 24, 25, 27, 28, 30; September 1, 3, 4, 7, 9, 10, 11, 14, 15, 16, 18, 19, 20, 21, 22; October 1

Praise
January 1, 20; May 26; June 8, 13; August 20, 23; September 5, 6, 17, 25; October 18, 21

Prayer
February 24; March 26; July 26; October 24; November 5, 16; December 17

Salvation
February 6, 12; March 4; April 10, 18; May 6; June 11, 12; July 24, 31; August 2, 7, 9; September 26; November 10, 23; December 2, 22

Servants
March 19; April 8, 21; May 16

Sin
February 11; March 7; May 2, 8, 20; July 12; October 31; November 3, 26; December 27

Spiritual Levites
January 10, 12, 13, 27; February 3, 4; March 3; May 7, 19; June 2, 3, 4, 5; July 1, 13

Spiritual Warfare
March 5; May 22, 30; June 21, 22

Teaching
March 17; April 20; June 26, 30; August 1, 8, 11

What To Say and What Not To Say
February 1; August 16, 17, 19, 22, 26, 29, 31; September 2, 12

Worship
August 12; December 13, 14, 16, 19, 20, 21, 24

About the Authors

Marsha Harvell

Marsha Harvell is passionate about her LORD and Savior Jesus Christ and treasures His Word. She loves to lead Bible studies and teach people how to study God's Word. As an international trainer for Precept Ministries, she has taught hundreds of people in Germany, France, Qatar, Bahrain, India, Malaysia, Indonesia, and Japan how to study the Bible and lead Bible studies. Marsha is dedicated to helping others discover the promises found in Scripture.

Marsha served as a missionary to the military as a chaplain's wife, appointed by the North American

Mission Board for 34 years. Her husband Ron recently retired from the United States Air Force. They now minister to college students and the faculty and staff at Charleston Southern University in North Charleston, South Carolina, where Ron is the Foundational Director of the Dewey Center for Chaplaincy. With a Bachelors in Education from Hardin-Simmons University and a Masters in Gifted and Talented Education from Texas Women's University, Marsha Harvell has taught in both public and private schools. She has helped plant churches and served as a worship leader and a women's ministry director. She is also a conference speaker; some of her favorite topics include: The Covenant Maker, Godly Relationships, Being a Godly Wife and Mother, Hearing and Heeding God, Being Complete in Christ, Knowing God, and How to Pray.

She is the author of *The Covenant Maker: Knowing God and His Promises for Salvation and Marriage*, co-author with Ron of *The Watchman on the Wall: Daily Devotions for Praying God's Word over Those You Love (Volumes 1, 2, 3 and 4)* and co-author with Ron and Wendy K. Walters of *50 Steps with Jesus: Learning to Walk Daily with the Lord (New Believer's and Shepherd's Guides)*.

Marsha and Ron have been married since 1984 and have two grown children, Stephanie, married to Jonathan, and Steven, married to Rachel. They have seven grandchildren: Nathan, Adilynn, Kik, Daniel, Kyro, Caleb, and Abigail.

Ron Harvell

Dr. Ron Harvell is the Foundational Director of the Charleston Southern University Dewey Center for Chaplaincy in North Charleston, South Carolina. The Dewey Center develops academic and functional training to help believers better serve their churches and communities by increasing their ministry skills. He is a retired Chaplain Brigadier General and former Deputy Chief of Chaplains for the United States Air Force where he was responsible for developing and supporting ministry to the entire Air Force community. Prior to that position, he was the Command Chaplain for Air Force Air Mobility Command, Air Force Global Strike Command, and Air Force Central Command, caring for all Air Force personnel serving in 22 countries of the Middle East.

Ron felt called to ministry when he was 17 years old. After being licensed to the Gospel Ministry by Circle Drive Baptist Church in Colorado Springs, he attended college where he met and married Marsha (1984). In June of 1985, he was ordained by Friendship Baptist Church in Weatherford, Texas. Following seminary, he pastored Northside Baptist Church in Kermit, Texas for four-and-a-half years. Since 1986, Ron and Marsha have lived in 22 locations around the world, serving as endorsed ministers of the North American Mission Board to the Air Force Chaplain Corps. They are excited now to be serving college students, faculty, and staff at Charleston Southern University

Ron is an award-winning church growth pastor in both civilian and military organizations and a visionary leader serving God in His transformation of individuals, communities, and institutions. He is the co-author with

Marsha of *The Watchman on the Wall: Daily Devotions for Praying God's Word over Those You Love (Volumes 1, 2, 3 and 4)* and co-author with Ron and Wendy K. Walters of *50 Steps with Jesus: Learning to Walk Daily with the Lord (New Believer's and Shepherd's Guides)*.

Ron has earned a Bachelor of Arts degree from Hardin-Simmons University in Bible and History, a Master of Divinity from Southwestern Baptist Theological Seminary, and a Doctor of Ministry from Asia Graduate School of Theology with a focus in Transformational Leadership for the Global City. He also has a Master of Science in National Security Strategy from National War College at the National Defense University and a Master of Arts in Organizational Management from The George Washington University. These academic experiences help shape ministry opportunities and capacities where his gifts and passions are: preaching, teaching, discipleship, church planting, and church growth.

Ron and Marsha have been married since 1984 and have two grown children, Stephanie, married to Jonathan, and Steven, married to Rachel. They have seven grandchildren: Nathan, Adilynn, Kik, Daniel, Kyro, Caleb, and Abigail.